ICONS
of
American
Popular
Culture

ICONS
of
American
Popular
Culture

From P.T. Barnum to Jennifer Lopez

Robert C. Cottrell

M.E.Sharpe
Armonk, New York
London, England

Library of Congress Cataloging-in-Publication Data

Cottrell, Robert C., 1950–
  Icons of American popular culture : from P.T. Barnum to Jennifer Lopez / Robert C. Cottrell.
    p. cm.
  ISBN 978-0-7656-2298-3 (cloth: alk. paper) — ISBN 978-0-7656-2299-0 (pbk.: alk. paper)
  1. Popular culture—United States—History. 2. Celebrities—United States—Biography. 3. Entertainers
  —United States—Biography. 4. National characteristics, American. I. Title.

  E169.1.C787 2009
  306.0973—dc22   2009010385

Printed in the United States of America

The paper used in this publication meets the minimum requirements of
American National Standard for Information Sciences
Permanence of Paper for Printed Library Materials,
ANSI Z 39.48-1984.

∞

IBT (c)   10   9   8   7   6   5   4   3   2   1
MV (p)   10   9   8   7   6   5   4   3   2   1

For Sue and Jordan

Contents

Introduction

A nation's story can be captured in numerous ways. Historical accounts of economic developments, military conflicts, domestic debates, and natural disasters all help to shape images of a land and its people; but so too does an appreciation of the sublime and the ridiculous, the heroes and heroines, and fads and frivolities that make up the popular culture of a mass society. Popular culture in an advanced, industrialized country such as the United States reflects the intellectual, social, cultural, political, and demographic currents of the time (see Chronology on page xiii). Using popular culture as a lens on history is enlivening and illuminating and recaptures something of the "lightning in the bottle" effect that characterizes particular individuals, events, and happenings. This is especially so with regard to the remarkable pantheon of American popular cultural figures, whose life stories, accomplishments, and difficulties often mirror those of the nation they represent. What follows is an admittedly abbreviated, subjective presentation of several of the most iconic individuals in American popular cultural history. Another historian undoubtedly would have chosen at least some other figures. This author reluctantly left out many personal favorites, including Mark Twain, Babe Ruth, Humphrey Bogart, Lucille Ball, Bob Dylan, Jane Fonda, Richard Pryor, Angelina Jolie, and Tiger Woods, to name a few.

Beginning nearly 200 years ago—when necessary technological advances, widespread literacy, affluence, and mythmaking coalesced—popular culture began to dramatically influence the course of events in the United States. It served to shape and then recast images of the American man and woman, the American experience, and the very idea of America itself. This volume attempts to explore some of the most striking developments involving popular culture from antebellum America to the very present by examining the roles played by key individuals in the unfolding of the notion of the American Dream. During this period the United States underwent tremendous alterations, as a rural, Calvinistic society and fledging democracy gave way to an urban, post-Victorian, and pluralistic order while wrestling with sectional, racial, class, and gender divisions. *Icons of American Popular Culture* profiles twenty prominent figures who helped to shape the imagination, hopes, and aspirations of countless numbers of their countrymen, as those transformations took place.

The first chapter, "Democratic Showmen: James Gordon Bennett and P.T. Barnum," introduces one of the originators of the penny press and the founder of the popular American Museum. Bennett and Barnum helped to democratize American popular culture in the very period when democracy largely emerged, imploded, and then flourished in nineteenth-century America. Next, "Exponents of the Culture of Consumption: Marshall Field and Horatio Alger Jr." grapples with other aspects of consumer culture in the last half of the nineteenth century, when a more affluent society welcomed department stores and the dime novel among other cultural amenities. Along the way Field and Alger forever altered perceptions of the American Dream. Chapter 3, "Stars of Vaudeville and Tin Pan Alley: Lillian Russell and Irving Berlin," features one of the early, great American actresses of live theater and an immigrant Jew who became perhaps the finest American popular songwriter. Both provided democratic entertainment to native-stock Americans and immigrants alike. The next chapter, "The Cinematic Artist and the Literary Lion: D.W. Griffith and Ernest Hemingway," focuses on the new industry of film and the American literary renaissance of the 1920s, particularly as associated with the so-called Lost Generation. Each used cinematic-styled techniques to offer his analyses of American life. The fifth chapter, "The 'New Woman' and the 'New Negro': Clara Bow and Bessie Smith," profiles Hollywood's "It Girl" during the heyday of silent films and the legendary blues singer who traveled the black theater circuit and recorded with Columbia Records. In the post-Victorian America of the Roaring Twenties, both exuded a sexuality that proved uncomfortable to many.

"Voices of Radical Culture: Margaret Bourke-White and Woody Guthrie," Chapter 6, relates the artistic accomplishments of the famous photojournalist and the folk balladeer and their appeals to social conscience. Bourke-White captured images of Dust Bowl America, fascist aggression, the Holocaust, postwar anticolonialism, and the early Cold War. Guthrie sang of the downtrodden, the dispossessed, and folk heading down the road "feelin'" bad. Chapter 7, "American Heroes: Hank Greenberg and Edward R. Murrow," traces the remarkable stories of the Jewish baseball slugger and the CBS broadcaster who initially made their marks during the Great Depression, then served their country in different ways during World War II, and remained important figures in the postwar era. Along the way Greenberg belied anti-Semitic stereotypes, while Murrow fearlessly reported what he saw to be true, whether overseas or at home. The eighth chapter, "American Rebels: Marilyn Monroe and Elvis

Presley," recalls the beautiful actress who challenged gender boundaries in her own fashion and the rock and roll pathfinder who helped to spawn a youth culture.[1] The "blonde bombshell" and the swivel-hipped singer vanquished the vestiges of Victorianism that remained part of mid–twentieth-century America. Chapter 9, "American Icons in a Time of Unrest: John F. Kennedy and Muhammad Ali," underscores the charismatic qualities of the young president and the heavyweight boxing champion who combined heroic and antiheroic characteristics in an era that proved unsettling to many but transformative for others. Both men expertly used mass media to shape images of themselves and of their nation. The final chapter, "American Dreamers: Michael Jordan and Jennifer Lopez," presents the stories of two individuals, one African-American and one Hispanic, who combined accomplishments in their respective fields with a business acumen that has made them powerhouses. They may well remain on the national stage for decades to come, evolving, along with American society, in ways as yet unforeseen.

Note

1. Monroe and Presley were paired in an earlier and quite different essay in Blaine T. Browne and Robert C. Cottrell, *Modern American Lives: Individuals and Issues in American History Since 1945* (Armonk, NY: M.E. Sharpe, 2008), Chapter 3.

A Chronology of Significant Events in the History of American Popular Culture

1800   Construction of the White House in Washington, DC, is completed.

1810   Construction of the U.S. Capitol is completed.

1815   Francis Scott Key publishes his poem "The Star Spangled Banner."

1823   James Fenimore Cooper publishes *The Pioneers*.

1828   Thomas Dartmouth "Daddy" Rice, appearing as Jim Crow, introduces minstrel dancing.

1835   James Gordon Bennett begins publishing *The New York Herald*.

1840   Edgar Allan Poe publishes his short story, "The Fall of the House of Usher."

Alexander Wolcott receives the first American patent pertaining to photography for his camera.

1841   P.T. Barnum's American Museum opens.

Blackface minstrelsy debuts at the Park Theatre in New York City.

1844   Henry David Thoreau begins living at Walden Pond.

1846   Merchant Alexander Turney Stewart establishes the "Marble Palace" on east Broadway in New York City.

John Plumbe Jr. takes the first-known photograph of the White House and President James K. Polk.

1848   Construction of the Washington Monument is completed.

1850   Nathaniel Hawthorne's novel *The Scarlet Letter* becomes a bestseller.

1851 Stephen Foster writes the tune "Old Folks at Home," also known as "Swanee River."

1852 Harriet Beecher Stowe publishes *Uncle Tom's Cabin.*

1853 The New York state legislature designates Central Park in New York City.

1855 Walt Whitman publishes *Leaves of Grass.*

1858 Rowland Hussey Macy founds Macy's as a dry goods store in New York City.

1861 Mathew Brady begins his photographic record of the Civil War.

1865 Field, Leiter & Palmer (later Marshall Field's) opens in Chicago.

Tony Pastor's Opera House opens on the Bowery in New York City.

1866 Mahon Loomis delivers the first radio transmission.

The musical play *The Black Crook* opens at a theater on lower Broadway.

1868 Horatio Alger publishes *Ragged Dick.*

Lydia Thompson and the British Blondes introduce burlesque theater in the United States.

1869 The Cincinnati Red Stockings comprise the first professional baseball team.

Rutgers and Princeton play in the first college football game.

1871 "P.T. Barnum's Grand Traveling Museum, Menagerie, Caravan & Hippodrome" begins operations.

The Great Chicago Fire sweeps across the city.

1872 Aaron Montgomery Ward publishes the first mail-order catalog.

1874 Alexander Graham Bell invents the telephone.

1876 Eight teams make up baseball's first organized professional circuit, the National League.

Mark Twain publishes *The Adventures of Tom Sawyer.*

1877 Thomas Edison invents sound recording.

1878   Thomas Edison receives a patent on the phonograph.

1881   Vaudeville impresario Tony Pastor's Fourteenth Street Theatre opens in New York City.

1883   Construction of the Brooklyn Bridge is completed.

1884   Mark Twain publishes *The Adventures of Huckleberry Finn*.

1885   Sharpshooter Annie Oakley and Lakota chief Sitting Bull join Buffalo Bill's Wild West traveling show.

1886   Coca-Cola is introduced in Atlanta, Georgia.

        The Statue of Liberty is dedicated.

1889   Commissioned by Thomas Edison, William Kennedy Laurie Dickinson devises the first motion-picture camera, the Kinetograph.

        George Eastman seeks a patent on motion-picture roll film.

1890   Jacob Riis's first photographs of New York City slums appear in the *New York Sun*.

1891   Carnegie Hall opens in New York City.

        James Naismith introduces the indoor game of basketball.

1892   Henry Ford produces his first car.

1893   Richard Warren Sears offers his first mail-order catalog.

        The World's Columbian Exposition Fair is held in Chicago.

1894   The first Kinetoscope parlor opens in New York City.

1895   Joseph Pulitzer's *New York World* prints comics by Richard Outcault, featuring a boy wearing a yellow nightshirt: "The Yellow Kid."

1896   The modern Olympic Games open in Athens, Greece, with the United States capturing the most gold medals.

        Ragtime becomes a popular musical genre.

1897   John Philip Sousa composes "Stars and Stripes Forever."

1897   Rudolph Dirks's *The Katzenjammer Kids* appears in William Randolph Hearst's *New York Journal*, the first comic strip to offer a story through a series of panels.

1899   Scott Joplin's "Maple Leaf Rag" is the first ragtime song to become a sheet music bestseller.

Walter Camp announces his first annual "All-American" football team.

1900   The Brownie is the first mass-marketed camera.

1903   Major league baseball's first World Series is held, pitting the Boston Americans against the Pittsburgh Pirates.

Orville and Wilbur Wright undertake their first successful plane flight.

Edwin S. Porter directs the silent film *The Great Train Robbery*.

W.E.B. DuBois publishes *The Souls of Black Folk*.

1904   George M. Cohan's Broadway hit *Little Johnny Jones* helps to initiate indigenous musical theater in the United States.

1906   Upton Sinclair publishes *The Jungle*.

1907   Florenz Ziegfeld presents *Ziegfeld's Follies* on Broadway.

1908   Henry Ford produces the first Model T automobile.

1909   The National Association for the Advancement of Colored People (NAACP) is founded.

Isabel Gordon Curtis publishes *The Good Housekeeping Woman's Home Cookbook*.

The first plastic bakelite is produced.

Frank Lloyd Wright builds the Robie House in the Hyde Park neighborhood of Chicago.

1910   Two billion dollars worth of Tin Pan Alley sheet music is sold.

Fanny Brice and Bert Williams make their first appearances in *Ziegfeld's Follies*.

1911   Songwriter Irving Berlin presents "Alexander's Ragtime Band."

1912   Songwriter W.C. Handy composes "Memphis Blues."

1913   *Billboard* magazine issues a list of the most popular vaudeville songs.

The Armory Show is held in New York City, introducing "modern art" to the American public.

Darktown Follies opens in Harlem.

1914   Charlie Chaplin appears as his film character The Little Tramp.

1915   D.W. Griffith's silent epic film *The Birth of a Nation* is released, leading to protest and even some riots.

The Ku Klux Klan is reorganized.

1917   The United States enters World War I.

The Original Dixieland Jazz Band releases the first jazz record, which sells 1 million copies.

The Pulitzer Prizes are established.

1918   A "red scare" sweeps across the United States in reaction to the Bolshevik Revolution.

1919   Chicago emerges as the jazz capital of the United States.

Several members of the Chicago White Sox agree to "throw" the World Series to the Cincinnati Reds.

1920   The Nineteenth Amendment to the U.S. Constitution is ratified, declaring "The right of citizens of the United States to vote shall not be denied or abridged by the United States or by any State on account of sex."

Prohibition begins in the United States.

Newspapers report the "sale" of Babe Ruth to the New York Yankees.

The first commercial radio broadcast airs.

F. Scott Fitzgerald publishes *This Side of Paradise*.

Eugene O'Neill's play *Beyond the Horizon* opens on Broadway.

1920   The Negro National League and the American Pro Football Association (later the National Football League) are formed.

1921   Rudolph Valentino stars in the silent film *The Sheik*.

Noble Sissle and Eubie Blake present *Shuffle Along*, an all-black musical, on Broadway.

The first Miss America beauty pageant is won by Margaret Gorman.

1922   Louis "Satchmo" Armstrong joins Joe "King" Oliver's Creole Jazz Band.

1923   Bessie Smith records "Downhearted Blues."

The Cotton Club opens in Harlem, featuring black performers and white audiences.

1924   George Gershwin composes *Rhapsody in Blue*.

1925   The "Scopes Monkey Trial" involving the teaching of evolution in public schools takes place in Dayton, Tennessee.

The WSM Barn Dance, later called The Grand Ole Opry, airs its first broadcast.

F. Scott Fitzgerald publishes *The Great Gatsby*.

Swedish film actress Greta Garbo and director Maurits Stiller relocate to Hollywood.

1926   Ernest Hemingway publishes *The Sun Also Rises*.

Modern dance pioneer Martha Graham presents her first performance in New York City.

1927   Italian anarchist immigrants Nicola Sacco and Bartolomeo Vanzetti are executed.

Charles Lindbergh undertakes the first solo trans-Atlantic flight in his plane *Spirit of St. Louis*.

The Jazz Singer becomes the first full-length motion picture "talkie."

1927   Based on a novel by Edna Ferber, *Show Boat*, with music by Jerome Kern and lyrics by Oscar Hammerstein, becomes an enormously popular musical.

General Electric produces the modern flashbulb.

Babe Ruth breaks his own single season home run record, belting sixty altogether.

Failing to head for a neutral corner, former champion Jack Dempsey loses in a rematch against Gene Tunney for the heavyweight boxing championship. The incident is referred to as "the long count."

1928   Philo T. Farnsworth demonstrates television transmission of motion pictures.

General Electric opens its first television station in Schenectady, New York.

Eastman Kodak offers color film for 16mm movie cameras.

Walt Disney releases the first Mickey Mouse cartoon, *Steamboat Willie*.

1929   The first Academy Awards ceremony is held in Hollywood.

Ernest Hemingway publishes *A Farewell to Arms*.

The New York Stock Exchange crashes, helping to trigger the Great Depression.

Abby Aldrich Rockefeller opens the Museum of Modern Art in New York City.

1930   The amateur Bobby Jones wins the Grand Slam of golf: the U.S. Open, the British Open, the U.S. Amateur, and the British Amateur championships.

1931   Construction of the Empire State Building is completed in New York City making it the tallest building in the world.

Of Thee I Sing, written by George S. Kaufman and Morrie Ryskind and scored by George and Ira Gershwin, becomes the first musical to win the Pulitzer Prize for Drama.

1932   Amelia Earhart becomes the first woman to fly solo across the Atlantic Ocean.

The Museum of Modern Art offers an exhibition on modern architecture, organized by Philip Johnson, referring to the "International Style."

Radio City Music Hall opens in New York City.

1933   President Franklin Delano Roosevelt delivers his first of thirty fireside chats broadcast nationally over radio.

1934   Folklorist John Lomax records Huddie "Leadbelly" Ledbetter at the Angola Prison Farm in Louisiana.

Singer Ella Fitzgerald debuts at Harlem's Apollo Theater.

1935   George Gershwin presents the opera *Porgy and Bess*.

Clarinetist Benny Goodman is called the "King of Swing."

The New Deal Works Progress Administration initiates the Federal Theater Project.

1936   Electric guitars debut.

Blues guitarist Robert Johnson makes his first recordings in San Antonio, Texas.

Dorothea Lange snaps the photograph "Migrant Mother."

Sprinter–broad jumper Jesse Owens wins four gold medals at the Berlin Olympics.

1937   Frank Lloyd Wright completes the house Fallingwater at Bear Run, Pennsylvania.

1938   Edward R. Murrow and William Shirer broadcast a "European News Roundup" for CBS radio, reporting on Nazi Germany's annexation of Austria.

Orson Welles's radio broadcast of *The War of the Worlds* causes national hysteria.

Cliquot Club ginger ale is the first canned soft drink.

Superman appears in *Action Comics* #1.

1938 Don Budge is the first tennis player to win the sport's Grand Slam: the Australian, French, Wimbledon, and U.S. Open championships.

1939 The World's Fair opens in New York City.

John Steinbeck publishes *The Grapes of Wrath*.

The epic film *Gone with the Wind*, based on Margaret Mitchell's novel, premieres in Atlanta.

WGY-TV in Schenectady, New York, becomes the first commercial television station.

New York Yankee first baseman Lou Gehrig, afflicted with the disease that would bear his name, ends his streak of 2,130 consecutive games played.

1940 Dizzy Gillespie helps to introduce bebop jazz.

Ernest Hemingway publishes *For Whom the Bell Tolls*.

Richard Wright publishes *Native Son*.

Edward R. Murrow reports from London during the Blitz.

1941 Japanese planes bomb Pearl Harbor, leading to an American declaration of war.

Orson Welles directs his film classic, *Citizen Kane*.

Detroit Tiger slugger Hank Greenberg is the first major league star to be drafted into the U.S. military during early World War II.

New York Yankee star Joe DiMaggio establishes a 56-game hitting streak, while Boston Red Sox slugger Ted Williams bats .406, the last major league player to hit .400 or better.

1942 The T-shirt is introduced.

The first electronic computer is built in the United States.

Casablanca premieres, starring Humphrey Bogart and Ingrid Bergman.

1943 Richard Rodgers and Oscar Hammerstein's *Oklahoma!* opens on Broadway.

1944   "Beat Generation" writers Allen Ginsberg, William S. Burroughs, and Jack Kerouac first meet in New York City.

1945   The United States drops atomic bombs on the Japanese cities of Hiroshima and Nagasaki.

Jackie Robinson signs a minor league contract with the Brooklyn Dodgers, breaking the twentieth-century color barrier in organized baseball.

Frank Lloyd Wright designs the Guggenheim Museum in New York City.

1946   The post–World War II "baby boom" begins.

Pediatrician Benjamin Spock publishes *The Common Book of Baby and Child Care*.

Bikini swimwear is introduced.

1947   Polaroid cameras and transistors are invented.

The first American television soap opera, *A Woman to Remember*, is broadcast.

The opening contest between the New York Yankees and the Brooklyn Dodgers is the first World Series game to be televised.

The House Committee on Un-American Activities initiates an investigation of the Hollywood film industry.

NBC's *Meet the Press* has its first television broadcast.

Tennessee Williams's *A Streetcar Named Desire* opens on Broadway starring Marlon Brando and Jessica Tandy.

1948   CBS-TV News with Douglas Edwards offers the first network nightly newscast.

Columbia Records introduces the long-playing 33-1/3 rpm record.

The first 35mm Nikon camera becomes available.

The first cable television systems in the United States appear.

1949   45-rpm records are sold in the United States.

1949 Hank Williams makes his debut on the stage of the Grand Ole Opry.

1950 Senator Joseph McCarthy claims he has discovered the presence of 205 known Communists in the U.S. State Department.

The United States enters the Korean War.

The first modern credit card is issued by Diners Club.

Charles Schultz draws his *Peanuts* comic strip.

1951 Color television is introduced.

Cleveland disc jockey Alan Freed talks about "rock and roll" music.

CBS broadcaster Edward R. Murrow hosts *See It Now*, a television documentary program.

I Love Lucy premieres, launching the American situation comedy.

1952 Car seat belts are introduced.

Sam Phillips opens Sun Records in Memphis, Tennessee.

The avant-garde musician-artist John Cage offers the silent composition *4'33"*.

Les Paul mass produces electric guitars.

1953 The New York Yankees, led by manager Casey Stengel and centerfielder Mickey Mantle, win their fifth consecutive World Series championship.

1954 In the case of *Brown v. Board of Education*, the U.S. Supreme Court asserts that racial segregation is impermissible in the field of public education.

"Rock Around the Clock" by Bill Haley and the Comets is the first rock and roll hit by a white band.

1955 Disneyland Park opens in Anaheim, California.

Actor James Dean dies in a car crash.

Ray Kroc opens his first McDonald's restaurant.

Singer-songwriter Chuck Berry records "Maybellene" for Chess Records in Chicago.

1955 The Museum of Modern Art presents the photographic exhibit "The Family of Man."

Beat poet Allen Ginsberg orchestrates the Six Gallery poetry reading and Lawrence Ferlinghetti establishes City Lights Bookstore, both in San Francisco.

1956 Elvis Presley's appearance on *The Ed Sullivan Show* causes a furor.

Tennis player Althea Gibson becomes the first African-American to win Grand Slam events, capturing the French Open, Wimbledon, and the U.S. Open championships.

Douglas Edwards and CBS News offer the first television program broadcast from tape.

1957 Dr. Seuss publishes the children's book *The Cat in the Hat.*

The Soviets launch *Sputnik.*

Leonard Bernstein presents *West Side Story* on Broadway.

Viking Press publishes Jack Kerouac's *On the Road.*

1958 *Billboard* presents its Hot 100 chart.

The Brooklyn Dodgers and the New York Giants begin the new major league season residing in Los Angeles and San Francisco, respectively.

The Baltimore Colts defeat the New York Giants 23–17 in the first overtime game in National Football League history, winning the NFL title.

1959 A scandal brews over the fixing of television quiz shows.

The National Academy of Recording Arts and Sciences bestows its first Grammy Award.

Berry Gordy Jr. founds Motown Records in Detroit.

The new American Football League is organized.

The Barbie doll debuts at the American International Toy Fair in New York.

1960 Demonstrators engage in sit-ins at lunch counters and bus stations to challenge Jim Crow racial segregation practices.

1960 The Student Nonviolent Coordinating Committee, Students for a Democratic Society, and Young Americans for Freedom are founded.

John F. Kennedy and Richard M. Nixon appear in the first televised presidential debates.

The Federal Drug Administration authorizes the sale of Enovid-10, the birth-control pill.

Timothy Leary and Richard Alpert initiate the Harvard Psilocybin Project.

Edward R. Murrow hosts the documentary *Harvest of Shame*, about migrant farm workers in the United States.

1961 Black and white civil rights activists participate in "freedom rides" to contest segregation in interstate transportation.

Henry Miller's *Tropic of Cancer* is published in the United States.

Marvel Comics presents Stan Lee's *The Fantastic Four*.

Roger Maris breaks Babe Ruth's thirty-four-year-old single season home run record.

1962 Actress Marilyn Monroe dies from an apparent drug overdose.

Pop artist Andy Warhol crafts his *32 Campbell's Soup Cans*.

Rachel Carson's *Silent Spring*, Edward Albee's *Who's Afraid of Virginia Woolf?*, and Ken Kesey's *One Flew Over the Cuckoo's Nest* are published.

Philadelphia Warrior star center Wilt Chamberlain scores 100 in a single game; he averages 50.4 points a game during the regular season.

1963 Betty Friedan publishes *The Feminine Mystique*.

Martin Luther King Jr. delivers his "I have a dream" speech to a crowd of 250,000 at the Washington Mall.

President John F. Kennedy is assassinated while riding in a presidential motorcade in Dallas, Texas. CBS anchor Walter Cronkite's reporting on the death and the subsequent shooting of the president's purported assassin helps Cronkite become the most respected figure on American television.

1963 Bob Dylan's "Blowin' in the Wind," sung by Peter, Paul, and Mary, becomes an iconic anthem for the civil rights movement.

Polaroid markets instant color film and instamatic cameras.

1964 The Beatles arrive at Kennedy Airport, fueling Beatlemania in the United States.

Cassius Clay wins the heavyweight boxing championship with a technical knockout of Sonny Liston. Clay soon proclaims himself a Muslim whose nonslave name is Muhammad Ali.

The 1964 Civil Rights Act is passed.

Race riots occur in Harlem and elsewhere, a recurrent event during the 1960s summers.

The Warren Report on the assassination of President Kennedy is released.

The Berkeley Free Speech movement begins.

Fiddler on the Roof opens on Broadway.

1965 Black Muslim leader Malcolm X is assassinated in New York.

In the case of *Griswold v. Connecticut*, the U.S. Supreme Court refers to the protection of privacy in overturning a state statute restricting the use of contraceptives by married couples.

The 1965 Voting Rights Act is passed.

President Lyndon B. Johnson dramatically escalates U.S. involvement in the Vietnam War.

Helen Gurley Brown, author of the 1962 bestseller *Sex and the Single Girl*, is named editor-in-chief of *Cosmopolitan* magazine.

Folk rock becomes popular thanks to groups like the Byrds, the Lovin' Spoonful, and the Mamas & the Papas. The Grateful Dead (first called the Warlocks) and Jefferson Airplane (first called the Great Society), two of the most important bands influenced by psychedelics, make their initial appearances.

E-mail or electronic mail is used to facilitate communication between various users of a time-sharing mainframe computer.

1966   The Black Panther Party is established.

Acid or psychedelic rock becomes increasingly popular.

Star Trek premiers as a television series.

The Boston Celtics, coached by Red Auerbach and led by center Bill Russell, win their eighth consecutive National Basketball Association championship.

1967   The first Super Bowl is played between the Green Bay Packers and the Kansas City Chiefs.

Approximately 200,000 attend the three-day Monterey International Pop Music Festival in Monterey, California, to hear The Who, Jimi Hendrix, Janis Joplin, and Otis Redding.

The media proclaim the "Summer of Love" in the Haight-Ashbury district of San Francisco.

Rowan & Martin's *Laugh-In* debuts as a television special.

1968   During the Tet Offensive in Vietnam, CBS television anchor Walter Cronkite editorializes that the war is not winnable.

Civil rights leader Martin Luther King Jr. is assassinated in Memphis, Tennessee.

Presidential candidate Senator Robert F. Kennedy is assassinated in Los Angeles, California.

Television cameras record as violence erupts in Chicago during the Democratic Party National Convention.

Sprinters Tommie Smith and John Carlos give a Black Power salute during the Mexico City Olympics.

Detroit Tiger pitcher Denny McClain wins thirty-one games, the first pitcher in thirty-four years to win at least thirty.

The rock musical *Hair* opens on Broadway.

Protest erupts during the Miss America beauty pageant, with feminists crowning a sheep and tossing away beauty devices, including bras.

1969   Astronaut Neil Armstrong is the first man to walk on the moon.

1969 Approximately 400,000 people attend the Woodstock music festival in upstate New York; many popular musicians and groups perform during the four-day event.

Over 500,000 demonstrators gather in Washington, DC, to protest the war in Vietnam.

The Altamont Free Concert erupts in violence at the Altamont Speedway in California.

The children's program *Sesame Street* first airs on PBS.

1970 Computer floppy disks are introduced.

Four students are killed during antiwar protests at Kent State University in Ohio, and two at Jackson State College in Mississippi.

Gary Trudeau's comic strip *Doonesbury* appears in daily newspapers.

1971 Videocassette recorders are introduced.

Ray Tomlison introduces the first network e-mail.

Alvin Toffler publishes *Future Shock.*

The Kennedy Center for the Performing Arts opens in Washington, DC.

1972 Swimmer Mark Spitz captures seven gold medals at the Summer Olympics in Munich, Germany, an event clouded by terrorism.

The first revelations of the Watergate scandal surface.

1973 The Supreme Court ruling in the case of *Roe v. Wade* allows for legalized abortion.

Billie Jean King and Bobby Riggs compete in a televised tennis match called "The Battle of the Sexes," won in straight sets by King.

Secretariat becomes the first horse in twenty-five years to win the Triple Crown of thoroughbred racing: the Kentucky Derby, the Preakness, and the Belmont Stakes.

John McCain returns home after five and a half years as a prisoner in North Vietnam.

1974   Newspaper heiress Patty Hearst is kidnapped by members of the Symbionese Liberation Army.

President Richard Nixon resigns in the midst of impeachment proceedings.

Singer Patti Smith issues her version of "Hey Joe," considered the first punk rock single.

Hank Aaron breaks Babe Ruth's lifetime home run record.

Notre Dame ends the eighty-eight consecutive game winning streak of UCLA, which is led by its legendary basketball coach John Wooden.

1975   Tennis star Arthur Ashe becomes the first black man to win the Wimbledon championship.

CBGB (Country Bluegrass & Blues) in New York City showcases punk rock.

Saturday Night Live debuts on NBC to replace reruns of *The Best of Carson.*

1976   The National Endowment for the Arts is established.

The United States holds its Bicentennial celebration.

Alex Haley publishes *Roots: The Saga of an American Family*, which is adapted as a television miniseries in 1977.

Country singer Willie Nelson releases *Wanted! The Outlaws.*

1977   Elvis Presley is found dead at his Graceland mansion.

The film *Star Wars* is released.

The film *Saturday Night Fever* helps trigger disco mania.

The Apple home computer is introduced.

1978   Hip hop dance emerges in the South Bronx.

The movie *Animal House* is released, starring John Belushi.

1979   Sony markets the Walkman, a portable audio-cassette player.

The Sugar Hill Gang releases "Rapper's Delight," the first commercial hit rap song.

1979   ABC News airs nightly coverage of *The Iran Crisis—America Held Hostage*, which later becomes the news program *Nightline* with Ted Koppel.

1980   Former Beatle John Lennon is assassinated in front of the Dakota apartments in New York City.

The United States and several of its allies boycott the Moscow Olympics in response to the Soviet invasion of Afghanistan.

Ted Turner establishes CNN, a twenty-four–hour news network.

Sony introduces the first camcorder for consumers.

1981   The AIDS epidemic becomes front-page news.

IBM introduces personal computers.

MTV begins operations on cable television.

1982   Singer Michael Jackson releases *Thriller*.

Cats opens on Broadway.

1983   *La Cage aux Folles* opens on Broadway as the AIDs crisis sweeps across the nation.

Motorola DynaTAC offers the first mobile phone, approved by the Federal Communications Commission (FCC), in the United States.

1984   Sony presents the first high-definition television system.

Sprinter–broad jumper Carl Lewis wins four gold medals at the Los Angeles Olympics, which is boycotted by the Soviet Union and several of its allies, in retaliation for the U.S. boycott of the Moscow Games in 1980.

Madonna's *Like a Virgin* tops the U.S. album chart.

1985   Pixar develops the first digital imaging processor.

The multi-venue Live Aid rock concert is held to provide relief for famine-ravaged Ethiopia, shortly followed by a Farm Aid benefit concert to save U.S. family farms from foreclosure.

1986   The *Challenger* space shuttle explodes after liftoff.

1988   Compact disks outsell vinyl records.

1988   The *Washington Post*'s Thomas Boswell charges that baseball slugger Jose Canseco is "the most conspicuous example of a player who has made himself great with steroids."

1989   The Loma Prieta earthquake interrupts the World Series between the San Francisco Giants and the Oakland Athletics.

1991   Nirvana's song "Smells Like Teen Spirit" helps spark the grunge movement.

        The Internet World Wide Web becomes public.

1992   Compact disks outsell cassette tapes.

        Michael Jordan heads a list of All-Star players on the Dream Team, the basketball squad representing the United States during the Barcelona Olympics.

1994   Former football star O.J. Simpson is arrested for murdering his former wife Nicole Brown Simpson and her friend Ron Goldman.

        Labor strife results in cancellation of the World Series.

        Blogging, through which individuals provide accounts of their personal lives, becomes popular on the Internet.

1995   The Murrah Federal Building in Oklahoma City is destroyed by a bomb that kills 168 people.

        The Rock and Roll Hall of Fame Museum opens in Cleveland, Ohio.

        Jeff Bezos launches the retail website Amazon.com.

        Pierre Omidyar launches an online auction site—the future eBay.

1996   The personal digital assistant, the PalmPilot, is manufactured.

        Rupert Murdoch's Fox News Channel premieres on cable with personalities including talk show host Bill O'Reilly.

1997   Tiger Woods becomes the first African-American golfer to win the Masters tournament.

        Princess Diana dies in an automobile accident in Paris.

        British author J.K. Rowling publishes *Harry Potter and the Sorcerer's Stone*.

1998   The online *Drudge Report* leaks news of a scandal involving President Bill Clinton and a White House intern.

St. Louis Cardinal Mark McGwire and Chicago Cub Sammy Sosa both break the single season major league home run record.

1999   The "Pop Lolita" trend soars with the success of teenage performers Britney Spears and Christina Aguilera.

Jon Stewart becomes the host of the Comedy Central cable network's satirical news program *The Daily Show*.

President Bill Clinton, impeached by the U.S. House of Representatives on December 19, 1998, is acquitted by the U.S. Senate on February 12.

2000   Widespread concerns center on the possibility of software problems that might disable computers when the calendar advances to the year 2000, or Y2K.

The 2000 presidential election results in a virtual tie, with the U.S. Supreme Court ultimately handing down a decision on December 12 favoring Texas governor George W. Bush over Vice President Al Gore.

2001   Jennifer Lopez becomes the first actress-singer to have both a movie, *The Wedding Planner*, and an album, *J.Lo*, positioned as #1 at the same time.

The reality show *Survivor* becomes the top-rated American television program.

Tiger Wood wins the Masters tournament, enabling him to become the first golfer to simultaneously hold all four of the men's professional majors: the Masters, the U.S. Open, the British Open, and the P.G.A. Championship.

Apple Inc. introduces iTunes.

Terrorists attack the World Trade Center and the Pentagon. President George W. Bush proclaims a "war on terror."

San Francisco slugger Barry Bonds breaks the single season home run record.

2001   Apple Inc. launches iPod, a portable media player.

The action-drama series *24* presents a tale of political espionage in real time over the course of the television season.

2002   Filmmaker Michael Moore's *Bowling for Columbine* examines the culture of guns and violence in the United States.

American Idol, the singing competition, debuts on the Fox television network.

Computer programmer Jonathan Abrams founds Friendster, an Internet social networking website.

2003   The United States sends military units to oust Iraqi strongman Saddam Hussein. Reporters are embedded with the troops.

MySpace provides a social networking website for teenagers and adults.

2004   The Facebook website is founded by a Harvard University student.

Illinois state senator Barack Obama delivers a well-received speech at the Democratic National Convention in Boston.

Filmmaker Michael Moore's *Fahrenheit 9/11* presents an embittered look at President George W. Bush and the war on terror.

2005   YouTube provides a video-sharing website.

The Colbert Report debuts on Comedy Central starring *The Daily Show* regular Stephen Colbert as a television pundit.

Hurricane Katrina hits the U.S. Gulf Coast and devastates the city of New Orleans.

2006   Nintendo releases the Wii in North America.

"Godfather of Soul" singer James Brown dies at age seventy-three.

2007   Filmmaker Michael Moore's *Sicko* explores the American health system, comparing it unfavorably with those in France, Great Britain, Canada, and Cuba.

Apple unveils the iPhone, a multimedia smart phone that is Internet-connected.

2007 The Mitchell Report, *The Report to the Commission of Baseball of an Independent Investigation into the Illegal use of Steroids and Other Performance Enhancing Substances by Players in Major League Baseball*, is released.

2008 Swimmer Michael Phelps wins eight gold medals at the Beijing Olympics.

Senator Barack Obama of Illinois defeats Senator John McCain and becomes the first African-American elected president of the United States.

2009 U.S. Airways pilot Captain Chesley Sullenberger III makes an emergency landing in the Hudson River, saving all 155 passengers, after his aircraft's engines are disabled by a flock of geese.

President Barack Obama's inauguration draws record crowds in Washington, DC, and media viewers around the world.

"King of Pop" Michael Jackson dies at age fifty.

General Motors, founded in 1908 and the world's second largest automaker, emerges from Chapter 11 bankruptcy reorganization planning to pare down U.S. production to four of its oldest brands: Buick, Cadillac, Chevrolet, and GMC.

Reader's Digest, founded in 1922 and still the best-selling general interest magazine in the United States, files for Chapter 11 bankruptcy protection to restructure its finances.

ICONS
of
American
Popular
Culture

ONE

Democratic Showmen

JAMES GORDON BENNETT AND P.T. BARNUM

The foundation for modern American popular culture emerged during the three decades before the Civil War. Antebellum America witnessed technological changes that dramatically affected leisure and work patterns alike. As historians have recognized, Americans increasingly became dependent on recreation provided by others as a kind of commodity. Technological and entrepreneurial genius enabled a type of "democratic entertainment" to prevail in the very period when the Age of the Common Man experienced sweeping transformations in the political realm. While even the earliest Puritan colonists in British North America had sought to enliven their existence through sports and games, Americans now expected figures like James Gordon Bennett and P.T. Barnum to enrich their lives through an association with both everyday affairs and the spectacular. Helpful of course was the weakening of the Protestant ethic or at least its harsh, Calvinist strain, which emphasized austerity, toil, and thrift, and the greater popularity of other versions of Christianity that offered a more hopeful, optimistic perspective. The latter proved more in keeping with the America of the Jacksonian period with its buoyancy, belief in progress, and entrepreneurial gamesmanship. Antebellum Americans, like their predecessors and successors, nevertheless battled over religious matters, including those that supposedly pertained to everyday affairs.

Still, heightened literacy, technological advances, and greater affluence, even in the midst of a volatile economic order, provided the backdrop in which popular culture thrived. The literacy rate, already relatively high during the colonial period and the era of early nationhood increased among whites and free blacks. Patrons readily encountered bookstores and libraries in the largest metropolitan areas. Major publishing houses first appeared. Technological improvements proved equally important, with the ushering in of inexpensive cloth bindings during the 1810s, then refined bookbinding mechanisms in the following decade. During the 1830s, Harper, Matthew Carey, and Thomas, Cummings and Hilliard became great publishing concerns. Helpful too was the appearance of improved oil lamps, then gas lighting, which lengthened the time available for reading. "Cheap publishing," however, awaited the 1840s, following the disastrous depression of 1837 that crippled the book industry. To reduce costs, publishers resorted to newspaper presses and took advantage of special mailing rates and free postal delivery. Weekly periodicals now contained fiction, which transformed the newspaper industry and attracted readers. This continued a trend begun the previous decade when newspapers underwent marked transformations from the staid, prosaic publications of previous eras.

Relying on printing presses, journalists like Bennett slashed prices, witnessed soaring circulations, and reaped considerable profits. The first penny newspaper, the *New York Sun*, appeared in 1833. That was soon followed by the *New York Herald*, published by Bennett, who initiated a new era of personal journalism and came to be viewed as the father of the modern American newspaper. Daily circulation figures multiplied fourfold to 300,000 by 1840, while twice as many weekly newspapers could be found. The interest of readers was piqued by the focus on human-interest tales involving vicious felonies and vagabond children. Helpful too was the manner in which newsboys aggressively hawked their wares on street corners. Bennett consequently helped to cement the popularity of the inexpensive, mass circulation newspaper. The mass publication of books, many of a cheap variety, led the poet Edgar Allen Poe to charge, "Certain books lately printed induce us to believe that some people think by machine."

Entertainment of a nonliterate variety also was available to antebellum Americans. P.T. Barnum bought a dilapidated museum in 1841 in New York City, soon renamed the American Museum. Barnum, in contrast to earlier museum owners, did not strive merely to educate patrons, displaying stuffed birds and animals, interesting rock formations, and paintings. Barnum instead sought to titillate, to arouse public interest by exhibiting the strange and the wonderful, including ventriloquists, magicians, and albinos. He also featured a young midget he called General Tom Thumb and the so-called Feejee Mermaid, which Barnum insisted had "been taken alive in the Feejee Islands." The American Museum was the best known of any in the United States by the end of the decade. Barnum later became identified with another popular cultural phenomenon, the "Barnum and Bailey Greatest Show on Earth," the largest circus enterprise in the nation's history.

JAMES GORDON BENNETT

Born in Keith, Banffshire, Scotland, James Gordon Bennett was the oldest son of devout Catholic parents. Spurning their desire that he become a priest, Bennett withdrew from a Catholic seminary at the age of nineteen. Influenced by Benjamin Franklin's *Autobiography*, Bennett sailed for North America, landing in Nova Scotia in 1819, where he toiled as a teacher before moving to Boston. Eventually, the six-foot-tall, slender, well-built young man settled in South Carolina, joining the staff of the *Charleston Courier.* He then worked for a number of other newspapers before becoming a reporter for the *New York Courier,* a Sunday publication. New York City was becoming the nation's leading metropolis and cultural center. Bennett came to believe that "no editor could break the mental and moneyed monopoly held by the old newspapers, except by adopting an extravagant and severe style. . . . People scolded and fretted . . . but they would read, and with most zest devoured those articles which were most declamatory and personal, and least instructive and valuable." He soon moved to the *New York Enquirer,* serving as its Washington correspondent. In 1829, after the *Enquirer* and the *Courier* merged, Bennett, who reasoned that "the world has been humbugged long enough," headed the paper. Operating in the very period when American democracy began to flower, Bennett asserted that "an editor must always be with the people— think with them—feel with them—and he need fear nothing, he will always be right—always be strong—always popular—always free." Following the paper's pronouncement of support for the Whigs, Bennett, who repeatedly encountered barbs that he was a "foreigner," resigned rather than oppose President Andrew Jackson.

In October 1832, Bennett began publishing a daily evening newspaper, the *New York Globe,* in which he expressed continued support for "the principles and nominations of the Democratic party." He favored the late Thomas Jefferson's emphasis on states' rights, in addition to sound economic policies, the "reduction of unnecessary taxes—and the advancement of human liberty and human happiness." Wanting the *Globe* to acquire distinctiveness, Bennett envisioned a newspaper that would be "moderate in size, but neat and manageable, printed on fine paper with beautiful type." The *Globe* soon went out of business. Still, it helped to initiate the penny press or the independent press that was not officially tied to any political organization. Bennett briefly served as an editor and co-owner of the *Pennsylvanian* in Philadelphia, hoping to encourage a drive to ensure that Martin Van Buren become the nominee of the Democratic Party at the close of Jackson's second presidential term. Financial difficulties that the Democrats failed to alleviate resulted in Bennett's estrangement from both the party and Van Buren.

Bennett foundered for a spell, failing to hook up with another paper, such as Ben Day's *New York Sun,* a newspaper that sold for a penny in contrast to its competitors whose editions sold for six cents a copy. Other penny papers had not succeeded, but Day's experiment proved financially lucrative. Moreover, as Bennett recognized, Charles Knight's *Penny Magazine* was thriving in England. After Day turned down his request for a job, the now forty-year-old Bennett, relying on a $500 investment and a pair of friendly printers and operating out of a basement in the Wall Street district, single-handedly put out the first issue of the *New York Herald* on May 6, 1835. The four-page newspaper, sized ten-and-a-half by fourteen inches, sold for a penny and proved enormously popular. It ushered in a new age of personal journalism while altering American journalism and reading habits. Fifteen daily newspapers catered to the reading whims of the 270,000 inhabitants of New York City. The timing proved propitious for Bennett's venture in personal journalism thanks to both the surge in the nation's population, abetted by high levels of Irish and German immigration, and advances in printing technology. Bennett delivered the following pledge in the first issue of the *Herald*:

> Our only guide shall be good sound practical common sense, applicable to the business and bosoms of men engaged in every-day life. We shall support no party, be the organ of no faction or COTERIE, and care nothing for any election or any candidate from president down to a constable. We shall endeavor to record facts on every public and property subject, stripped of verbiage and coloring, with comments suitable, just, independent, fearless and good-tempered.

Bennett sought to appeal to a wide spectrum of New Yorkers, including "the great masses of the community" ranging from businessmen to workers. His first issue offered book reviews, a story on spring apparel, news of events in Europe, theatrical information, a look at the population of New York City, a police court account, political tidbits, listings of marriages and deaths, advertising, poems, and fictional pieces, among other items.

The second issue appeared following a short delay, along with Bennett's promise to provide "a correct picture of the world," including Wall Street, the Stock Exchange, police operations, the theater, and the opera, or "wherever human nature and real life best displays their freaks and vagaries." Unlike other editors, Bennett offered greater variety, more international coverage, "theatrical chit-chat," stock market reports, and his own, often sharply drawn editorials. He tracked political machinations involving the fledgling Tammany Hall. He discovered "the hollow-heartedness and humbuggery of . . . political associations and political men." He initially covered all such stories himself, producing reports that piqued public interest and angered Wall Street operators. While offering the financial news and presenting stock lists, he strove to "tell what Wall Street really is and what is done there."

During the *Herald*'s first year of publication, a fire destroyed the plant that printed the newspaper, which was promptly suspended for nineteen days. A promise to advertise Brandreth's Pills, a patent medicine, possibly helped save Bennett's publication. Once the *Herald* was back in circulation, it would be "larger, livelier, better, prettier, saucier, and more independent than ever," he promised. The *Herald* attained a circulation of 40,000 within fifteen months, with newsboys helping to deliver the paper, but its editor's ambitions remained greater still. As he soon indicated, "Shakespeare is the great genius of the drama, Scott of the novel, Milton and Byron of the poem—and I mean to be the genius of the newspaper press." Other newspaper publishers, Bennett wrote, were "lazy, ignorant, indolent, blustering blockheads," while he awakened at five in the morning, knocking out editorials and reports before breakfast. He scoured through the papers of competitors and correspondence starting at nine o'clock, seeking "facts, thoughts, hints, and incidents sufficient to make up a column of original spicy articles." He also met with visitors ranging from businessmen to "some of the loveliest ladies in New York." He sauntered down to Wall Street in the early afternoon before returning to his office, where he completed the paper's edition by four o'clock.

The advent of the independent penny press, as best exemplified by the *Sun* and the *Herald*, proved to be of no little import. In the spirit of an age when reform movements were in vogue, Bennett imagined the daily newspaper becoming "the greatest organ of social life," surpassing books, the theater, and religion in importance. A newspaper, he wrote, "can send more souls to Heaven, and save more from Hell, than all the churches or chapels in New York—besides making money at the same time." As for his part, Bennett promised to "speak on every occasion the words of truth and soberness," even if that involved an examination of "human depravity to the core." He did so even in regular Sunday editions, to the chagrin of offended ministers. A mere nine months after the *Herald* included advertisements for Brandreth's Pills, Bennett sought to warn "the public throughout the country, from being any longer deceived and cheated by the quackeries of this most impudent charlatan."

Like other penny newspapers in New York City, the *Herald* rhapsodized about sexual affairs and sporting events, covering boxing matches and horse races, along with other sports. The paper played up the murder of Ellen Jewett, a beautiful young prostitute, slain with a hatchet in April 1836. The *Herald's* circulation tripled in a manner of days. Accused of "poor taste," Bennett strove to expand his audience, relying on jaunty humor. He subsequently was credited with or blamed for "having invented news as we know it today. . . . None of the existing taboos or sacred cows were respected by this irrepressible reporter." The sometimes racy nature of the paper led Park Benjamin of the *New York Signal* to initiate a "Moral War" against the *Herald*, decrying its purported "indecency, blasphemy, libel, and blackmail." The *Herald's* determination to print the news in a manner befitting Bennett also resulted in numerous libel actions, requiring him to retain an "abundance of counsel." Bennett's doggedness and emphasis on crime, vice, and sex also made him, his biographer Oliver Carlson suggests, "the real father of 'yellow journalism.'"

The *Herald*'s exhibitionism helped to make Bennett a rich man but alienated many, including a former employer, James Watson Webb, who supported the Whig position and scuffled with the publisher at one point. Not about to pass up the opportunity to relay such news, Bennett reported that Webb had come "up behind me, cut a slash in my head about one and a half inch in length, and through the integuments of the skull." Bennett insisted he would not be intimidated nor would he alter his approach. He bluntly wrote, "Neither Webb nor any other man shall, or can, intimidate me. I tell the honest truth in my paper, and leave the consequences to God. Could I leave them in better hands?" He then asserted, "I may be attacked, I may be assailed, I may be killed, I may be murdered, but I never will succumb. I never will abandon the cause of truth, morals, and virtue." Hubris continued to characterize Bennett, as when he referred to himself as "the NAPOLEON of the newspaper press."

The ever-controversial Bennett continued to expand his news operations while becoming financially comfortable enough to hire first a police reporter and then a managing editor, Frederic Hudson. Bennett initiated the employment of foreign correspondents for the *Herald* as early as 1838, hiring a team of six reporters after a trip to Europe. The next year, Hudson had the *Herald* report on religious conclaves, which led to condemnations of Bennett's "atheism." He took time off from his news operations to marry Henrietta Agnes Crean, an attractive, young Irish woman, on June 6, 1840; the Bennetts eventually had four children, although two died while still youngsters. The controversial nature of her husband's journalistic venture led Henrietta to spend much of her time in Europe. She was evidently much distressed by events such as the "Great Moral War," initiated by publications associated with Wall Street, some of Bennett's competitors in New York, and Whig newspapers, which denounced Bennett, the *Herald*, and its readers as "impious and immoral." Public establishments were pressured not to feature the paper while merchants were threatened with the loss of business if they continued to advertise in the *Herald*. A journalistic assault targeted the *Herald*, which was associated with a "Filthy sheet," "Mass of trash," "Infamous Scotchman," "Prince of darkness," "Contemptible libeler," "Depraved appetite," "Humbug," "Vulgar attacks," "Blasphemy," "Obscenity," "Reckless depravity," "Moral pestilence," "Slanderous abuse," and "Insidious poison," among other infamies. He certainly was a peddler, Bennett admitted, just as Shakespeare and "every great intellectual" had been. He also had been "a wayward, self-dependent, resolute, self-thinking" individual from his youth onward. Yet he adhered to "lofty principles of morals, honor, philosophy, and religion, that the contumely of the world can not shake, or all the editors or bankers in Christendom intimidate." He saw himself as participating "in a great cause—the cause of truth, public faith and science, against falsehood, fraud, and ignorance." His opponents, "these blockheads," Bennett noted, "are determined to make me the greatest man of the age."

The Great Moral War soon withered as the *Herald* continued to prosper: the paper was earning $100,000 annually by 1841. That year, during a special congressional session, Bennett attempted to hire a group of Washington reporters for the then lordly sum of $200 weekly. An infuriated Bennett discovered that Senator Samuel Southard of New Jersey refused to allow the *Herald* correspondents entrée. Bennett proceeded to unveil information about government payments to various local newspapers. The *Herald*, Bennett bristled, would perform the same services free of charge instead of seeing "public money thrown away."

Patriotic and jingoistic, Bennett indicated in 1843 that "the Anglo Saxon race is intended by an over-ruling Providence to carry the principles of liberty, the refinement of civilization, and the advances of the mechanic arts through every land, even those now barbarous. . . . Mexico, too, must submit to the o'erpowering influence of the Anglo Saxon." Favoring the annexation of Texas, he insisted that the United States expand its boundaries to encompass "the whole of North America." Bennett saw a means to convey information more quickly during the Mexican-American War, which would result in a massive expansion of his nation. He believed that the telegraph would only extend the reach of American journalism, soon "more influential than ever" as it offered "tidings of great events" more rapidly. During the Mexican-American War, Bennett turned to the overland express as a newspaper war developed with the *New York Sun*. Linking up with the *Journal of Commerce* and the *New Orleans Crescent City*, Bennett sped up transmission of news reports about the fighting. He also began publishing an overseas edition of the *Herald* in 1846.

Bennett throughout this period continued seeking an edge over competitors. The *Herald* by October 1847 indicated that it had obtained "the long-looked-for intelligence from the city of Mexico." However, the *Herald* acknowledged that the overland express had relayed that information for a host of newspapers, with the expectation that it would be passed on to Washington, DC, and widely disseminated throughout the nation. The newspaper combination thereby reduced expenses but hardly diminished the journalistic war. The *Herald* obtained a scoop regarding a speech on the Mexican-American War by former presidential aspirant Henry Clay. A group of newspapers, including the *Herald*, eventually agreed in 1848 to establish the Harbor News Association and the New York Associated Press. As the gold rush developed out west, the *Herald*, like other eastern newspapers, began printing a California edition.

Bennett's ambitions for his frequently controversial journalistic venture remained as large as ever. As he acknowledged:

> My ambition is to make the newspaper Press the great organ and pivot of government, society, commerce, finance, religion, and all human civilization. I want to leave behind me no castles, no granite hotels, no monuments of marble, no statues of bronze, no pyramids of brick—simply a name. The name of JAMES GORDON BENNETT, as one of the benefactors of the human race, will satisfy every desire and every hope.

No matter his lofty determinations, assaults continued to come Bennett's way. While walking with his wife on Broadway in New York City, Bennett was physically attacked by a recently defeated candidate for district attorney, who joined with his brothers in beating the editor with whips. The *Herald*'s editorial slant perhaps resulted in the attempt in late 1852 to send a bomb to Bennett at his newspaper building. The *Herald*—now eight pages long and sporting three full pages of advertisements—nevertheless remained a popular newspaper, surpassing even the *Sun*'s circulation by the close of the decade. Bennett employed a large network of correspondents, including ones based in the nation's capital, Albany, Europe, Cuba, and Mexico. He offered his own accounts of extensive trips throughout the United States and overseas.

When first South Carolina and then other Southern states opted to secede from the Union, Bennett referred to the "right of revolution" and blasted President Abraham Lincoln and his top advisers for "selfishness, fanaticism, and suicidal imbecility." A mob, containing thousands of Unionists, stood ready to burn down the new building that housed the *Herald* after the Civil War began. Bennett now insisted that the Confederacy be suppressed and he instructed his son to enter the Union navy. The *Herald* remained highly critical of Lincoln and opposed the emancipation of the slaves; Bennett believed in the basic inferiority of African-Americans. Lincoln responded to critical editorials in the *Herald* by writing to Bennett and thanking him for his "able support." The growing power of the daily press also was evidenced when Secretary of War Edwin M. Stanton, a frequent subject of criticism, felt compelled to inform Bennett about "some observations respecting the present state of things as they appear to me." Notwithstanding his earlier criticisms, Bennett eventually backed Lincoln's reelection. Lincoln subsequently proposed in February 1865 that Bennett become the U.S. minister to France, an offer that was declined. Bennett continued to have the *Herald* cover the events of the Civil War on a "day to day" basis. He later contended that he expended half a million dollars in covering the conflagration, using woodcuts and as many as sixty-three reporters in the field. He allegedly ordered his reporters "to obtain the most accurate information by personal observation, and forward it with utmost dispatch, regardless of expense, labor, or danger." The subscriptions figures of the *Herald* soared.

James Gordon Bennett Jr. replaced Frederic Hudson as the *Herald*'s managing editor after the war, before taking over business operations from his father. When the senior Bennett retired in 1867, his famed newspaper had a circulation of 90,000 and annual profits amounting to $400,000, thanks in part to advertising revenues surpassed only by the *London Times*. A contingent of would-be investors offering $2.2 million sought to purchase the *Herald* from the Bennett family by 1869. Bennett established the Pension and Annuity Fund Association of *New York Herald* employees that same year, setting aside $10,000 for medical and death benefits. The workers in turn allowed small amounts to be taken from their weekly paychecks to help ensure the plan's solvency. Bennett died in 1872, only a short while before his longtime competitor Horace Greeley, whom he had earlier referred to as "crazy" and a "monster." An editorial in a rival newspaper insisted that Bennett's career particularly exemplified "prosperous infamy." Bennett was "shrewd, enterprising, audacious, liberal." He was "a quiet-mannered, courteous, and good-natured old gentleman." But, the editorial continued, Bennett still lacked "the sense of truth and honor, public spirit, and patriotism" and "was, in fact, an utterly unscrupulous person" who "peddled" in "obscenity and personal defamation." Other eulogies credited Bennett with having established the modern American newspaper, while Greeley affirmed that the longtime *Herald* editor "was the first journalist who went to meet the news half-way." Following his father's death, James Gordon Bennett Jr. continued to guide the *Herald* into the days when Charles Anderson Dana, William Randolph Hearst, and Joseph Pulitzer again revitalized the newspaper industry. Dana, like Bennett, practiced personal journalism, while Hearst and Pulitzer, again in the fashion of the *Herald* founder, strove for mass audiences, drawing on sensationalistic accounts and human-interest stories.

P.T. BARNUM

America's greatest showman of the nineteenth century, Phineas Taylor Barnum, was born on July 5, 1810, in Bethel, Connecticut, to Irena Taylor and Philo F. Barnum, who at various times farmed, ran a tavern and a livery stable, and operated a country store, among other enterprises. Barnum acquired limited formal education, often remaining out of school in order to help his family on the farm. He attended the Congregational Church with his family, but the Calvinistic fire-and-brimstone sermons appalled him. He subsequently adopted Universalism with its notion of a benevolent deity, which his grandfather favored. Seemingly adverse to manual labor, Barnum acquired his "organ of acquisitiveness" early, conducting small business ventures, even joining in a cattle drive that took him to New York City for the first time when he was perhaps twelve years old. Recognizing that his son "generally contrived to shirk the work altogether, or by slighting it, get through with the day's work," Philo Barnum stopped requesting that he work on the farm, requiring him instead to clerk at the family country store in Bethel.

When business was slow, Barnum spent his time with "six to twenty social, jolly, story-telling, joke-playing wags and wits, regular originals . . . relating anecdotes, describing adventures, playing off practical jokes upon each other, and engaging in every project out of which a little fun could be extracted." Barnum also sold lottery tickets. After his father died, the fifteen-year-old lad attempted to financially care for his mother and five siblings. At one point, however, the drudgery of his work drove Barnum to Brooklyn, where he established a porterhouse pub before becoming a bartender in New York City. As Barnum later acknowledged, "My disposition is, and ever was, of a speculative character, and I am never content to engage in any business unless it is of such a nature that my profits may be greatly enhanced by an increase of energy." On returning to Bethel, Barnum set up a fruit and confectionery store, which succeeded commercially, and he also headed a series of lottery offices across the state. In 1829, the six-foot-two, blue-eyed Barnum, already boasting receding curly hair, married twenty-one-year-old Charity Hallet, "a fair, rosy-cheeked, buxom-looking girl with beautiful white teeth," whom many considered to be "altogether too good" for him but with whom he had four daughters. Following a series of early business setbacks, he began the *Herald of Freedom*, a liberal weekly newspaper, in Danbury, Connecticut, in 1831. He promised to contest "Bigotry, Superstition, Fanaticism, and Hypocrisy" and demanded the separation of church and state. The *Herald of Freedom* championed Andrew Jackson's fledgling Democratic Party, declaring that "the hard-working, tax-paying people have been governed by the aristocracy long enough." A series of libel actions culminated in a fine of $100 and Barnum's incarceration after he charged that a church deacon was "taking usury of an orphan boy." During his sixty-day jail time, Barnum received numerous visitors, including the Danbury Universalist minister.

In late 1834 the Barnums moved to New York City, where he, along with a partner, John Moody, opened a grocery store. To supplement their income, the Barnums also operated a boarding house. Barnum's life and that of American popular culture began to alter dramatically in late July of the following year.

At that point he encountered another native of Connecticut, Coley Bartram, who possessed a bit of experience in show business. Bartram pointed to a copy of the *Pennsylvania Inquirer* that contained an advertisement for "one of the greatest natural curiosities ever witnessed . . . JOYCE HEITH, a negress aged 161 years, who formerly belonged to the father of Gen. Washington" and was about to appear at the Masonic Hall in Philadelphia. The present owner of Heith hoped to sell her. Barnum rushed off to see the blind, toothless Heith, who claimed to have raised George Washington himself. Scraping together $1,000, Barnum purchased the services of the old slave, whom he planned to exhibit at Niblo's Garden, an open-air saloon, in New York City. As he later remembered, "I saw everything depended on getting people to think and talk and become curious and excited." Heith was, Barnum exclaimed in newspaper advertisements, "unquestionably the most astonishing and interesting curiosity in the world." The *Evening Star*, a popular New York newspaper, compared her appearance to that of "an Egyptian mummy just escaped from its sarcophagus." As attested by weekly receipts of $1,500, Heith proved a sensation and Barnum soon displayed her at sites in other large, northeastern cities, including Boston's Concert Hall. Befitting his later career, controversy and charges of fraud swirled about Barnum's exhibit. When Heith died in early 1836, it was apparent that she was no more than seventy years old. His immersion into popular entertainment and the riches that followed nevertheless appealed to Barnum, who later reflected this was "the business for which I was destined."

During an exhibition in Albany, Barnum encountered "Signor Antonio," an Italian immigrant who twirled plates, walked on stilts, and engaged in various balancing acts. Barnum signed the performer, whose name he changed to Signor Vivalla, to a year-long contract, paying twelve dollars weekly along with expenses. Extolling Vivalla's "wonderful qualities and performances," Barnum sent word of his latest find's deft skills to New York City. Barnum's eye for entertainment again appeared keen: audiences packed into the Franklin Theatre to watch the juggler, and performances in Boston were also well received. An engagement in the nation's capital proved far less successful, however, as snow kept crowds down and a financial debacle threatened. Barnum realized that "something must be done to stimulate the public. And now that instinct . . . which can arouse a community and make it patronize . . . came to my relief, and the help, curiously enough, appeared in the shape of an emphatic hiss from the pit!" Attendance in Philadelphia at first proved no better until Barnum came across a circus juggler, Roberts, whom he convinced to compete against Vivalla in a "great trial of skill." The show ran for a month, but engagements in other communities hardly covered expenses. Barnum and Vivalla then linked up with Aaron Turner's circus, which took them from state to state. Barnum just escaped a lynching in Maryland after Turner, determined to pique interest, declared Barnum to be a clergyman who had recently been acquitted on a murder charge. After collecting $1,200 within six months, Barnum began to conduct his own circus, having purchased a tent, wagons, and horses and employed musicians, a dancer, a black singer, and a juggler. After his singer ran away, Barnum donned blackface makeup and performed minstrel songs such as "Zip Coon" and "The Raccoon Hunt, or Sitting on a Rail." As the troupe continued migrating southward, Barnum began calling his show "Barnum's Grand Scientific and Musical Theatre." He purchased a steamboat at one point, offering entertainment as it coursed down the Mississippi River.

"Thoroughly disgusted with the life of an itinerant showman," Barnum returned to New York City in mid-1838. Placing advertisements in local newspapers, Barnum indicated that he had $2,500 to invest in a business that he hoped would be "respectable, permanent." Solicitations poured forth and Barnum chose to back a German manufacturer, Proler, who produced cologne water, bear's grease, and paste-blacking. The two rented a building in the Bowery, but the business quickly foundered. Barnum was left holding a worthless note for $2,600 as his erstwhile partner absconded to Europe. With little capital remaining, Barnum offered a series of performances at Vauxhall Gardens, but the effort flopped badly. Then he came across John Diamond, a terrific black dancer, whom Barnum paired with another dancer from Kentucky. His latest endeavor came to an inglorious end after Diamond ran off. Barnum replaced him with a blackfaced white dancer and a lawsuit pitted the showman against his former employee. The angry judge dismissed the case, terming both parties vagabonds. Barnum next hired agents to sell thousands of copies of Sears' Pictorial Illustration of the Bible, but he reaped few profits from that venture. He was soon "at the foot of fortune's ladder," reduced to crafting advertisements and articles for newspapers.

Having bounced around for the last several years, Barnum discovered in mid-1841 that a $50,000 "collection of curiosities" from across the globe known as Scudder's Museum was for sale. Early museums in the United States were a bit staid even when they contained paintings and "oddities" amassed from far-flung travels. By 1830 John Scudder had relocated the old Tammany Museum to the City Hall and then to its later location at Broadway and Ann Streets, where he operated the American Museum. Lacking showmanship, Scudder nevertheless amassed stuffed birds and reptiles, along with waxwork displays of notorious and celebrated figures. The early American Museum also featured Scudder's "living collection of animals and freaks," ranging from a card-playing dog to a three-foot-tall midget, as Barnum biographer Irving Wallace notes. After early successes and following Scudder's death, the

American Museum experienced financial difficulties. Hearing that the museum was for sale, Barnum went to check it out, determining "that only energy, tact, and liberality were needed, to give it life and to put it on a profitable footing." When asked by a friend what he would purchase the five-story marble building with, Barnum replied, "Brass, for silver and gold I have none." With backing by Francis W. Olmstead, a wealthy retired businessman, Barnum bought the American Museum in late December 1841, opening its doors on New Year's Day. It transformed American popular entertainment and soon became "the ladder by which I rose to fortune," Barnum recalled.

At the time Barnum took control of the American Museum, only three theaters could be found in New York City: the Park, the Bowery, and Mitchell's Olympic. Renowned performers such as Edwin Forrest, Edmund Kean, and Junius Booth appeared, but the theater possessed a less than savory reputation with upper galleries reserved for those deemed less than respectable: prostitutes, hooligans, and blacks. The American Museum with its dark interior was fortunately located in the very heart of New York. The well-regarded Astor House was situated on the other side of Broadway. Only blocks away could be found Delmonico's, considered New York's finest restaurant. Even closer were City Hall Park and St. Paul's Church. The young photographer Mathew Brady, the *New York Herald*'s James Gordon Bennett, and the *New York Tribune*'s Horace Greeley resided in the neighborhood.

The American Museum thrived under Barnum's stewardship. The opening session of the new American Museum featured holdovers from Scudder's operation, but Barnum added his own touch. In an effort to garner a larger audience, he sought out "industrious fleas, automatons, jugglers, ventriloquists, living statuary, tableaux, gypsies, albinos, fat boys, giants, dwarfs, rope-dancers, dioramas, panoramas, models of Niagara, Dublin, Paris and Jerusalem . . . Punch and Judy . . . fancy glass-blowing, knitting machines . . . dissolving views, American Indians, who enacted their warlike and religious ceremonies on the stage." The price of admission was twenty-five cents for an adult, half that for children. Crowds began flocking to the American Museum, whose proprietor created a carnival-like atmosphere. The outside of the building displayed bright lights or an array of color, with windows displaying paintings of animals, birds, or snakes. The "lecture room" held performances each afternoon and evening, eventually accommodating 3,000 patrons. Barnum offered "moral dramas" of "Moses," "Joseph and His Brethren," and "The Drunkard," with celebrated actors and actresses like Edward Sothern, Barney Williams, and Mary Gannon. The American Museum featured a former jockey turned clown, Dan Rice, who appeared on stage as Uncle Sam. Also appearing at Barnum's theater was Tony Pastor, later American vaudeville's leading promoter. The fare was appropriate for women and children with no "third tier" gallery present, as was the case in other theaters. Among the early visitors to Barnum's American Museum was Charles Dickens, the young but already celebrated author of *The Pickwick Papers* and *Oliver Twist.*

Barnum offered new exhibits when interest in one area slackened. He presented white whales, the first hippopotamus in the United States, colored tropical fish from the Caribbean, and Native Americans. As Harvey W. Roots records, Barnum came across "dwarfs and giants, fat women and thin men, and freaks and monstrosities of all kinds." A Jerusalem-born Arab, Colonel Routh Goshen, stood eight-foot-two and sported just under 600 pounds, while a Belgian, Monsieur Bihin, was a mere six inches shorter. The American Museum also offered shows that celebrated babies, flowers, birds, dogs, or chickens. In one early season alone, Barnum presented a magician-ventriloquist, a "mysterious Gypsey" girl, an armless man, an impersonator, an individual covered with tattoos, a singer of ballads, and an albino woman, along with striking backdrops such as "The Great Model of Niagara Falls, With Real Water." During the summer of 1842, Barnum obtained a strange looking preserved creature from overseas that he called the Feejee Mermaid, a three-foot-long, blackened figure with the head of a monkey and misshapen arms. When one visitor to the American Museum indicated that he had lived on the Fiji Islands and had never encountered a mermaid, Barnum retorted, "There's no accounting for some men's ignorance." In a letter to his friend Moses Kimball, who ran the Boston Museum, Barnum admitted not knowing if the Fejee Mermaid were "the work of nature or art." No matter—"it is decidedly the most stupendous curiosity ever submitted to the public for inspection." The exhibit continued and helped to make the American Museum, by year's end, the most popular amusement spot in New York City.

Returning from a trip to Albany in the fall of 1842, Barnum stopped off in Bridgeport, Connecticut, where he encountered "the smallest child" he "ever saw that could walk alone." Around two feet high, weighing a mere fifteen pounds, and possessing a three-inch foot, Charles S. Stratton turned out to be only five years old. Barnum signed him for a limited engagement, announcing him as eleven-year-old General Tom Thumb, a perfectly proportioned midget, not a dwarf, as his employer referred to him. After a year of displaying Tom Thumb, who had learned to sing and dance or been dressed as Yankee Doodle, Cupid, and Hercules, to approximately 80,000 visitors, Barnum determined to take him overseas. He also hoped to encounter additional curiosities. Thousands headed for the docks to see off Tom Thumb, while one newspaper predicted, "Our little countryman will astonish the citizens of the Old World!" Tom Thumb's appearance at the Egyptian Hall in London led to meetings with Edward Everett, the U.S. ambassador to England, and, along with Barnum, encounters with the Baroness Rothschild and her husband, the world's wealthiest banker. Barnum also received an invitation to accompany Tom Thumb to Buckingham Palace, where the two met Queen Victoria, Prince Albert, the Duchess of Kent, and several other members of the English nobility, whom Tom Thumb entertained with "songs, dances, and imitations." During two later meetings with the queen, Tom Thumb was introduced to the three-year-old Prince of Wales and King Leopold of Belgium. Emperor Nicholas of Russia sent an invitation to Tom Thumb, who had become a sensation in London. *Punch* referred to Tom Thumb as the "Pet of the Palace," while Barnum had a carriage built for him by the queen's carriage-maker. Barnum eventually took Tom Thumb with him to Paris, where they met King Louis-Philippe, Queen Marie Amalie, and other members of the French royalty. The acclaim that "General Tom Pouce" received in Paris was the greatest yet, followed by a visit to Spain, where he was brought before Queen Isabella, a stopover in Belgium to entertain King Leopold and other members of the Belgian royalty, and a successful return to London's Egyptian Hall. Except for two trips back home, Barnum remained in Europe for three years of "unbroken pleasure and profit." During that period Barnum also took his charge across Scotland, and to Belfast and Dublin.

Barnum was a wealthy man by the time he returned home in February 1847. He began building Iranistan, an oriental palace situated on seventeen acres in Bridgeport, Connecticut, which cost more than $150,000. He announced the return of the now internationally acclaimed "GENERAL TOM THUMB, The Smallest Man in Miniature in the known world . . . who has been patronized by all the CROWNED HEADS of Europe, and been seen by over 5,000,000 persons." Tom Thumb would appear in "his CITIZEN'S DRESS" while sharing "his History, Travels," and "sing a variety of songs, dance the polka, Sailor's Hornpipe, give representations of NAPOLEON, FREDERICK THE GREAT, GRECIAN STATUES." The midget also would be attired "in his magnificent COURT DRESS" received from Queen Victoria, and his "BEAUTIFUL SCOTCH COSTUME" as he performed "the HIGHLAND FLING." Tom Thumb soon toured across the United States and in Havana, Cuba, while Barnum became the nation's leading showman. He extended his lease of the American Museum for $10,000 a year and expanded its size and operations. He intended "to make the Museum a permanent institution in the city." A top guidebook of the city termed the American Museum "the most popular" of its kind in the United States.

Striving to maintain interest in his operations, Barnum had sought, albeit unsuccessfully, to purchase Shakespeare's home, a tree with Lord Byron's carving, and Madame Tussaud's Waxworks. The American Museum now housed more of Barnum's curiosities, including Tom Thumb's carriage and presents from European royalty and a diorama of Napoleon's funeral. Barnum advertised Major Littlefinger, smaller even than General Tom Thumb, and regularly presented melodramas. One critic charged that Barnum's purported delivery of morality tales was but a "miserable trick." Undaunted by such criticism, Barnum continued seeking out new curiosities, promising a beauty contest to uncover "the handsomest women in America." Appearing at the American Museum were Old Blind Tom, an imitative African-American piano player; a black inventor who supposedly could employ a weed to whiten African-Americans; the nearly eight-foot-tall Anna Swan, who married the still taller Captain N.V. Bates; and the fully bearded Madame Josephine Fortune Clofullia. A supposedly irate customer sued Barnum for fraud, charging that Madame Clofullia was an impostor, but it turned out that the showman had instigated the suit for publicity's sake. Fans also flocked to the American Museum to see Chang and Eng, the so-called Siamese Double Boys, conjoined at birth.

The most successful of Barnum's commercial ventures involved his extended presentation of the Swedish Nightingale, the former operatic star Jenny Lind, who delivered more than ninety concerts for him. He later wrote, "It was an enterprise never before or since equaled in managerial annals. As I recall it now, I almost tremble at the seeming temerity of the attempt. . . . I risked much but I made more." Barnum paid Lind $1,000 for each performance but soon sweetened that contractual agreement in addition to covering expenses, which he did by mortgaging his property and obtaining a loan from a friend. With the tour about to begin, Barnum encountered a train conductor whom he informed about the visit. The conductor stunned Barnum by exclaiming, "Jenny Lind! Is she a dancer?" Barnum felt compelled to initiate an unprecedented press campaign to publicize "the greatest songstress in the world." Lind possessed an "intrinsic worth of heart and delicacy of mind," Barnum extolled; "it is her pure and intense feelings that abide her potency." When Lind docked in New York Harbor on Sunday, September 1, 1850, "the wildest enthusiasm prevailed," he reported. Then, 20,000 people gathered in front of the Irving House, where Barnum had rented an apartment for his guest performer.

As he later acknowledged, Barnum conducted what he considered "the first attempt in this country to 'work the press.'" The *London Times* reported that New Yorkers, during Lind's visit, "cannot help being proud of their city, of their visitor, of themselves, and of their singular good taste." James Gordon Bennett's *New York Herald* exclaimed, "Jenny Lind is the most popular woman in the world at this moment—perhaps the most popular that ever was in it." Five thousand people, who had paid as much as $225 for a ticket, congregated at Castle Garden, a large auditorium in the Battery district of New York City, to witness Lind's first concert in America. The *Herald* rhapsodized that the brilliant soprano's visit to America was "as significant an event as the appearance of Dante . . . Raphael, Shakespeare, Goethe . . . or Michael Angelo [sic]." Word that Lind was donating lavishly to charity led Bennett to ask when Barnum would follow suit. Bennett charged, "Jenny Lind does all the generous acts, and Barnum perpetrates all the mean doings." The Lind tour traveled up and down the eastern seaboard, with President Millard Fillmore, Senator Daniel Webster, and Senator Henry Clay attending performances. The concerts continued all the way down south into Charleston and then on to Havana before heading back to New Orleans and then up the Mississippi River. Return engagements in New York City and Philadelphia also followed when Lind opted to continue without Barnum as manager. She had delivered ninety-three concerts that earned her approximately $250,000, while Barnum amassed at least that much in profits.

Barnum undertook another tour of Great Britain after the Lind excursion, this time featuring child performers. He also sponsored Barnum's Gallery of American Beauty and agreed to serve as president of the financially strapped New York Crystal Palace, a decaying exhibition hall that began serving as a world's fair by 1853. Realizing after three months that "the dead could not be raised," Barnum warded off expectations that he would personally honor the debts of the Crystal Palace by submitting his resignation. He continually received proposals to invest large sums of money in various operations, schemes, stock companies, and the like, invariably guaranteed to produce large returns on his money. Although he sometimes blundered badly, Barnum usually responded to such suggestions in the following fashion: "You are much mistaken in supposing that I am so ready or anxious to make money. On the contrary, there is but one thing in the world that I desire—that is, tranquility."

Although Barnum continued to run the American Museum, he became less enthusiastic about operating the museum and hosting other exhibits. As he indicated to Moses Kimball in mid-1854, he was "weary, fagged, tired, tired, and almost sick." He spent most of his days at Iranistan. Contemplating retirement, Barnum now acknowledged, "I was an ass for having anything to do with the Crystal Palace." In 1855 Barnum presented an early autobiography, *The Life of P.T. Barnum Written by Himself*, which revealed various deceptions he had committed, including those involving the ages of both Joyce Heith and Tom Thumb. The book sold 500,000 copies, including at least one to Mark Twain, who remained "up nights to absorb it" and rose "early . . . to follow the career of the great showman," the man who insisted that "the American people like to be humbugged."

Barnum lost a great amount of money in real estate and commercial transactions, particularly one involving the Jerome Clock Company of New Haven. Driven into bankruptcy and denounced as a swindler and a fraud, Barnum nevertheless received support from countless business luminaries, including

Cornelius Vanderbilt and Robert Stuyvesant. Declining a suggestion that his family take advantage of several public benefits, Barnum instead managed to sell his museum collection while his wife, who held the lease on the property site of the American Museum, drew an annual income of $19,000. Barnum admitted, "The situation is disheartening but I have experience, energy, health, and hope." He also prevailed in a series of legal suits with creditors and soon began purchasing real estate in East Bridgeport, Connecticut. To get away from his problems at home, Barnum undertook another European adventure in 1857, carrying along General Tom Thumb and Cordelia Howard, a child actress. Having returned home at the end of the summer, Barnum was residing in New York when he received word that the too lightly insured Iranistan had completely burned. Money from the sale of the grounds on which Iranistan had stood ended up in the hands of creditors; Barnum would soon build the more modest Lindencroft. Back in England the next year, Barnum spoke on "The Art of Money-Getting." In literary form, the subject garnered a considerable sum while Barnum obtained new curiosities for his museum during his latest trip overseas.

Financially solvent once more, he repurchased his museum collection and heralded the reopening of the American Museum, announcing, "Barnum on His Feet Again." Barnum met the buckskin-attired, wolf-head-sporting James C. "Grizzly" Adams, who possessed scores of animals from California, including grizzly bears, wolves, buffaloes, lions, tigers, elk, and a sea-lion. The two men began displaying the animals in a tent located at Broadway and Thirteenth Street. Less successful was Barnum's exhibiting of whales, which died in captivity. His experiment with a hippopotamus, displayed as "The Great Behemoth of the Scriptures," proved happier. So did Barnum's celebration of a twenty-nine-inch–tall dwarf, George Washington Morrison Nutt, renamed Commodore Nutt, whom the showman took to meet Abraham Lincoln at the White House. Barnum acquired still greater notoriety after he helped introduce Tom Thumb to Lavinia Warren, who stood twenty-four inches high. The two appeared as an engaged couple at the American Museum and married in early 1863. Barnum escorted the pair to see President Lincoln. The paper of his now longtime antagonist, James Gordon Bennett, assailed Barnum for his role in bringing Tom Thumb and Lavinia Warren together. The *New York Herald* charged, "The American press and public have been exceedingly lenient with Barnum. They have allowed him to make money by humbugging innocent people, and more money by selling a book telling how well his humbugs have succeeded."

In 1865 Barnum released *The Humbugs of the World*, which did not extol cheats, impostors, counterfeiters, or confidence men but did discuss spiritualists, adulterators of food and drink, auctioneers, lottery moguls, stock swindlers, speculators, promoters of patent medicine, and proselytizers of "heathen" religions. A fire swept through the American Museum that same year, destroying the animals, costumes, and various curiosities. The *New York Times* bemoaned the loss of the museum, which notwithstanding "its humbugs and exaggerations still deserved an honorable place in the front rank of the rare and curious collections of the world." Indeed, the museum, the *Times* continued, was "a landmark of the city; has afforded us in childhood fullest vision of the wonderful and miraculous; has opened to us the secrets of the earth and revealed to us the mysteries of the past; has preserved intact relics of days and ages long since gone." Barnum rented another site on Broadway close to Spring Street, where on November 13, 1865, he initiated Barnum's New American Museum. In the meantime, he delivered his existing eleven-year lease on the lot that had housed the American Museum to James Gordon Bennett for $200,000; Bennett purchased the land itself for $500,000 but another battle ensued between the two men because the newspaper publisher had hoped that the lease money would be deducted from the sale price. Long a Jacksonian Democrat, but one who had converted to the Republican Party of Abraham Lincoln, Barnum made an unsuccessful run for a congressional seat from Connecticut in 1867. Barnum suffered yet another setback in March 1868 when the New American Museum burned down, leading its proprietor to announce his retirement and promise to concentrate on "serious reflections on the ends and aims of human existence." He sold Lindencroft and moved into a home on Long Island Sound, having already purchased a town house on Fifth Avenue.

By early 1871, however, Barnum kicked off a large traveling show that was called P.T. Barnum's Grand Traveling Museum, Menagerie, Caravan, and Circus. Ten thousand people gathered in Brooklyn to witness wax displays, dioramas, a Sleeping Beauty, a Bearded Boy, Fiji Cannibals, and a giraffe. Advertised widely by W.C. Coup, Barnum's circus, soon dubbed "The Greatest Show on Earth," appeared in large cities and small towns alike. The circus could be found on Fourteenth Street in New York City during the winter season at the Hippotheatron, although fire destroyed it too in late December 1872. The Barnum show became the nation's first two-ring circus; later, another ring was added. Barnum was informed of the death of his long ailing wife while traveling through Europe in 1873. Within a year he wedded Nancy Fish, the twenty-four-year-old daughter of an English compatriot. After he returned to Manhattan, Barnum's circus became associated with the Great Roman Hippodrome at Madison Square Garden, which was attended by President Ulysses S. Grant, King Kalakau of Hawaii, and other dignitaries. Barnum became mayor of Bridgeport in 1875, asserting that "Honesty is always the best policy" and promising, as a longtime proponent of temperance, to do battle with saloon operators. Serving in public office for only one year, Barnum joined in the centennial celebration of the Declaration of Independence, complete with a Goddess of Liberty and revolutionary uniforms, while continuing to feature what was long known as "Barnum's Great Moral Show," which purportedly contained "nothing that professed Christians do not approve." His circus was obtaining receipts of over $400,000 annually by the end of the decade, but profits were decreasing. Barnum had increasingly relinquished the actual operations of the circus to others. He soon agreed to form a partnership with his toughest competitor, James A. Bailey, and Barnum & Bailey became "The Greatest Show on Earth." Profits soared, the greatest attraction proving to be Jumbo, a massive elephant acquired from the London Zoo to the chagrin of many, including Queen Victoria. The Barnum & Bailey circus appeared in London to great acclaim in 1889. His flagging health compelled him to return home and the eighty-one-year-old Barnum died on April 7, 1891. The *Boston Herald* noted the passing of "the foremost showman of all time." The *New York Times* acknowledged that "there has been no showman to be compared with him." The *Times* insisted that "what distinguished Barnum from other public entertainers of equal or nearly equal conspicuousness was really the absence of humbug. . . . Barnum was never under any illusions, nor did he ever encourage illusions, about the nature of his function. He did not pretend to be an evangelist or an artist, but simply a showman." The *London Times* sang his praises too: "He created the métier of showman on a grandiose scale. . . . He early realized that essential feature of a modern democracy, its readiness to be led to what will amuse and instruct it."

Bibliography

Barnum, *P.T. Barnum*. New York: Cosimo Classics, 2007.

Cook, James W. *The Arts of Deception: Playing with Fraud in the Age of Barnum*. Cambridge, MA: Harvard University Press, 2001.

Crouthamel, James L. *Bennett's* New York Herald *and the Rise of the Popular Press*. Syracuse, NY: Syracuse University Press, 1989.

Dennett, Andrea Stulman. *Weird and Wonderful: The Dime Museum in America*. New York: New York University Press, 1997.

Fitzsimons, Raymund. *Barnum in London*. New York: St. Martin's Press, 1970.

Harris, Neil. *Humbug: The Art of P.T. Barnum*. Boston: Little, Brown, 1973.

Hudson, Frederic. *Journalism in the United States from 1690 to 1872*. New York: Harper and Brothers, 1873.

Kunhardt, Philip B.; Philip B. Kunhardt III; and Philip B. Kunhardt. *P.T. Barnum: America's Greatest Showman*. New York: Knopf, 1995.

Lee, Alfred M. *The Daily Newspaper in America*. New York: Macmillan, 1937.

Levine, Lawrence. *Highbrow/Lowbrow: The Emergence of Cultural Hierarchy in America*. Cambridge, MA: Harvard University Press, 1988.

Mott, Frank Luther. *American Journalism: A History 1690–1960*. 3rd ed. New York: Macmillan, 1962.

Pray, Isaac C. *Memoirs of James Gordon Bennett and His Times*. New York: Stringer and Townsend, 1855.

Reiss, Benjamin. *The Showman and the Slave: Race, Death, and Memory in Barnum's America*. Cambridge, MA: Harvard University Press, 2001.

Root, Harvey W. *The Unknown Barnum*. New York: Harper and Brothers, 1927.

Saxon, Arthur H. *P.T. Barnum: The Legend and the Man*. New York: Columbia University Press, 1995.

Seitz, Don C. *The James Gordon Bennetts*. Indianapolis: Bobbs-Merrill, 1928.

Tebbel, John. *The Compact History of the American Newspaper*. New York: Hawthorn Books, 1969.

Wallace, Irving. *The Fabulous Showman: The Life and Times of P.T. Barnum*. New York: Knopf, 1959.

Werner, M.R. *Barnum*. New York: Harcourt Brace, 1923.

Exponents of the Culture of Consumption

MARSHALL FIELD AND HORATIO ALGER JR.

During the last four decades of the nineteenth century the United States underwent a period of rapid modernization, experiencing marked industrial growth and urbanization. The nation consequently became infinitely wealthier, as did the richest of all Americans, while the middle class grew in size and importance. Large numbers of workers—including many so-called new immigrants from southern, eastern, and southeastern Europe—became members of a new industrial proletariat. Farmers also entered the marketplace that tied them, however indirectly, to giant corporations. Numerous people of color, such as African-Americans and Native Americans, were run roughshod over as market forces became more predominant.

Other changes affecting the workplace also were ushered in. The length of the average workweek decreased between 1860 and 1900, with a much sharper reduction (from sixty to forty-seven hours) occurring during the following two decades. An adequate labor supply, greater affluence, and labor-saving mechanisms—which affected both American industry and agriculture—resulted in extended leisure time. Many white-collar workers put in fewer than ten hours a day and received the weekends off. Others, of course, proved far less fortunate, toiling long hours into the weekend and possessing neither the time nor the resources for leisure. Nevertheless, more diversions became available to more Americans than ever before. Moreover, a key portion of the American economy was now based on the providing and enjoyment of entertainment. This was possible thanks to the expansion of the American infrastructure through the railroad, telegraph, and telephone, which allowed for a consumer-oriented society. Significant too was the giving way, to a certain extent at least, of the older focus on thrift and saving to the amassing of material possessions. In highlighting the quality and inexpensive nature of their products, merchandisers helped to assuage any residual guilt experienced by prospective consumers. They also suggested that consumption allowed less affluent individuals to share in America's material bounty.

The culture of consumption increasingly became a dominant force in American life. In the great urban centers, palatial department stores catered to the whims and cultivated the commercial habits of wealthy and upper-middle-class women in particular. Starting in the 1850s, commercial pleasure houses like Macy's, Wanamaker's, and Marshall Field cropped up in New York, Philadelphia, and Chicago, respectively. For the well-heeled clients who coursed through the plush showrooms, encountering salespersons seemingly ready to meet their every commercial need, shopping at such establishments was an experience in itself. Helping to get customers in the proper spirit befitting spending sprees were signs indicating rock-bottom prices or end-of-the-season sales and full-page advertisements that began appearing in leading newspapers. Patrons easily discarded their older, puritanical notions regarding thrift and their Victorian sensibilities about fashion, shopping to please themselves, not for practical reasons alone, and concerning themselves with new airier, less restrictive styles. The shopping mania that seemingly afflicted good portions of the American upper crust also affected other segments of American society, as mail-order houses and chain stores reached out to rural and small-town inhabitants. Marshall Field reigned by the 1880s as one of the nation's merchant princes and as proprietor of "The Great American Store," having helped turn Chicago's State Street into a magnet for the new consumer culture. For their part, Aaron Montgomery Ward and Richard Warren Sears drew on entrepreneurial genius to devise catalogs containing thousands of items, many costing little, and ranging from agricultural implements to clothes and toys. The advent of rural free delivery and parcel post ensured the commercial viability of their enterprises in the very period when chain stores on the order of Woolworth and the Great Atlantic and Pacific Tea Company (A&P) carried the consumer culture to pockets around the nation.

The gospel of consumption spread rapidly in the last several decades of the nineteenth century thanks to these commercial endeavors, the tremendous growth of advertising, and the celebration of such developments by newspapers, magazines, and books. Mass-circulation publications continued to shape the sensibilities of the average American and to create lasting images about the American experience. During the antebellum era, the penny newspaper, poetry, and early novels grabbed the attention of city dwellers and, sometimes, of their rural counterparts. The post–Civil War period witnessed the proliferation of cheap, sensational, paperbacked novels, like those published by Beadle & Adams. These dime novels featured stories of the American West, presenting stock images of the cowboy and the outlaw that retain their hold on the American imagination.

Another literary sensation appeared during this period: Horatio Alger, a former clergyman who wrote rags-to-riches tales of bootblacks and others who through pluck and luck began to spiral up the socioeconomic ladder. The Alger tales became caught up in the swirl of ideas that amounted to a business ethic. These included laissez-faire, the notion that government should not encumber the marketplace, and social Darwinism, the idea of survival of the fittest, derived appropriately or not by the British philosopher Herbert Spencer and his American counterpart William Graham Sumner from the evolutionary theory articulated in Charles Darwin's *The Origin of the Species* (1859). Softening some of the hardest edges of these two components of the business ethic was Andrew Carnegie's call for wealthy individuals to practice the "gospel of wealth," a voluntary decision to give back to society some of the riches garnered in the industrial age in the form of philanthropic endeavors. Alger's novels at least touched on portions of these aspects of the business ethic, albeit not always favorably, while particularly reinforcing the long-standing American belief in self-reliance and individualism. At the same time his brief literary treatments provided many of his readers with a means to explore something of the economic condition of American cities in the last stages of the nineteenth century.

MARSHALL FIELD

Marshall Field was born on September 18, 1834, on a farm outside Conway, Massachusetts, to John and Fidelia Field, hardworking but not notably successful Congregationalists. As a youngster, Marshall, the fourth of eight children, helped in his family's fields and attended local schools. He demonstrated little fondness for academics, other than mathematics, and frequently fought with other boys. At the age of sixteen, Marshall convinced his father to let him serve as an apprentice at Henry G. Davis's general store in Pittsfield, thirty miles away. Residing in a room above the store, Marshall would awake early and clean the downstairs before his boss began operations. The ambitious young lad pored over *Godley's Lady's Book* and *Hunt's Merchant's Magazine* in between toiling long hours from Monday through Saturday. He did so "with the dry passion of a genius," Field later acknowledged. He watched as a number of local residents moved to Chicago, a booming metropolis. Field eventually followed suit, receiving an unqualified recommendation from his employer, who deemed him "a young man of unusual business talent worthy of the confidence of any who would employ him."

The slender, five-foot-nine Field, carrying nearly $1,000 in savings, arrived during the spring of 1856 in Chicago, which had received its charter of incorporation less than twenty years earlier. Initial growth proved steady but became explosive in the first half of the 1850s, encouraged by Chicago's emergence as a boom city thanks to its strategic location along the Great Lakes and in the path of the westward movement, its connection to the Mississippi River through the Illinois & Michigan Canal, and the opening of the Galena and Chicago Union Railroad. The *Chicago Tribune* in late 1850 referred to the city's "future commercial importance" and "the brilliant prospect of its future greatness." A pamphlet drafted in 1852 asked whether it should be "wondered at" that Chicago's population had doubled within the past three years and "that men who were trading in small seven-by-nine tenements, now find splendid brick or marble stores scarcely large enough to accommodate their customers." Indeed, beginning in the 1850s, Chicago was on the way to becoming the nation's industrial capital and America's second city.

New to Chicago, twenty-one-year-old Marshall Field became a clerk for Cooley, Wadsworth, & Company, a leading wholesale dry-goods firm that paid him an annual salary of $400. "Silent Marsh," as the taciturn young man was known, proved highly ambitious and hardworking. He toiled long hours and studied merchandising practices, particularly those involving retail sales, during his spare time. Junior partner John Villiers Farwell recognized that Field "had the merchant's instinct. He knew how to show off a stock to its best advantage, and he always knew what was in stock. He lived for it, and it only." Not surprisingly then, Farwell made Field a traveling salesman sent to visit new towns outside Chicago. Then, as a severe economic depression swept across the American landscape in 1857, Field helped bring about a tightening of credit and a reduction of inventory that prevented Cooley, Farwell, and Wadsworth from suffering the fate that bankrupted hundreds of other wholesale businesses. He also followed the opening of a new store at 139 Lake Street by Potter Palmer, fresh from Lockport, New York, who began to draw comparisons to Alexander Turney Stewart, operator of New York City's largest wholesale and retail dry-goods business, the Marble Palace. A previously unsuccessful merchandiser, Roland Hussey Macy, visited Palmer's new commercial establishment after setting up his own "fancy dry goods" store at Sixth Avenue and Fourteenth Street in Manhattan.

Chicago meanwhile continued to experience tremendous growth, boasting a population of 109,000 by 1860. The outbreak of the Civil War ironically only heightened Chicago's economic prosperity as demands for farming implements increased, factories opened up to produce equipment for the Union army, and railroad profits soared. Palmer's commercial operations received a boost after he affirmed a money-back guarantee in late November 1861. To retain Field's services, Cooley and Farwell made him a junior partner and paid him $3,000 a year, along with a share of the thriving company's profits. Focusing on sales and credit operations, Field became a full partner in 1863, paying $15,000 for that privilege. His success enabled Field to marry Nannie Scott, with whom he subsequently had two children, Marshall Jr. and Ethel. Late in the war, the reshuffled company, now named Farwell, Field, & Company, supplanted Potter Palmer at the top of the Chicago dry-goods trade. The *Chicago Tribune* noted, "Outside of New York, Chicago is the market of the West."

In 1865 Field severed ties with Farwell and, along with Levi Leiter and the $300,000 they had amassed, became senior partners alongside Palmer. Among the salespersons hired by the reconstituted firm were Field's brothers, Henry and Joseph, along with a young man from Chatham, New York, Montgomery Ward. Field, Palmer, & Leiter continued Palmer's policy of allowing unwanted merchandise to be returned, posting the following notice: "IF, WHEN YOU GET YOUR GOODS HOME, AND DO NOT FIND THEM ENTIRELY SATISFACTORY, PLEASE RETURN THEM AND YOUR MONEY WILL BE REFUNDED." The partners promised to undersell other retail establishments in Chicago and to match any in New York City. The fledgling business also employed women clerks in the lingerie department while offering low prices and quality merchandise. First-year sales amounted to $8 million, with $300,000 of that profit. Field and Leiter bought out the ailing, overworked Palmer within three years and relocated as Field, Leiter, & Company in 1868 to a six-story marble store on State Street, rented from Palmer for $50,000 annually; State Street soon supplanted Lake Street as the city's finest shopping district. Field and Leiter promised to accept back any items "if not entirely approved" and at their expense. They also guaranteed "the very lowest prices upon every article."

Deemed "a Dazzling Assemblage of Wealth, Beauty and Fashion" and "the Largest and Finest in America," the new store catered to both merchants and retail customers. It featured an upper floor with wholesale items, but also an elegant main floor that drew upper-middle-class and wealthier patrons. Awaiting them were walnut counters, frescoed walls, and gas lighting. The cloak department contained satin and striped silk cloth, silk robes, and both velvet and sealskin cloaks. The shawl department offered expensive Persian cashmeres, Paisleys, and shawls. A Gents' Furnishing Goods section held scarves, ties, cardigans, and tweeds. A Ladies' Suit Department exhibited Parisian styles. Field and Leiter advertised "THE MOST ATTRACTIVE GOODS FOR ONE DOLLAR EVER OFFERED IN THIS CITY!", but also sold lace tablecloths for $1,000 and shawls for $750. Sales clerks and customers could spot Field passing through the retail section each morning. On one occasion, after witnessing a clerk arguing with a customer, Field exclaimed, "Give the lady what she wants," providing his store's motto. He instructed his employees "to do the right thing at the right time, in the right way" while doing "some things better than they were ever done before." To stay ahead of his competitors on Lake Street, Field sent representatives to Europe to obtain information about fashion trends across the Atlantic. That enabled him and his partner to trumpet their "unparalleled foreign imports."

By 1870 Chicago was a bustling metropolis with 300,000 residents. A member of the British Parliament reported, "This place is the wonder of the Wonderful West. . . . [I]t is one of the handsomest cities I ever saw." But the "Great Conflagration," the worst fire in American history, soon transformed the city altogether. For three months, Chicago, with its rickety wooden buildings and streets, had experienced only an inch of rainfall, and for several days a potent wind blew in from the Southwest. The *Chicago Tribune* warned, "The absence of rain . . . has left everything in so flammable a condition that a spark might set a fire that would sweep from end to end of the city." On Sunday, October 8, 1871, a fire ignited at 9:45 p.m. in a cow barn in back of a cottage at 137 DeKoven Street on the West Side. A gale swept the fire across the southern branch of the Chicago River and into the business district within three hours. In the *Tribune*, editor in chief Horace White reported tens of thousands of people in the North Side fleeing "in mortal terror before the flames." White witnessed "a shower of water" pouring onto "the immense store of Field, Leiter, & Company" from its "own fire-apparatus." Later, White saw that a burning roof had crippled those "great pumping engines" and that goods were being transported out of the building. After raging for a day and a half, the Great Chicago Fire left the city devastated, with magnificent hotels like the Palmer House, the Tremont, and the Sherman ruined, and Field, Leiter, & Company, along with many other businesses, "reduced to blazing ash." Chicago suffered the loss of $200 million worth of property; 100,000 people became homeless, and 300 died as a consequence of the fire. Within days, Chicagoans began to rebuild their city and the *Tribune* exclaimed, "CHICAGO SHALL RISE AGAIN!"

Field and Leiter managed to get $200,000 worth of goods out of the store before it was destroyed, and insurance covered all but $750,000 out of the $2.5 million loss of merchandise. After only two weeks their store reopened in a temporary location at State and Twentieth streets in dilapidated horse barns owned by the Chicago City Railway Company. A second move followed to Market and Madison at the former site of the burned-out Garden City Hotel, with the grand opening taking place on April 25, 1873. Some 30,000 visitors arrived with women especially exploring the fine items on display on the ground floor. Sales unfortunately soon lagged at the new location as they had at State and Twentieth. To ward off competition from A.T. Stewart, Field and Leiter subsequently signed a three-year lease on a five-story store, possessing a great central glass dome, located on State Street. The annual rent for the building, constructed by the Singer Sewing Machine Company, was $75,000. Clerks toiled long hours for approximately $10 a week while again being expected to cater graciously to the needs of customers. The new store began operations on October 9, 1873, only a month before the country headed into an economic tailspin. Chicagoans witnessed the collapse of five banks, the closing of numerous businesses, and the loss of countless jobs, but Field & Leiter instructed its customers that there was "no cause for general alarm." The store soon even expanded deliveries inside the city, paying boys a nominal sum to transport packages to residences and then using horses and wagons to reach out to the suburbs and other merchants. Field and Leiter confronted a price war, pitting their store against the A.T. Stewart Company. Field felt compelled to hire more traveling salesmen, but soon Stewart's operations out west began to wither. Field in contrast felt comfortable enough to have famed architect Richard Morris Hunt build a $100,000 mansion for him on stately Prairie Avenue. Field's wife, Nannie, spent a considerable time in Europe while the entrepreneur and his children occasionally traveled with her on an ocean liner. At other times Field made the voyage on his own for commercial purposes.

A fire beset the Singer Building in mid-November 1877, with employees of Field & Leiter again saving about $200,000 worth of merchandise. Four times that amount was lost but Field and Leiter had $1 million in insurance coverage. Within two days, Field rented the Inter-State Industrial Palace on Michigan Boulevard for a mere $750 a month. During this period, an ongoing struggle between Field and Leiter intensified. Field desired to renew retail operations, but Leiter pointed out that wholesale trade had proven far more profitable for their business. During the past half-dozen years, Field & Leiter had amassed retail profits approximating $300,000, but wholesale profits were almost eighteen times greater. The two partners finally reached a deal with Singer to purchase the rebuilt store for $700,000. They had to come up with an additional $100,000 to convince another company to relinquish the lease on the Singer property it had just signed.

The new Field & Leiter building, devised by the famed architect Daniel Burnham, opened in April 1879, featuring "brilliant white" walls, large windows, a great light well in the middle of the building, more expansive aisles, plush carpets, a magnificent staircase, ornate designs, and more dignified operations, with a greeter welcoming ladies as they departed from horse-drawn carriages. A ventilating system was soon added along with electric lights. Like Wanamaker's and Macy's, the store soon provided customers with telephone, telegraph, and postal service and a theater ticket office, along with fashion displays. Field & Leiter's leading competitors on State Street eventually included Carson, Pirie, & Company, The Fair, and Mandel Brothers. Field bought out Leiter for $2.5 million in 1881 although the store was taking in receipts of $25 million annually. Field attempted to reach beyond his affluent clientele, offering low-cost items in addition to luxurious ones and demanding that the sales staff—initially composed mostly of men—be "polite and attentive to rich and poor alike." Harry Gordon Selfridge, eventually a junior partner, initially orchestrated the store's bargain basement that Robert Hendrickson refers to as "the first of its kind" and later was considered "the world's largest single salesroom." At first Field hired women to work in the ready-to-wear and lingerie departments, and although more slowly than some of his national competitors, such as Wanamaker's and Macy's, he began to welcome a large number of female employees. Young women flocked to work at Marshall Field's, a respectable establishment where female employees had toilets set aside for them, a recreation center, a lunchroom, and the liberty to come to work a half-hour after their male counterparts did and to leave thirty minutes before the men could. At the same time, Marshall Field's treated women customers with great respect during this era of Victorian America. He allowed patrons to roam freely through the store, to meet friends there, and, finally, to purchase items for cash or on credit.

Field's own workday seldom varied, beginning with an eight o'clock breakfast when he examined the financial sections of various newspapers, including the *Chicago Tribune*. His carriage dropped off Field, impeccably attired in a tailored suit and white gloves, several blocks from the store, and he briskly walked the rest of the way. Field's own offices, both at the retail store and at the wholesale house, were spare. The latter amounted to "a plain box of a place, fenced off in a corner of the store," one visitor suggested. Field generally had lunch at the Chicago Club, where other regulars at the "millionaires' table" included George Pullman of railroad sleeping car fame, N.K. Fairbank, the president of the club, and Lyman Gage, who headed the First National Bank and later served as U.S. Secretary of the Treasury. Not one to engage in small talk either at the club or his commercial establishment, the steel-gray-eyed Field usually departed shortly after lunch to either a bank where he was majority owner or his wholesale house. He regularly delivered pithy, pointed advice to employees, declaring, for instance, "Quality is remembered long after price is forgotten." He informed one of his executives that business success required "the four C's—character, courage, courtesy, and capacity." Field insisted on the need to do "business on a 'cash basis,'" sell goods more quickly than one's competitors, sell the same quality goods at lower cost, and ensure that customers met their obligations. He became the dominant figure in wholesale trade and a pathfinder in retail operations, striving to make his store a full-service commercial enterprise.

Another policy that Field adhered to amounted to paying low salaries to employees, other than top executives. At the same time he expected that his often hard-pressed workers would save even "five, ten, or fifteen cents a day." Seconding Field's approach was "Mile-a-Minute Harry" Selfridge, the retail general manager who became a junior partner and helped pitch the gospel of Marshall Field's. Field amassed greater and greater wealth through his retail and warehouse operations, investments in railroads, holding of stocks and bonds, and purchase of real estate. Like many other extremely wealthy individuals of his era, Field's political philosophy was decidedly conservative as he viewed with abhorrence "anarchists" and "socialists." His worldview was in keeping with that of his contemporaries and acquaintances, individuals such as John D. Rockefeller, J.P. Morgan, and Andrew Carnegie. Field applauded the death sentence meted out to eight anarchists following a bombing at Chicago's Haymarket Square that resulted in several casualties. The *Chicago Tribune* reported Field's response: "Law has triumphed. Anarchy is defeated." In contrast to several other Chicago luminaries, including Potter Palmer, Lyman Gage, and Lyman Trumball, former law partner of Abraham Lincoln, Field argued against clemency. Field purportedly rose and expressed his opposition during a meeting of top business leaders. That led to a breakup of the gathering for "none cared to take issue with him."

In 1887 Field moved his store to a new, nine-story building, situated on an entire block in downtown Chicago at the corner of Washington and Wabash, and constructed a new wholesale house. Six years later, with the World's Columbian Exposition approaching, Marshall Field's was expanded to accommodate the anticipated influx of tourists. As company biographers Lloyd Wendt and Herman Kogan indicate, at Marshall Field's could be found Oriental silks, Belgian laces, French lingerie, Irish linens, Bohemian glassware, rugs, drapes, and household ware. Following the Columbian Exposition, Marshall Field imported nearly $3 million worth of goods annually. His store continued to cater to women shoppers, who were treated like royalty when they came to the store's entrance on Washington Street. Other visitors included Spanish princess Infanta Eulalia, Prince Henry of Prussia, President Grover Cleveland, Theodore Roosevelt, President-elect William McKinley, and Mary Todd Lincoln, Abraham Lincoln's widow. Writing in O.S. Marden's *Success*, Theodore Dreiser sang Field's praises, indicating that the career of "the celebrated Western merchant, sprung from rugged Eastern soil," provided a model for American youth and businessmen alike. When asked how he became a business tycoon, Field replied, "I was determined not to remain poor." Others viewed the operations of giant retail establishments like Marshall Field's less favorably. They bemoaned the entrenchment of the "Department Store Octopus" and decried the low wages paid employees of such enterprises.

Field was clearly Chicago's wealthiest citizen and largest taxpayer at the turn of the century. The city where he had made his fortune, however, acquired a reputation for its urban sprawl, industrial exploitation, and political corruption. As Lincoln Steffens indicated in 1902, Chicago "was first in violence, deepest in dirt, loud, lawless, unlovely, ill-smelling, irreverent, new, an overgrown gawk of a village, the 'tough' among cities, a spectacle for the nation." To rectify some of Chicago's ailments, the nation's leading retail merchant helped to found the Civic Federation, which supported civic reforms pertaining to gambling, prostitution, and corrupt politicians. At the same time, Field, like many of his counterparts, readily worked with Charles Tyson Yerkes Jr., who had been imprisoned for swindling bonds but helped to initiate an elevated railway system that financially benefited Field. Longtime mayor Carter Harrison charged, "The people who constitute the most desirable class of buyers in the city of Chicago and its suburbs are deposited at the doors of Marshall Field & Co., or within sight and easy walking distance of the big store."

In the June 1902 issue of *The Cosmopolitan*, the journalist Charles S. Gleed offered his own analysis of Field, whom he termed "the greatest merchant in the United States," albeit a figure "as quiet and undemonstrative as a bashful preacher." Temperance guided Field, whether that involved dietary habits or his abstention from both alcohol and tobacco. The *Cosmopolitan* article indicated that Field followed all his company's business operations, but he did so like "a cold, calm, calculating machinist." Away from the office, Field dwelled in a spacious but unostentatious abode, had a few close friends, and belonged to a number of clubs but attended very few of them. Field traveled abroad frequently, particularly to England, where he possessed a dwelling close to Leamington, southeast of Birmingham. Gleed noted that Field did not deem himself to be wealthy notwithstanding the great fortune he had amassed from his far-flung business enterprises, massive real estate holdings, and large investments in railroads, banks, and factories. Field's annual income eventually reached $40 million during a period when the wages of American workers averaged only a few hundred dollars a year and often proved sporadic at best.

Field's commercial success led to the construction of a new, twelve-story building that covered an entire city block connecting Washington, State, Wabash, and Rudolph streets and opened on September 29, 1902. Advertisements proclaimed that the new Marshall Field's was "Everybody's Store." The pitch continued: "We have built this great institution for the people, to be their store, their downtown home, their buying headquarters, where their best interests might be considered!" Among those visiting was John Wanamaker, who backed off on plans to construct a branch of his own store in Chicago when Field threatened to extend his own reach into Wanamaker's home base in Philadelphia. Amassing large annual profits, Marshall Field's, like much of Chicago, less happily became ensnared in a major labor strike during the summer of 1905. Strikebreakers and police battled against union operatives, leading to twenty-five deaths, 400 injuries, and millions of dollars in lost business and wages. Field emerged out of the conflict more bitterly anti-union than ever. Labor leaders in Chicago referred to National Guardsmen as "Marshall Field's boys."

In 1905, twelve years after his first wife's death, Field, called "the first merchant of the United States," married for a second time, wedding Delia Caton. Less than three months later, his son Marshall Field Jr. died in a mysterious fatal shooting that may well have been a suicide. The loss proved shattering to Field, who soon suffered pneumonia and died on January 16, 1906. Field, who had donated generously to the University of Chicago and the Chicago Museum of Natural History (first called the Field Museum), left behind, through a 22,000-word will, the city's greatest estate, some $118 million altogether (about $2 billion in present dollars) that would be invested in real estate before reverting to his grandson Marshall Field III nearly forty years later with $8 million set aside for the museum. The January 17, 1906, issue of the *New York Times* discussed the death of "the richest merchant in the world, the largest individual taxpayer in the United States, and, perhaps, the third wealthiest citizen in the country." The *Times* editorialized that Field's life suggested what could be accomplished by "every beginner of native or foreign birth in this great and happy land." *World's Work* seconded that notion, celebrating the fact that Field initiated his business career as a penniless boy who mastered "the science of buying and selling things . . . to become the largest merchant in the whole world."

HORATIO ALGER JR.

Boasting ancestors dating back to the Plymouth Pilgrims, Horatio Alger Jr. was born in Chelsea, Massachusetts, on January 13, 1832, to Olive Feeno Alger, whose own father was a wealthy merchant and landowner, and Horatio Alger Sr., a graduate of Harvard College and the Theological School in Cambridge. The senior Alger's paltry salary as the Unitarian minister of the First Congregational Church and Society required him also to serve as the town's initial postmaster, a farmer, and a teacher. Financial difficulties beset the family, which eventually included five children, resulting in the sale of the Alger property and relocation in 1844 to Marlborough, located between Boston and Worcester. Afflicted with nearsightedness and asthma, Horatio initially received tutoring from his father, who taught him algebra and Latin, while the youngster read "whatever came in my way," he remembered, including the *Arabian Nights*, Josephus's *History of the Jews*, and "Jack the Giant Killer." Despite an early stuttering problem, Alger proved to be a star student, attending prep school at Gates Academy before entering Harvard at the age of sixteen. That experience proved delightful as he later recalled: "No period of my life has been of such unmixed happiness as the four years which have been spent within college walls." He covered some of his expenses at Harvard by serving as "President's Freshman," which required carrying out various errands for the college president, and he also received financial support from the industrialist Cyrus Alger, a cousin of Horatio Alger Sr. Alger sat in the classrooms of various luminaries at Harvard such as the poet Henry Wadsworth Longfellow, received a number of academic awards, and also began writing, becoming the class poet before graduating Phi Beta Kappa. He took classes from Unitarian professors who emphasized the importance of both intellectual accomplishments and moral uplift.

In 1853, the diminutive Alger enrolled in Harvard Divinity School but soon departed, accepting a job as assistant editor of the *Boston Daily Advertiser*. He remained for a few uneventful months before becoming an assistant teacher at a boarding school in East Greenwich, Rhode Island. In 1856, Alger headed a boys' academy in Deerfield, Massachusetts, but left the following year to become a private tutor and to write editorials for the *True Flag*, a Boston newspaper. He returned to Harvard Divinity School in 1857, graduating three years later. Alger published a collection of poems and stories, *Bertha's Christmas Visions: An Autumn Sheaf*, and an extended poem, *Nothing to Do: A Tilt at Our Best Society*, while a small number of his writings appeared in *Putnam's* and *Harper's New Monthly Magazine*. Shortly following his graduation from divinity school, Alger joined a cousin and a classmate on a tour of Europe that took them from the British Isles to Italy. Alger served as "a foreign correspondent" who offered various "European Letters" to the *New York Sun*, the penny paper. Following a year abroad, Alger returned home in the midst of the Civil War. He preached for a spell as a Unitarian minister, served as a private instructor, taught in Nahant, Massachusetts, and was drafted but avoided service in the Union army because of his asthmatic condition or because at five-foot-two he failed to meet the minimum height requirement. Several of his stories and poems now appeared in *Harper's New Monthly Magazine*, *Harper's Weekly*, and *Putnam's Magazine*, among other publications.

Alger's literary work at this point included crafting a pair of novels: *Frank's Campaign; or, What Boys Can Do on the Farm for the Camps* and *Paul Prescott's Charge*. The bookseller Aaron K. Loring agreed to publish *Frank's*

Campaign, Alger's first boys' book. The sixteen-year-old hero, Frank Frost, convinces his father to enlist in the Union army and he himself, a star pupil, quits school to run the family farm. Urging that bounties be paid to men who agree to fight on behalf of the Union, Frank battles against his small town's wealthiest individual, who objects that taxes will consequently increase. Frank eventually encounters a wealthy stranger, Henry Morton, who helps to rescue the Frost farm from the financial stranglehold of Frank's antagonist. Morton also promises to pay for Frank's college education. The delighted publisher handed Alger a fifty-dollar advance for the book, promising royalties of five cents for each copy sold. Alger's novel sold out within a month of its publication and a larger printing was issued. Loring urged his new author to deliver another novel as soon as possible.

"The high moral tone" of *Frank's Campaign* helped convince the hiring committee of the First Unitarian Church and Society of Brewster, Massachusetts, to offer Alger a ministerial post, paying $800 annually. In late 1864 he began his service as a minister there. He resigned after two years, indicating that "physical necessity" demanded he "leave his position in Brewster & the profession and . . . take some more healthful occupation." In fact, he had been accused of sexually abusing young male congregants, a charge he failed to refute, admitting that he had been "imprudent." Parish committeemen of the Unitarian Church indicated that if Alger had not resigned, "an arrest or something worse might have occurred," such as a lynching. They informed the American Unitarian Association that the scandal involved "gross immorality and . . . the abominable and revolting crime of unnatural familiarity with *boys*."

Alger now determined to make his living as a writer. His second novel, *Paul Prescott's Charge*, centers on a thirteen-year-old orphan, Paul Prescott, who feels compelled to pay off his late father's $500 debt. Forced into a poorhouse, where he has to rise at five each morning and work all day, Paul escapes. He ends up in New York City, where he is soon homeless but is taken in by a church's sexton and his wife. Paul subsequently displays his innate intelligence in school and obtains a job in a store. Paul saves enough to pay off his father's debt, ensuring that his father's "memory is free from reproach," and begins to thrive financially. Alger now obtained ten cents for each copy of *Paul Prescott's Charge* that was sold, the same royalty that Louisa May Alcott, author of *Little Women*, received.

Having left the ministry behind, Alger himself headed for the nation's largest metropolis, which, along with Boston, was already one of America's leading literary centers. He found comfortable lodging on Tenth Street, close to University Place, and awaited publication of his most recent books, *Helen Ford* and *Timothy Crump's Ward; or the New Year's Loan and What Came of It*, his first adult novel. *Helen Ford* features a young woman who performs song recitals to care for her flighty father, while *Timothy Crump's Ward* presents a poor family that takes in an abandoned baby girl. Alger soon completed another novel, *Charlie Codman's Cruise*, another boys' book, along with a series of short stories. His latest novel, Alger offered, was "more adventurous than its predecessors," with its protagonist compelled to endure trials more taxing than even Frank Frost or Paul Prescott had. The indigent, fourteen-year-old Charlie Codman is pirated out of Boston on the ship *Bouncing Betsey*. Charlie eventually manages to jump ship and return home, where his long-suffering mother marries a banker and Charlie appears to be heading "into smoother waters." Alger wrote, "The sky above him is cloudless. His character has been strengthened by his combat with adversity." The author sermonized, "Let us hope that his manhood may redeem the promise of his youth, and be graced by all the noblest attributes of humanity."

In 1867, Alger, now determining to focus on boys' books, produced the tale of "Ragged Dick," a so-called street Arab who lives on the streets of New York City. The story appeared in serialized fashion in *Student and Schoolmate*, a monthly periodical that presented moral tales for boys. The timing was propitious for Alger was experiencing financial difficulties, feeling compelled to move to a less expensive apartment in Greenwich Village. The first issue of "Ragged Dick or Street Life in New York" appeared in January 1867 and contained an illustration of the poor young bootblack. Charles Loring Brace, the social worker who founded the Children's Aid Society, informed Alger, "Young man, I can't sufficiently tell you how very important your story is to my work. 'Ragged Dick' has called the attention of many, many thousands to a situation most of them didn't know exists, and that many simply ignore." Brace spoke to Alger about the Newsboys' Lodging House, insisting that there the author would encounter "sufficient material for a hundred *Ragged Dicks*." Alger became involved in efforts to establish other large boardinghouses that offered a cot and an inexpensive meal for street Arabs.

The novel arrived the next year. It opens with a porter awakening Dick as he lies in the street. Dick talks of staying at a flophouse in the Old Bowery, in the southern sector of Manhattan where actors like Junius B. Booth and Edwin Forrest had once performed. When asked where he got the money to do so, Dick answers, "Made it by shines, of course." His guardian, the young lad continues, failed to provide any money for him to attend theatrical performances so he has "to earn it." When the porter counters, "Some boys get it easier than that," Dick retorts, "You don't catch me stealin,' if that's what you mean." The surprised porter asks, "Don't you ever steal, then?" and Dick replies, "No, and I wouldn't," although lots of the boys he knows do. Readying for his day of work, Dick is not troubled by the rags he wears or the dirt on his face. Despite his poverty, "there was something about Dick that was attractive," even "decidedly" so, the author wrote. In contrast to some of his counterparts who are "sly" and apparently distrustful, Dick possesses "a frank, straight-forward manner" that appeals to prospective customers. Dick charges ten cents but his first customer of the day, Mr. Greyson, has nothing less than a quarter and tells the boy to return the change to his office on Fulton Street.

Greyson wonders if "the little scamp" will show up, failing to understand Dick. The lad certainly possesses vices, including a readiness to swear on occasion, to play tricks on unknowing country boys, and to deliver wrong directions to gentlemen unfamiliar with New York City. Dick also can be extravagant, spending his earnings carelessly at the Old Bowery Theatre or Tony Pastor's vaudeville establishment. He smokes fairly expensive cigars. He gambles on Baxter Street. Although hardly a "model boy," Dick is "above doing anything mean or dishonorable. He would not steal, or cheat, or impose upon younger boys." Rather he is "frank and straight-forward, manly and self-reliant." Indeed, Dick possesses a "noble" nature that "saved him from all mean faults." After breakfast, Dick shines the shoes of a stylishly attired young man who hands him a two-dollar bill and asks him to get change. The clerk takes the bill when Dick enters a store but refuses to return it, declaring it counterfeit. Dick informs his customer about the incident and the two head back to the store, where the clerk is forced to relinquish the bill. Dick's customer pays him fifty cents for his troubles. Delighted, Dick thinks about going to Barnum's American Museum so he could "see the bearded lady, the eight-foot giant, the two-foot dwarf, and the other curiosities."

Overhearing a middle-aged gentleman and a thirteen- or fourteen-year-old boy named Frank talking about New York City, Dick offers to show the latter around. The gentleman, Mr. Whitney, considers the proposal "novel" and feels that Dick looks "honest." His new acquaintances guide Dick into a hotel where they give him a somewhat worn gray suit that Frank is ready to discard. Mr. Whitney admonishes Dick to clean up before he puts on the suit. After Dick bathes, Frank hands him a shirt, stockings, and shoes. Dick soon looks "quite handsome" and could pass "for a young gentleman" but for his worn, dirty hands. Dick calls Frank "a brick . . . a jolly good fellow" for treating him so kindly. The two set out to explore the city, soon spotting A.T. Stewart's department store on Tenth Street, the largest on Broadway. The Bowery is "a great place for shoppin'," offering goods "cheaper'n anybody else," Dick informs Frank. When asked about Barnum's Museum, Dick says that is where "lions, and bears, and curiosities generally" can be found. "It's a tip-top place," Dick affirms. "It's most as good as the Old Bowery, only the plays isn't quite so exciting."

Dick later appears eager when Frank promises to teach him how to read properly if he moves to New York City. Dick hopes he can "get somethin' else to do" eventually: "I'd like to be a office boy, and learn business, and grow up 'spectable.'" Dick again expresses appreciation for how kindly Frank has treated him, who has been called "Ragged Dick" and told that he would "grow up to be a vagabond . . . and come to the gallows." Frank denies that such a fate is likely to befall Dick, asserting, "If you'll try to be somebody, and grow up into a respectable member of society, you will." He continues, "You may not become rich,—it isn't everybody that becomes rich, you know,—but you can obtain a good position, and be respected." Dick promises that he will make the effort, admitting, "I needn't have been Ragged Dick so long if I hadn't spent my money in goin' to the theatre, and treatin' boys to oyster-stews, and bettin' money of cards, and such like."

Dick subsequently conveys his life story to Frank, explaining that his mother died when he was three years old and his father then headed off to sea. After boarding with a family until he was seven, Dick was on his own, selling matches and working as a newsboy in the days when Horace Greeley and James Gordon Bennett competed in the newspaper business. He has known difficult times. He has been hungry and cold but "there's one thing I never could do. . . . ," Dick revealed. "I never stole. It's mean and I wouldn't do it." By the time he departs from Frank, Dick has agreed to attend night school and to give up gambling. After dining out at a somewhat better restaurant than he is accustomed to, Dick rents an apartment, however spare and dirty, on Mott Street in the neighborhood of the Five Points, the mythic slum area.

He determines to show Frank that "I can do something." Dick goes to a savings bank where he deposits five dollars and receives a book indicating the name of the holder, Dick Hunter; he departs "with a new sense of importance." He feels "himself a capitalist" but also recognizes that he requires education to be considered respectable. The next morning, Dick remembers that he has not yet returned the change to his customer of two days earlier, Mr. Greyson. He heads for 125 Fulton Street, meets up with Greyson, and hands him fifteen cents in change. Remarking that Dick is an honest lad, Greyson asks who taught him to be that way. "Nobody," Dick replies. "But it's mean to cheat and steal. I've always knowed that." Greyson responds, "Then you've got ahead of some of our business men." When asked if he reads the Bible, Dick admits that he has not but has "heard it's a good book." After expressing his willingness to attend Sunday School, Dick receives an invitation to attend Greyson's church, located on Fifth Avenue.

That evening at a restaurant on Chatham Street, Dick encounters another bootblack, Henry Fosdick, sitting next to him. Dick buys him dinner and the two converse, Henry revealing that he has recently suffered the death of his father and thus cannot attend an academy as planned. The two agree that Henry will teach Dick to read and write and, in exchange, share Dick's room. On returning to Dick's apartment, the two immediately begin the first of many lessons. After the lesson ends, Henry teaches Dick, who is "not naturally irreligious," a prayer. The two boys now work side by side, with both depositing funds in savings accounts by the end of the week. Dick and Henry attend service at Greyson's church that Sunday morning. They then depart with the Greyson family down Fifth Avenue to have lunch at the Greyson brownstone on Twenty-fourth Street.

"A new life" begins for Alger's protagonist over the course of the next several weeks. Dick stops frequenting the Old Bowery and Tony Pastor's theater, studying instead for two hours each evening, proving to be "gifted with a natural quickness." Dick encourages Henry to take the bulk of the evergrowing savings the two have compiled and purchase new clothes. Henry soon obtains a position as an errand boy at a hat and cap store on Broadway, thanks to a recommendation by Greyson. Nine months later, Henry convinces Dick, whose speech has become more refined, to begin searching for a job himself. One day while walking with Henry along the South Ferry, Dick hears a man cry out when his child falls in the water. Dick rescues the six-year-old boy, returning him to his father. James Rockwell sends a new outfit of clothes to Dick and asks to see him at his office on Pearl Street the next day. Rockwell hires Dick as a clerk in his counting-room, paying a weekly salary of $10 and promising to promote his new employee "as your progress will justify it." Alger's novel concludes with Dick and Henry's determination to rent another apartment in a better part of town. The two agree that Dick should now consider himself "Richard Hunter, Esq." or, as Henry indicates, "a young gentleman on the way to fame and fortune."

Alger and the rags-to-respectability theme of *Ragged Dick* resonated with many readers in this period immediately following the Civil War, when economic opportunity seemed limitless for some in the midst of urban sprawl, industrial development, and heightened income disparities. The novel appeared on May 5, 1868, with the initial edition of several thousand copies quickly selling out and another edition released that summer. Reviews were highly favorable, with the *Boston Transcript* applauding "the courage, the ambition, the struggling nobility" of youngsters like Ragged Dick and proclaiming that Alger himself was "something more than a mere writer of juvenile books"— rather, he was "the philanthropist." Between 1868 and 1870, publisher Aaron K. Loring convinced Alger to write another handful of novels, a "Ragged Dick Series," which obtained little literary acclaim but sold well. In *Fame and Fortune*, Dick and Henry dwell on Bleecker Street, while Dick becomes first a bookkeeper and then a junior partner at Rockwell's firm. He also marries Ida

Greyson, his benefactor's daughter. In the years ahead, Alger wrote several more books for a "Luck and Pluck Series" that featured indigent country boys, intending to verify "that a manly spirit is better than the gifts of fortune." He also produced "The Tattered Tom Series," focusing on "other classes of street Arabs," and a "Brave and Bold Series," highlighting juvenile heroes including *The Western Boy.* Alger tutored a number of boys to supplement his income, including the children of the international banker Joseph Seligman, and wrote for *Ballou's, Harper's New Monthly Magazine, New York Weekly,* and *Young Israel.*

His fame enabled the balding Alger, sometimes decked out in a wig and cape, to meet Harriet Beecher Stowe, P.T. Barnum, Mark Twain, and President Ulysses S. Grant, among others. Shared interest in the Newsboys' Lodging House led to an acquaintanceship between Barnum and Alger. Barnum frequently gave out free passes to his New American Museum at the Newsboys' Lodging House. Alger would go along with several of the boys to Barnum's establishment. The two men believed that diligence, perseverance, and temperance would serve boys well. Alger resided in a room in a brownstone mansion on Thirty-fourth Street (at the future site of the Empire State Building) near the great Barnum home on Fifth Avenue, and the two sometimes shared a ride in the great showman's carriage.

Various controversies regarding American juvenile fiction developed in the 1870s and 1880s. During a sensational murder trial, the prosecutor charged that dime-novel westerns had induced the defendant to commit the crime. Self-styled moral arbiters already worried that dime novels wrongly influenced their young audience. At the Boston Public Library in late 1877, a speaker denounced the "endless reams" of "drivel poured forth by . . . Alger" and another popular writer. Librarians expressed concerns about "the freedom which most of our public libraries afford for the daily supply and exchange of this class of books among school children." Another librarian, however, contended that such literature served a purpose, that if young readers were not able "to read the stories of Messrs. Alger and [William T.] Adams," they would likely have "sought worse reading." Hopefully, that librarian acknowledged, "a boy begins by reading Alger's books. He goes to school. His mind matures. He outgrows the books that pleased him as a boy." In 1896 Alger himself admitted, "Sensational stories . . . do much harm, and are very objectionable. Many a boy has been tempted to crime by them."

Altogether Alger wrote more than 100 books, many of them celebrating poor boys who strove to make their mark in the changed American society of the late nineteenth century. During the 1880s, Street and Smith released paperback editions of his books, which continued to increase in volume, while A.L. Burt Publishing Company initiated a Boy's Home Library featuring

Alger's work. The sweep of his characters widened as they headed out west and then to Australia, experiencing adventure, violence, bad guys, and wealth along the way. By the end of the nineteenth century, Alger's books increasingly were out of vogue, although his rags-to-respectability message never wholly lost its allure. Various authors, including Edward Stratemeyer, considered Alger an inspiration for their own work. Stratemeyer delivered series about the adventurous Rover Boys and the Motor Boys, while Gilbert M. Patten created the Frank and Yale Merriwell characters who excelled in sports and experienced college life. Stratemeyer received plaudits for producing "the sort of book that used to come from the pen of Horatio Alger, Jr."

Publisher Aaron K. Loring once asserted, "Alger is the dominating figure of the new era. . . . he has captured the spirit of reborn America. The turmoil of the city streets. . . . Above all you can hear the cry of triumph of the oppressed over the oppressor. . . . the ambitious soul—of the country." As Russell Nye notes, Alger emphasized belief in self-reliance, reinforced middle-class values, and, better than other authors of his ilk, appreciated the altered nature of urban America. While urbanization and industrialization swept across the nation, Alger's protagonists once again celebrated time-honored "values of Puritan and Franklinian individualism." His novels underscored the American dream that hard work, pluck, and perhaps a little luck could enable even unfortunate individuals to thrive. Seemingly all that was required was honesty, intelligence, ambition, morality, and opportunism. In 1928 the *New York Times* referred to Alger's ability to craft "successful protagonists, ambitious boys who, through one variation or another of an ever-efficient formula, found their way up the ladder of achievement." The *Times* indicated during the midst of the Great Depression, "It was Alger's comforting thesis that virtue and industry are always rewarded." As his star rose, fell, and then ascended once more, Alger's books sold hundreds of millions of copies while preaching the gospel of perseverance and stick-to-itiveness.

Bibliography

Alger, Horatio. *Ragged Dick and Mark, the Match Boy.* New York: Collier Books, 1978.

Benson, Susan Porter. *Counter Cultures: Saleswomen, Managers, and Customers in American Department Stores, 1890–1940.* Champaign: University of Illinois Press, 1960.

Ferry, John William. *A History of the Department Store.* New York: Macmillan, 1960.

Gardner, Ralph D. *Horatio Alger or the American Hero Era.* New York: Arco, 1978.

Hendrickson, Robert. *The Grand Emporiums: The Illustrated History of America's Great Department Stores*. New York: Stein and Day, 1979.

Hoyt, Edwin. *Horatio's Boys: The Life and Works of Horatio Alger, Jr.* New Castle, DE: Oak Knoll Books, 1974.

Madsen, Axel. *The Marshall Fields: The Evolution of an American Business Dynasty*. New York: Wiley, 2002.

Scharnhorst, Gary. *Horatio Alger, Jr.* New York: Twayne, 1980.

Scharnhorst, Gary, with Jack Bales. *The Lost Life of Horatio Alger, Jr.* Bloomington: Indiana University Press, 1985.

Tebbel, John. *From Rags to Riches: Horatio Alger, Jr. and the American Dream*. New York: Macmillan, 1963.

Weiss, Richard. *The American Myth of Success: From Horatio Alger to Norman Vincent Peale*. Champaign, Illinois: University of Illinois Press, 1988.

Wendt, Lloyd, and Herman Kogan. *Give the Lady What She Wants! The Story of Marshall Field & Company*. New York: Rand McNally, 1952.

THREE

Stars of Vaudeville
and Tin Pan Alley

LILLIAN RUSSELL AND IRVING BERLIN

During the last part of the nineteenth century and the early stages of the twentieth, vaudeville and Tin Pan Alley dominated the American theatrical and musical fields. As the consumer culture became more embedded in the nation's economic, social, and psychic fabric, those brands of popular entertainment offered both live performances and audio recordings. Vaudeville and Tin Pan Alley reached across ethnic, class, and, occasionally, racial barriers during the very era when a massive influx of immigration was taking hold. The theatrical and musical offerings both highlighted and downplayed ethnic differences, often doing so in good-natured fashion, while racial restrictions and stereotypes sometimes proved as heavy-handed as before.

The economic depression that began in 1873 weakened blackface minstrelsy, which was further crippled by artistic stagnation and its association with racism. Minstrelsy did not die out altogether nor did the live shows offered in concert salons and variety halls. Nevertheless, something different clearly began to emerge on the evening of October 24, 1881, when Tony Pastor— later acclaimed the "father of vaudeville"—opened his Fourteenth Street Theater in New York City. Like P.T. Barnum, Pastor envisioned attracting a broader clientele than the often-boisterous sorts who frequented the saloons and male-oriented variety centers. Pastor instead sought to attract both men and women, including affluent members of the American middle class, by providing a less bawdy brand of entertainment. Indeed, he highlighted the fact that his theater would be "catering to the ladies" while providing entertainment for "the cultivated and aesthetic." It was believed that the presence of women would ensure a certain level of civility and basic decency. The first evening's show at the Fourteenth Street Theater included comedy, burlesque, acrobatics, blackface comedy, loftier fare, and a male impersonator. Similar performances appeared on stage at the other vaudeville houses that sprang up in Manhattan and in urban centers around the country. Typical offerings included displays of athletic prowess by musclemen and sports stars, magic acts, animal tricks, operatic deliveries, gymnastics, and lectures by well-known figures.

Vaudeville houses welcomed immigrant and native-stock patrons alike, generally excluding or at times segregating dark-skinned individuals, particularly African-Americans. As more vaudeville theaters appeared, patrons included not merely the well-heeled, but also working-class individuals seeking relief from the tedium of their labor or an escape from the oppressive tenements they inhabited. Chains of vaudeville houses appeared, with Benjamin Franklin Keith, a one-time grafter, setting the pace after operating out of a storefront museum in Boston. Keith soon established theaters along the eastern seaboard, keeping admission prices low and advertising widely in newspapers in an effort to attract more patrons. Vaudeville theaters came to be open six days a week, providing afternoon and evening shows while attracting crowds by operating hour after hour. To outdo competitors, some vaudeville managers and performers challenged what was considered to be fitting and proper through off-color deliveries and sensual skits. Those same managers tried at the same time to snare adults and kids, with children enthralled by animal acts and families drawn by promises of wholesome entertainment. Vaudeville performers were heralded as Irish, Jewish, German, or "colored," with appropriate dialects and apparel. Stars included theatrical performers such as Lillian Russell and Sarah Bernhardt, singers as famed as Eddie Cantor and Al Jolson, comedians on the order of Fanny Brice and Weber & Fields, and African-American artists as skilled as Bert Williams and George Walker, billed as The Two Real Coons.

At the end of the nineteenth century no vaudeville performer appeared more luminous than the lovely Lillian Russell, the star of Pastor's comic operas and the longtime acquaintance of Diamond Jim Brady, the financier, philanthropist, and celebrant of Broadway. The great soprano accepted lead roles in *H.M.S. Pinafore, Patience, The Sorcerer*, and *The Brigands*, among other productions, as she helped to popularize musical theater in the United States. Russell embodied a standard of feminine beauty in keeping with Victorian America. With middle age setting in, "The American Beauty" suffered the fate of many female performers in the United States but was applauded as the American theater's *grande dame* while appearing at Weber & Field's Music Hall and establishing the Lillian Russell Opera Company. Russell later generously supported the Actors' Equity strike that followed World War I and backed chorus girls from the Ziegfeld Follies who established the Chorus Equity Association.

The heyday of Tin Pan Alley did not coincide with the peak of Russell's career, but other vaudeville luminaries excelled both in the live theater and through recordings of their work. Commercial popular music increasingly

45

found a home in New York City. Tin Pan Alley began cropping up on West Twenty-eighth Street between Broadway and Sixth Avenue by the 1890s, with music publishers setting up shop. They sold sheet music, as many as 200 million copies annually by the end of World War I. Early million sellers included "Let Me Call You Sweetheart," "Daisy Bell (The Bicycle Built for Two)," "Bill Bailey, Won't You Please Come Home?" and "Down by the Old Mill Stream." The proliferation of vaudeville theaters helped to advertise particular singers, various composers, and their tunes. Leading songwriters included Ernest R. Ball, Gus Edwards, and Harry von Tilzer, who wrote both "Take Me Out to the Ball Game" and "I Want a Girl Just Like the Girl Who Married Dear Old Dad." The scientific genius of Thomas Edison helped set the stage for the recordings of Tin Pan Alley songs. By the first decade of the twentieth century, a fierce competition existed between Columbia and the Victor Talking Machine Company.

In 1911 von Tilzer's stardom dimmed somewhat as a new songwriter catapulted to the top rung of American balladeers. A young Russian Jewish immigrant with the Anglicized name of Irving Berlin became known as the King of Ragtime Songs following the release of his "Alexander's Ragtime Band." Berlin's "Oh, How I Hate to Get Up in the Morning" proved enormously popular during World War I. When peacetime returned Berlin established his own music-publishing company and helped to set up the Music Box Theater in New York, where he featured his own revues. While the sale of sheet music plummeted with the introduction of radio, Berlin continued to write popular songs, including several that became featured in Hollywood or later on television. These included "Blue Skies," which was featured in *The Jazz Singer* (1927), the first motion picture with sound, and the scores for such films as *Top Hat* (1935) and *Holiday Inn* (1942). Two of Berlin's most beloved tunes were "God Bless America" and, ironically enough, "White Christmas."

LILLIAN RUSSELL

Lillian Russell was born Helen Louise Leonard, the youngest of five daughters of Charlie Russell, a mild-mannered newspaper publisher, and his wife Cynthia, attractive, hard driving, and ambitious, in Clinton, Iowa, in 1861. An ardent feminist, the frustrated Cynthia worked diligently to establish schools and churches in booming Clinton and performed as a musician and soloist for the local Baptist church. The family moved to Chicago when Russell was two years old. Charlie became a printer and Cynthia engaged in reform efforts of all kinds, including those pertaining to women's rights. The author of a pair of novels, Cynthia also attended to the needs of her children, including her youngest, who, as the nuns at the Sacred Heart school recognized, was a gifted singer. Cynthia, having determined to abandon her husband, spirited off the blonde-haired, blue-eyed, shapely Russell to New York City in 1878 to pursue a stage career. Charlie remained in Chicago, soon acquiring notoriety as the man who published the books of Robert G. Ingersoll, America's leading proponent of free thought, also known as "the Great Agnostic."

In New York, Cynthia placed her daughter under the tutelage of a voice instructor, Leopold Damrosch, with the expectation that an operatic career would be forthcoming. Little inclined to devote the time such an undertaking would require, Russell envisioned another venue altogether: the popular theater. In mid-November 1878 Russell made her initial appearance in a production of *H.M.S. Pinafore*, the Gilbert and Sullivan operetta presented by Edward E. Rice at the Boston Museum. *Pinafore* proved a smash hit, as did the buxom young singer, who quickly caught the attention of orchestra leader Harry Braham. The two married and soon had a son who died following injuries suffered while under a nurse's care. The still teenaged Russell got her big break as her already troubled marriage disintegrated. While singing at the home of a friend, the five-foot-six Russell encountered the diminutive Tony Pastor, the vaudeville producer, who asked, "How would you like to sing those songs every night in my theater for seventy-five dollars a week?" As she returned to her own room, an appreciation that her "hopes were about to be realized rushed over" Russell.

"The beautiful girl with the golden voice and golden hair" showed up at Tony Pastor's Theater in Manhattan the following day. Russell likened Pastor to "a little general," with his black hair, waxed and pointed mustache, immaculate attire, and polished manners. The theater sparkled as well, offering seats for a dollar and a half in an effort to attract more customers. Smoking was prohibited. The audience appeared in dress clothes, thus creating an atmosphere equally attractive to men and women. Little did Russell know that the most beloved theatrical figures of their generation, including Gus Williams, Jenny Yeamans, Flo Irwin, May Irwin, and Dan Daly, regularly performed at Pastor's Theater. Pastor indicated that Russell would start the next week but she responded, "Oh! I can't. I forgot. I haven't anything to wear on stage and I don't want my mother to know what I'm doing. I want to wait until I've done something big and then surprise her." Taking fifty dollars from Pastor, Russell purchased a beautiful, white satin dress. To avoid having her mother discover that she was performing on the vaudeville stage, she worked under the name of Lillian Russell.

The billing for her first performance included the Irwin sisters, while the soprano Russell herself was referred to as an "English Ballad Singer," offering "a vision of loveliness and a voice of gold." Pastor gave her a raise within two weeks and soon delivered yet another one as his patrons commended her "sparkling genius." Russell performed nightly at his theater for a month, leaving the boardinghouse where she lived with her mother, who was invariably busy with the suffragist campaign. However, one evening, a newspaperman who resided in the same house began explaining to Cynthia "that there is a girl named Lillian Russell, who sings at Tony Pastor's Theater, who looks enough like your little Nellie to be her sister." He proceeded to invite Cynthia to attend a performance there. Discovering that her daughter was the popular Lillian Russell, Cynthia initially sat in stunned silence but soon joined the rest of the crowd in offering "tumultuous applause." After Russell revealed how much money she had already saved from her earnings, a pleased Cynthia enthusiastically backed her daughter's new career.

Russell appeared in Pastor's adaptation of W.S. Gilbert and Arthur Sullivan's *The Pirates of Penzance*, renamed *The Pie Rats of Penn Yann*, which included Flo Irwin, May Irwin, and Russell in the cast. After seeing Russell on stage, Gilbert, Sullivan, and their manager D'Oyly Carte tried to steal her away from Pastor. She declined, soon receiving a lead role in Pastor's presentation of *Olivette*, which began in early March 1881. A critic at the *Dramatic Mirror* sang her praises: "Miss Lillian Russell . . . acted and sang most charmingly, and was faultlessly costumed. If the young woman does not allow adulation to conquer her ambition and elevate her too high in her own esteem, she will become a bright and shining star light on the lyric stage." Pastor soon sent Russell out west with a troupe headed by the comedian Willie Edouin, to appear in *Babes in the Woods* and *Fun in a Photography Gallery*. To the delight of male patrons in San Francisco, Russell displayed her legs in purple tights and encountered admirers eager to spirit her off to lavish parties. Returning to New York in the fall of 1881, Russell received more kudos thanks to her performance as D'Jemma in *The Snake Charmer*, an adaptation of Edmond Audran's comic opera, *Le Grand Mogul. The Spirit of the Times* noted, "Lillian Russell's looks, costumes, singing and acting create a furor. A year ago we noticed this little lady at Tony Pastor's; now she is a bright particular star of *opera bouffe*. There is nothing to compare with her in this country." The *Dramatic Mirror* praised her as well: "Lillian Russell is a charming singer, and as pretty as a posy." With her natural beauty and stage presence, Russell had become representative of the new American woman who threatened to emerge in the post–Civil War era. She was soon to begin a nearly forty-year reign "as queen of the American musical comedy stage" and "the best-known woman in America."

Although Russell's salary remained relatively low at this point, admirers handed her riches ranging from fruit and roses to jewelry and cash. She later acknowledged that one ardent fan sent presents costing $100,000 during a three-month period. Russell nevertheless proved increasingly dissatisfied with her financial arrangement with Pastor, and in the midst of the run of *Billee Taylor*, she left her mentor's fold. Receiving a raise to $250 a week, Russell starred in John A. McCaull's presentation of *The Sorcerer*, the Gilbert and Sullivan play, which proved a big hit at the Bijou Opera House and helped to cement her stardom. The *Dramatic Mirror* waxed eloquent: "Lillian Russell is charming; she sings music like a transmigrated nightingale, acts like a materialized grace, and looks like Venus after the bath." A theater critic in the *New York Herald* proclaimed, "Miss Russell had a beautiful face, a rare figure and a delightful voice that has not been sufficiently trained. If this lady learns to bring her acting up to the level of her other accomplishments, she will be invaluable in comic opera."

A major celebrity by this point, Russell remained constantly in the limelight in part because of her often-turbulent personal life. At the Bijou Opera House, she fell for another orchestra leader, the Englishman Edward Solomon. After another show that Russell starred in completed its run, Solomon convinced her to ignore a series of contracts she had signed and appear instead on the London stage. Receiving some of her worst press ever, Russell sailed for England along with her lover, whom she soon married. Gilbert and Sullivan hoped to feature her in one of their productions, although a personal spat prevented that from occurring. Although rumors spread that Russell was difficult to handle and all too ready to break contracts, she starred as Virginia in *Virginia and Paul* at the Gaiety. Her daughter Dorothy was born in 1884 and Russell appeared in another operetta, *Polly, the Pet of the Regiment*, with Solomon's musical score, and then as *Pocahontas*.

Russell returned to the States the following year for a New York rendition of *Polly* with her stardom reaffirmed. A scandal soon erupted. News emerged that Solomon was guilty of bigamy. Quickly moving on, Russell performed in Newport, Rhode Island, before initiating an extended run at the Broadway Theater in *The Queen's Mate*. A court case soon unfolded in which the producer of her latest show sued Russell, who, perhaps due to concerns about her broadening figure, refused to appear in tights. The resulting publicity merely heightened interest in Russell's stage performances, while garnering a generous contract for her at the magnificent Casino Theater at Thirty-ninth Street and Broadway. The top light opera house in the country, the Casino put on shows attended by General William T. Sherman and Diamond Jim Brady, among others. Now called the "Queen of Light Opera," Russell starred at the Casino in *Nadjy*, *The Brigands*, *The Grand Duchess* (her biggest hit), and *Poor Jonathan*. Her performance in *Nadjy* led one critic to proclaim, "She never looked so handsome, nor sang with such force and brilliance. Unquestionably, she is the Queen of Comic Opera in this country." Remembering having seen Russell on stage, the writer Clarence Day recalled, "There was nothing wraithlike about Lillian Russell; she was a voluptuous beauty, and there was plenty of her to see. We liked that. Our tastes were not thin, or ethereal. We like flesh in the Nineties. It didn't have to be bare, and it wasn't, but it had to be there."

As the new decade began Russell remained America's preeminent light operatic performer. This proved difficult at times. She complained, "The stage is so exacting. It demands your whole life. There is no pleasure in it." No matter—the actress Marie Dressler noted how audiences responded to Russell: "I can still recall the rush of pure awe that marked her entrance on the stage. And then the thunderous applause that swept from orchestra to gallery, to the very roof." Her performance in *The Grand Duchess* led the *Dramatic Mirror* to assert that "not even the Frenchwomen ever sang as well or looked as handsome as our own Lillian." Signing with T. Henry French, Russell now earned $1,250 a week, along with a percentage of box office and concession receipts, surpassing the amount paid to any other Broadway star of the era. She purchased a three-floor brownstone on West Seventy-seventh Street, between the fashionable West End Avenue and Riverside Drive.

In the midst of a four-month-long engagement in Chicago during the Columbia Exposition in the summer of 1893, Russell met Diamond Jim Brady, subsequently establishing a long-standing relationship. Brady enjoyed taking Russell out on the town, while invariably providing her with diamonds and other jewelry. In January 1894 she wedded Signor Giovanni Perugini, a tenor who actually hailed from rural Michigan and was originally named Jack Chatterton. The newlyweds apparently never consummated their marriage, and Perugini proved verbally and physically abusive. Although her third attempt at nuptial bliss had proved the most disastrous yet, Russell could always turn to Jim Brady for support. Russell soon performed in London yet again before returning to the Broadway Theater. She suffered another blow when a critic indicated that she was "affable, kindly . . . as filling as a plum pudding." Now drawing $1,500 a week in salary, Russell also confronted comic opera's waning popularity. Nevertheless, during a tour in Germany she was able to demand twice that salary, in addition to expenses, while drawing the unwanted attention of Prince Henry of Pless. Russell appeared at the court of Kaiser Wilhelm II, but also suffered scathing critiques of her fading beauty. More happily or not, she conducted an affair with Jesse Lewisohn, a scion of American copper magnates. In Saratoga, Russell and Brady, along with their lovers, served as "the uncrowned rulers of the spa."

At the end of the 1890s, when the aura that surrounded her had waned a bit, Russell's career underwent a much-needed transformation. She seamlessly became a featured player in the popular burlesque company of Joe Weber and Lewis Fields at their Music Hall on Twenty-ninth Street. The unlikely partnership lasted for six years. During this same period Russell's standing as the classic American beauty faded. The new model was the Gibson Girl, the younger, slender, athletic version of Russell drawn by Charles Dana Gibson. This updated version of American femininity appeared to possess the facial features of the young Russell, but also boasted the hourglass shape that the great singer no longer did. Dieting did enable Russell to drop several pounds and even join Brady in the bicycle-built-for-two craze that had taken hold. With her youthful sex appeal diminishing and her voice exhibiting strain, Russell now became something of the great lady of the American stage, acquiring a different kind of iconic status in the period when musical comedies supplanted light operas as the dominant American theatrical genre. During the production of *Twirly Whirly* in 1902 Russell sang "Come Down, Ma Evenin' Star," which John Stromberg wrote for her. It became a trademark song of Russell's and she recorded it ten years later. The Weber and Fields troupe continued to pack in the crowds, undertaking a transcontinental trip to San Francisco in 1904 before the male stars terminated their partnership.

A subsequent attempt by Russell at straight comedy in *Barbara's Millions* flopped. Now in her mid-forties, Russell starred in *The Butterfly*, no artistic success but still a well-paying venue. The April 20, 1907, edition of the *Dramatic Mirror* sang her praises, indicating that Russell had again demonstrated "the existence of that good nature, which, after her beauty, is the greatest of her charms." She determined to leave the musical theater behind but when called on to deliver a speech after a production of *The Butterfly*, Russell said, "I can't make a speech, but if you want me to I will sing a song." Russell then delighted the crowd with a version of "Ma Cherie," "Evening Star," and another tune from an earlier operatic performance.

The depression of 1907 resulted in the collapse of a bank where Russell was a customer, costing her $75,000 and compelling her to sell her townhouse. Investing in a road company, Russell traveled in a Pullman car. She returned to the New York stage in 1908 to appear in *Wildfire*, which ran at the Liberty Theater for two years. After a troubled couple of years, Russell reunited with Weber and Fields to star in *Hokey Pokey*, which opened on February 8, 1912. That summer she married an old flame, Alexander P. Moore, publisher of the *Pittsburgh Leader* and later the U.S. ambassador to Spain. Shortly after her latest wedding, Russell retired from the theater although she participated in a small number of vaudeville revues over the next few years.

Along with her husband, Russell supported another presidential bid by Theodore Roosevelt, speaking on behalf of the former chief executive, insisting that a victory for his Bull Moose Party "means an advancement of one hundred years for women in this country and the world." Following the 1912 presidential campaign, Russell wrote a column for the *Chicago Tribune* that focused on women's issues, but was hardly designed to serve as a feminist forum. Russell offered such words of wisdom as these: "I believe that all beauty is a gift from God and that it is given to all women." She also produced articles for the *Pittsburgh Leader* and delivered lectures on health and beauty. Russell backed the prohibition movement, writing an article, "Drink and Be Ugly." In 1915, she starred, alongside Lionel Barrymore, in the film production of *Wildfire*, which hardly equaled the theatrical version. Russell devoted herself once more to social causes, offering a column for the *Chicago Record-Herald*, a newspaper that afforded her greater freedom. In 1915 she joined with 50,000 women in a display of feminist solidarity, marching up Fifth Avenue to Central Park. She opposed child labor, called for free lunches for poor children who attended public schools, and insisted that women be represented in the judicial system. Following the entrance of the United States into World War I two years later, Russell joined in recruitment drives and Liberty Bond rallies.

Russell in her fifties and early sixties remained a strikingly beautiful woman, as attested by photographs of her. One Broadway observer indicated how the actress generally managed to overcome the ravages of time:

> Lillian Russell took better care of herself than any stage star I ever knew. She was never seen in Rector's or Shanley's after the show. She never indulged in any midnight parties. Night life meant nothing to her. When her performance was over, she went straight home and to bed. Perhaps she would have a bite of supper and a glass of champagne with a few friends in her apartment, but that was the extent of her 'dissipation.'

Nevertheless, as the 1920s began, Russell hardly still represented the ideal feminine beauty, not with the advent of the flat-chested, narrow-hipped flapper.

Following the election of Warren G. Harding as president, Russell received an appointment as special commissioner of immigration, which required her to tour Europe for several months. In the report she delivered to Secretary of Labor James Davis, Russell recommended that American diplomatic officials be allowed to test the mental capacities of potential immigrants, that American physicians check on their physical condition, and that immigration to the United States be suspended for five years. Russell claimed, "Our melting-pot has been overcrowded, it has boiled too quickly, and is running over. . . . If we don't put up the bars and make them higher and stronger, there no longer will be an America for Americans."

Returning home from Europe, Russell experienced internal injuries after a fall. She died in Pittsburgh on June 6, 1922. On receiving word of her death,

President Harding, several members of his cabinet, senators, governors, business leaders, journalists, and authors sang Russell's praises, extolling her "wonderful personality" and insisting that this "truly good woman" had served as a "symbol of the imperishable in feminine charm." An editorial in the *New York World* asserted that "Russell had a good time with life. This and her beauty are the facts that dominate the thought when one sits down to write of her in terms of farewell." The *American Review of Reviews* affirmed that Russell was "one of the most beautiful of stage women throughout the world" while *The Literary Digest* declared that she was among a handful of "distinctly American stage personalities of the past half-century."

IRVING BERLIN

On May 11, 1888, Irving Berlin was born Israel Isidore Beilin in Mohilev, 125 miles from the city of Minsk, which served as the capital of White Russia. The impoverished town of Mohilev was situated in the Pale of Settlement where Czar Alexander III insisted that Jews—who were saddled with numerous restrictions in his empire—reside. Alexander's policy fostered anti-Semitism, leading to a series of pogroms that compelled many Jews to escape to central or western Europe, Palestine, or the promised land of America. Like most of their Jewish brethren in Mohilev, Berlin's parents, Lena Jarchin and Moses Beilin, a cantor, practiced Orthodox Judaism. Their young Izzy witnessed the burning down of his family home when a pogrom swept through the town. In 1893 Moses and Lena opted to take their family of eight across the Atlantic aboard the *Rhynland*. Like many European Jews of that era, they passed through Ellis Island before settling in a three-room tenement basement in the heavily Jewish Lower East Side of New York City. Soon, however, the Beilins moved to a brownstone at 330 Cherry Street, where they, along with a boarder, occupied the third floor.

Life in the great American metropolis was not easy for the Beilins, who spoke only Yiddish and stood apart with their "Jew clothes," even in the lower sector of Manhattan where so many Jews resided. Moses was reduced first to serving as a kosher poultry inspector and then to giving Hebrew lessons and working as a house painter. The family never went hungry, however, as Lena worked as a midwife, three daughters obtained work on occasion wrapping cigars, and the oldest son ended up in a sweatshop. Like many young boys during that era, Berlin ran errands, delivered telegrams, toiled in a sweatshop, and sold newspapers, including William Randolph Hearst's sensationalistic *Evening Journal*, on the street corners of New York City. He also attended public school, proving to be an indifferent student at best; one teacher complained, "He just dreams and sings to himself." Berlin went to religious school too, readying for his bar mitzvah ceremony, and honed his singing skills at the local synagogue. Berlin later suggested that "singing in *shul* . . . gave me my musical background. . . . It was in my blood." In 1901 his fifty-three-year-old father died and the family's circumstances threatened to darken further. The now thirteen-year-old Berlin left school and soon "went on the bum," departing from his home. Like the vagabond children in Horatio Alger's novels, Berlin stayed in lodging houses or worse in the Bowery for two years. The Bowery contained an array of popular cultural venues, including saloons, bars, concert halls, dance halls, and theaters, with admission inexpensive and performers catering to immigrant audiences. Coming from a long line of cantors and rabbis, Berlin realized that singing might provide a means out of the ghetto. He headed into various saloons as a "street busker," hoping to earn enough money to stay in a flophouse rather than having to sleep on a park bench. Berlin witnessed the underbelly of America and wanted "only . . . to get the hell out of" there.

In 1902 Berlin landed in the chorus of a theatrical production, *The Show Girl*, but his role was cut before the musical ran on Broadway. He soon determined to head for Tin Pan Alley, the music publishing houses situated on West Twenty-eighth Street. Emboldened by his brief theatrical stint or desperate about his still precarious economic condition, Berlin managed to meet Harry Von Tilzer, the top Tin Pan Alley publisher. Von Tilzer hired the short, skinny Berlin as "a singing stooge," who would sit in Tony Pastor's Music Hall at Union Square and generate applause for a musical-comedy team, The Three Keatons, Ma, Pa, and Buster. Berlin also sang in movie houses, as movie reels were changed, and became friendly with Chuck Connors, the so-called Mayor of Chinatown. Connors possibly introduced Berlin to "Nigger Mike" Salter, a Jew with an olive complexion, who ran the Pelham Café, a dance hall and bar at 12 Pell Street in Chinatown, which both Irish-Italian and Jewish gang members frequented. Salter hired the likable Berlin as a singing waiter who put in long hours and received seven dollars a week along with tips often tossed by inebriated patrons. Exhibiting an ability to parody popular songs, Berlin sang well-known ballads by George M. Cohan such as "Ring to the Name of Rosie" and "Yankee Doodle Boy." To accommodate Salter's wishes for a song that would attract more tourists, Berlin crafted the lyrics for "Marie from Sunny Italy," the songsheet of which was released by Joseph W. Stern, a noted music publisher, on May 8, 1907, and earned the fledgling songwriter thirty-seven cents during the first year of its release. The song also resulted in his name change following the misprinting of "Israel Balin" and its replacement by "I. Berlin."

The ambitious Berlin, all of five feet, six inches packed on a frame carrying less than 125 pounds, departed from Chinatown and the Lower East Side, obtaining another job as a singing waiter at Jimmy Kelly's restaurant at 212 East Fourteenth Street, closer to Tin Pan Alley. Berlin now shared an apartment at East Eighteenth Street with Max Winslow, who worked for Von Tilzer and had earlier attempted to hire Irving as a lyricist. Berlin continued writing songs, co-authoring "Queenie, My Own," which motion picture mogul Carl Laemmle purchased, but the song failed to attract customers. The star performer Marie Cahill bought another song with Berlin lyrics, "She Was a Dear Little Girl," which she sang in the stage production *The Boys and Betty*. Berlin co-wrote "Wait, Wait, Wait," which netted a couple of hundred dollars in royalties. With the public wanting more than "old 'coon' songs," Berlin agreed to produce lyrics for a performer at Tony Pastor's for a ten-dollar payment. Berlin used as an inspiration the tale of Dorando Pietri, who appeared to have locked up the marathon gold medal at the 1908 Olympic Games in London before collapsing near the finish line. Berlin's "Dorando" proved a hit, garnering him $4,000 in royalties. A scandal concerning a production of *Salome*, the opera by Richard Strauss, led to one of his next songs, "Sadie Salome—Go Home." This tune, which helped to launch the career of Fanny Brice, sold 3,000 copies, leading the new publishing team of Henry Waterson and Ted Snyder to offer Berlin a position as a staff lyricist. He instead agreed to produce lyrics for their company for a twenty-five-dollar weekly salary plus royalties.

Then, in 1909, the twenty-one-year-old Berlin had another commercial hit, "My Wife's Gone to the Country," which sold 300,000 copies, becoming a national sensation. The lines, "My wife's gone to the country! Hurrah!" produced a kind of joyous hilarity that resonated with the American public. A subsequent song, "That Mesmerizing Mendelssohn Tune," proved an even bigger smash, selling over half a million copies and garnering $6,000 in royalties. Berlin was about to truly make his mark in the pantheon of leading American songwriters, who included the ill-fated Stephen Foster, the brilliant composer of "Oh! Susanna" and "Jeanie with the Light Brown Hair"; Foster had died penniless. Berlin attempted to break into the Broadway theater, linking up with Ted Snyder, who crafted melodies to go along with Irving's lyrics. A new production, *The Girl and the Wizard*, began its run in September 1909, complete with a Berlin and Snyder number, "Oh, How That German Could Love." More Berlin-Snyder pieces wafted through Broadway the following year and the *New York World* applauded him as "the most successful songwriter of the year." Berlin traveled with Henry Waterson to meet the company's British representative in London, where he was treated as something of a celebrity. Back home, Berlin continued pumping out songs, including ethnic and racially drawn ones called "'coon' songs." Berlin's "Call Me Up

Some Rainy Afternoon" offered his lyrics and music while doing fairly well commercially.

Berlin drew on lyrics from Stephen Foster and the ragtime phenomenon earlier associated with Scott Joplin to produce "Alexander's Ragtime Band" in 1911, after the music to the song sat in his "desk unpublished for a year." As vaudeville performers around the country, including Al Jolson, began crooning Berlin's latest hit, a young George Gershwin reportedly said, "This is American music. This is the way an American should write." The song that became, as Berlin referred to it, "a 'riot,' both here and in Europe," sold 2 million copies by the end of 1912, proving an international sensation in England and on the European continent. "Alexander's Ragtime Band" was reportedly "the biggest song hit ever known." It was certainly the best-selling song the industry had yet presented and transformed American music with the new melody drawn from honky-tonks. Songs like "Alexander's Ragtime Band" challenged American Victorianism altogether. Some charged that Berlin had not written his latest hit song, which purportedly had been delivered by a black pianist. Berlin felt compelled to declare, "When they told me about it, I asked them to tell me from whom I had bought my other successes—twenty-five or thirty of them. And I wanted to know, if a Negro could write 'Alexander,' why couldn't I?" Rumors still persisted that Joplin had crafted the popular hit.

No matter—Berlin had become something of a popular cultural industry, referred to as "the Hit Maker." Berlin was now considered one of the nation's leading songwriters, had produced a number of top commercial hits, and had appeared in vaudeville revues, in which he performed his own compositions. He also began to deliver songs for Broadway producer Florenz Ziegfeld Jr. Determined to have a lengthy career and to avoid the misfortunes of Stephen Foster, Berlin remained driven. In late 1911 he produced "Everybody's Doin' It Now," which fit in perfectly with the dance craze associated with the revival of ragtime music. Acclaimed "the Ragtime King," Berlin continued pumping out songs, purchased a house in the Bronx for his mother, and married the lovely Dorothy Goetz. While honeymooning in Cuba, twenty-year-old Dorothy was afflicted with typhoid fever and she remained ill shortly after the Berlins moved to their apartment at Seventy-second Street and Riverside Drive on Manhattan's Upper West Side. She died on July 17, 1912, a mere five months after having met Irving. During the period of his mourning, Berlin wrote "When I Lost You" a million-copy seller that was the last ballad he devised for many years. George M. Cohan referred to it as "the prettiest song I've ever heard in my life."

Returning to Europe a year after Dorothy's death, Berlin discovered that his acclaim had become greater still. The *Daily Express* exclaimed, "Go where you will, you cannot escape from the mazes of music he has spun"; in

European capitals from London to Venice his songs were played. The paper then explained, "Ragtime has swept like a whirlwind over the earth and set civilization humming. Mr. Berlin started it." The audience's response during his appearance at the Hippodrome in London, where he offered "The International Rag," "Alexander's Ragtime Band," and, of course, "When I Lost You," convinced Berlin that his fame as the Ragtime King was deserved. Back home Berlin received accolades in the popular press, including *The American Magazine*, which in its October 1914 issue referred to the fact that he had received royalties amounting to a quarter of a million dollars over the past five years and had surpassed $100,000 in one year alone. Berlin's tunes contained "infectious rhythms and syncopations [that] set first America and then England and the Continent to swaying," writer Ralph Brock Pemberton suggested. Moreover, Berlin "established the song hit as a money-making institution."

Broadway now beckoned more than ever, to Berlin's delight. He completed the "syncopated" musical score for a new production of Charles Dillingham, *Watch Your Step*, which opened on December 8, 1914. Berlin considered this "the first time Tin Pan Alley got into the legitimate theater" and was thrilled by the experience. The show starred the husband-and-wife team of Irene and Vernon Castle, the most renowned ballroom dancers during the era of the bunny hug, the fox trot, the Texas Tommy, and other leading social dances. Indeed, Philip Furia suggests that the Castles did for American dance the same thing "Alexander's Ragtime Band" did for ragtime, making it respectable by tempering its verve and sensuality. Berlin for his part captured the carefree sensibility characteristic of the social dance. As for *Watch Your Step*, it achieved critical acclaim, with one chronicler praising Berlin as "one of the greatest lyrical writers America has ever produced." The *New York Times* asserted, "More than to any one else, 'Watch Your Step' belongs to Irving Berlin. He is the young master of syncopation, the gifted and industrious writer of words and music for songs that have made him rich and envied." In 1915 the Globe Theatre featured another Dillingham production, *Stop! Look! Listen!*, which contained another Berlin score with songs like "The Girl on the Magazine Cover" and "I Love a Piano." By now Berlin amassed still greater royalties through the newly established music publishing company of Waterson, Berlin and Snyder, which released his songs. In 1916 Berlin and another leading composer of the era, Victor Herbert, crafted tunes for Florenz Ziegfeld's latest revue, *The Century Girl*, an ode to the American woman.

That same year *Literary Digest* highlighted Berlin in an article titled "The Birth of Our Popular Song." New York's Bowery district, the magazine noted, served as "the nursery of our popular songs," with figures like Stephen Foster, Harry Von Tilzer, Gus Edwards, L. Wolfe Gilbert, and Irving Berlin getting their start "there or thereabouts." According to the *Digest*, Berlin was now as well known on the continent as several European musical stars. "For a full season," his "Alexander's Ragtime Band" had "kept the hearts and the feet of several million foreigners dancing to his syncopated melody." Berlin had knocked out "hit after hit" in addition to a pair of Broadway musical scores. He possessed his own automobile, had a personal secretary, and headed his own musical firm, but remained "the same modest, unassuming fellow that he was when a dollar looked big to him." Berlin appeared to know little about music's complexities but "melodies just bubble out of his system. He has an ear for harmony, and can recognize a catchy strain the second he hears one."

The outbreak of World War I produced a conundrum for Tin Pan Alley songwriters. Al Piantadosi, an old compatriot of Berlin's, wrote "I Didn't Raise My Boy to Be a Soldier," a huge hit, and Berlin responded with his own "Stay Down Here Where You Belong." That antiwar song proved a dud and Berlin later presented more martial fare following U.S. entrance into the conflagration. He became an American citizen on February 6, 1918, and soon was drafted into the U.S. Army. Sergeant Berlin's *Yip! Yip! Yaphank!*, featuring 350 soldiers, opened at Broadway's Century Theatre in June; the *New York Times* proclaimed it "A Rousing Hit." Berlin sang a pair of tunes himself, including the much beloved "Oh, How I Hate to Get Up in the Morning." The song was somewhat autobiographical and a retort to the rose-colored quality of "The Star-Spangled Banner," Berlin later admitted. "There were a lot of things about army life I didn't like, and the thing I didn't like most of all was reveille. I hated it. I hated it so much I used to lie awake nights thinking about how much I hated it." Berlin intended to offer "a protest written from the heart out" with no anticipation "that it would ever earn a cent." "Oh, How I Hate to Get Up in the Morning" and a number of Berlin's other songs became favorites among the doughboys, the American soldiers stationed in Europe. Berlin had considered including another number in *Yip! Yip! Yaphank!* but decided against doing so. That song was "God Bless America," which he held back from publication for another twenty years. Nevertheless, the show proved enormously popular, garnering $83,000 for the U.S. Army, far more than had been envisioned, to finance a community house for friends and family members of soldiers at Camp Upton in Yaphank, Long Island.

After completing his military service in early 1919, Berlin formed his own publishing company at 1607 Broadway and proceeded to purchase as many of his old songs as possible. He also provided the musical score for the *Ziegfeld Follies of 1919*, reviving "Mandy" and writing "A Pretty Girl Is Like a Melody," Berlin's ode to American womanhood sung by John Steel. The October 1920 issue of *The American Magazine* contained a lengthy article on Berlin. It referred to him as "the most successful song writer living or that has ever lived" whose songs had "taken both his country and Europe by storm." Berlin was quoted as declaring that "the syncopated, shoulder-shaking type of vocal and instrumental melody, which now has been dignified internationally as 'typical American music' is not wholly, or even largely, of African origin, as is popularly supposed." Rather "those who label our popular dance and song music as 'typical American music' hit the bull's-eye in so naming it. For it is the syncopation of several lands and centuries 'Americanized.'"

On September 22, 1921, the Music Box, a new, million-dollar theater that sat just over 1,000 patrons, opened on Forty-fifth Street, financed by Berlin and his friend Joe Schenck. The *Music Box Revue of 1921* cost almost $190,000, over three times the expense of comparable revues. For that initial production, Berlin wrote "Say It With Music," sung by Joe Santley and Wilda Bennett. The healthy profits of the *Music Box Revue of 1921*, which ran for forty-one weeks, evidently convinced Berlin that he could depart from his apartment on Riverside Drive. He purchased a full building complete with a grocery store and tenants at 29 West Forty-sixth Street, located only a short walk from his own theater. Berlin's songs now produced royalties of about $160,000 a year, but he continually fretted about the Music Box's financial solvency.

Berlin's songs received wider play thanks to the advent of commercial radio and the popularity of recordings, coupled with continued sales of sheet music and piano rolls. His songs appeared to provide a perfect musical backdrop for the so-called Jazz Age, as he informed the *New York Times* in an interview in 1924:

> It was no more than being able to recognize what rhythm meant, and being with the times. It was the age of the automobile. The speed and snap of American jazz music is influenced by the automobile's popularity. . . . All the masters of music knew the value of movement. Crashing out to us come the songs of triumphant armies, or perhaps the changing notes tell of twilight with lovers dancing on the village green. All these sounds speak of action. The automobile, however, is a new method of movement. All the old rhythm is gone and in its place is heard the hum of an engine, the whirr of wheels, the explosion of an exhaust. The leisurely songs that men hummed to the clatter of horse's hoofs do not fit into this new rhythm. The new ages demands new music for new action.

Berlin also informed the *Times*, "Jazz is the only great contribution of the twentieth century to the music annals of the world. . . . It will thrive because there is nothing artificial about it."

That same year Berlin offered the *Music Box Revue of 1924*, the last of his own shows to appear at his theater during the decade. The Music Box continued to present new productions of other composers. When he was not residing in his penthouse apartment or working at the Music Box, Berlin could often be found at the nearby Algonquin Hotel, situated in the theater district. Berlin participated in the Round Table there, which included Dorothy Parker, Robert Benchley, Ring Lardner, Heywood Broun, Robert E. Sherwood, and Edna Ferber. He also met Ellin Mackay, a spirited, literate young woman whose wealthy Catholic father resided on a massive estate on Long Island and proved displeased about his daughter's relationship with an immigrant Jew.

The April 1925 issue of *Current Opinion* sang the praises of "a Great Song Maker." The publication suggested that Berlin was famous not because his "Alexander's Ragtime Band" had "set a new fashion in American music," but rather because he then crafted "a long succession—some three hundred—of equally far-spreading songs." *Current Opinion* reflected whether Berlin should be "considered as a force of nature or as a spring of melody or as a master of rhythm." In 1925 Berlin contributed several songs, including "When My Dreams Come True," for the Broadway production of *The Cocoanuts*, starring the Marx Brothers. *The Literary Digest*, in late January 1926, noted that this show had served Berlin well. He was pulling in about half a million dollars a year from his royalties, his publishing company, and the Music Box. The journal also discussed the romance between the songwriter and Ellin Mackay, which culminated in their marriage on January 4, 1926. The pair spent several months abroad, returning shortly before the birth of their daughter, Mary Ellin, which resulted in Berlin's wistful writing of "Russian Lullaby." The Berlins eventually had three other children, although Irving Berlin Jr. died in infancy. In late 1926 Berlin wrote "Blue Skies," which Al Jolson sang in *The Jazz Singer*, the first talking motion picture.

Berlin continued to write hit songs but his involvement with cutting-edge Broadway musicals had seemingly passed, despite his producing all the songs for the *Ziegfeld Follies of 1927*. Richard Rodgers, Lorenz Hart, George Gershwin, Ira Gershwin, Jerome Kern, and Oscar Hammerstein all supplanted him, working on productions like *A Connecticut Yankee in King Arthur's Court*, *Funny Face*, and *Show Boat*. Berlin opened an office in Hollywood and his songs could be heard in a number of films as the 1920s neared an end. In spite of Jolson's delivery of "Blue Skies," other Berlin tunes did not fare as well in the early talkies. Berlin suffered another setback when he lost millions as the stock market crashed, beginning in October 1929, and he himself endured anxiety and depression. Nevertheless, the Berlins remained quite comfortable financially since Berlin owned the copyrights to his vast array of songs and Ellin possessed a large trust fund. They built a new townhouse, which cost $200,000, at 66 East Ninety-third Street, saw the Gershwins' operetta, *Of Thee I Sing*, soar at the Music Box Theatre, and watched Berlin's musical magic return with his crafting in 1932 of "How Deep Is the Ocean?," "Let's Have Another Cup O' Coffee," and "Soft Lights and Sweet Music." The next year Berlin wrote "Heat Wave," "Easter Parade," and "Harlem on My Mind," which Ethel Waters sang for *As Thousands Cheer*, the second of Berlin's own shows at the Music Box during the 1930s and a smash hit on Broadway. Clifton Webb and Marilyn Miller performed "Easter Parade," a song Berlin reworked from his 1917 debacle, "Smile and Show Your Dimple." In May 1934 Berlin appeared on the cover of *Time* magazine, which featured an article on the songwriter and his quarter-century in the business and paired him with George Gershwin and Jerome Kern as "the important triumvirate in the U.S. songwriting industry." NBC radio presented a five-part examination of his career, playing scores of his hit songs. In 1935, Berlin, working for $75,000 and a sizable percentage of the profits, wrote several songs for the film *Top Hat*, starring Fred Astaire and Ginger Rogers. These included "Isn't This a Lovely Day to Be Caught in the Rain?" and "Cheek to Cheek." In 1938 the film *Alexander's Ragtime Band* featured Berlin's great early hit and much of his professional life as well.

International events increasingly attracted Berlin's attention. Having followed developments in Munich in October 1938 that led to the carving up of portions of Czechoslovakia, Berlin decided to rework the song he had failed to include in *Yip! Yip! Yaphank!* twenty years earlier. He soon handed "God Bless America" to Kate Smith, who sang it on Armistice Day. While criticized and even reviled by some, "God Bless America" found numerous champions too, including the poet Carl Sandburg, and Berlin donated the royalties to the Boy Scouts and the Girl Scouts of America. The *New York Times* soon coupled "God Bless America" with George M. Cohan's World War I offering, "Over There," as patriotic anthems.

Berlin returned to the Broadway theater in 1940, delivering a host of songs for *Louisiana Purchase*, which would be made into a film the following year. Then in 1942, after the United States entered World War II, Berlin produced several songs for both *Holiday Inn*, a film starring Bing Crosby and Fred Astaire, and the Broadway show *This Is the Army*. *Holiday Inn* featured "Easter Parade" and, more important, "White Christmas," which became the song many associated with that occasion. Happily received by American GIs stationed overseas, "White Christmas" became, as Berlin later suggested, "a peace song in wartime," which he had hardly intended. It also proved the top-selling song of all time. Boasting 300 soldiers, *This Is the Army* was Berlin's intended sequel to *Yip! Yip! Yaphank!*, with the Army Emergency Relief receiving $2 million in proceeds. To the delight of Broadway audiences, Berlin himself sang "Oh! How I Hate to Get Up in the Morning." The *Saturday Evening Post* called Berlin "the happiest man on Broadway." His company toured around the country, then traveled to Europe, North Africa, Italy, Egypt, Iran, and the South Pacific, to the delight of Generals Dwight D. Eisenhower and George Marshall. President Harry S. Truman subsequently awarded Berlin the Army's Medal of Merit, with the citation reading, "He has set a high standard of devotion to his country." Berlin considered this "the biggest emotional experience" of his life.

In 1946 Berlin provided the musical score for the Broadway show *Annie Get Your Gun*, including the songs "There's No Business Like Show Business" and "Anything You Can Do." Two years later Hollywood released *Easter Parade*. Over the next several years, Berlin, whom *Time* referred to as "the world's foremost writer of popular songs," continued crafting both pop and show songs, again delivering a series of songs for *There's No Business Like Show Business* and *White Christmas*, a pair of films released in 1954. *White Christmas* featured "Count Your Blessings," the last hit song Berlin wrote. Explaining his legendary success, Berlin reported, "'Easy to sing, easy to say, easy to remember and applicable to everyday events' is a good rule for a phrase." On May 11, 1958, the British Broadcasting Corporation (BBC) celebrated Berlin's seventieth birthday with a ninety-minute biography sprinkled with his music. An exhausted Berlin soon suffered a breakdown, triggered by depression, which lasted for about five years. Berlin briefly returned to the Broadway stage and Hollywood, albeit not terribly successfully, then moved into an uneasy retirement during which he jealously guarded his privacy. With no songs to his credit in the past dozen years, Berlin died on September 22, 1989, having just turned 100 years old. He had indeed become an American institution.

Bibliography

Bergreen, Laurence. *As Thousands Cheer: The Life of Irving Berlin.* New York: Viking, 1990.

Burke, John. *Duet in Diamonds: The Flamboyant Saga of Lillian Russell and Diamond Jim Brady in America's Gilded Age.* Kirkwood, NY: Putnam, 1972.

Crawford, Richard. *America's Musical Life: A History.* New York: W.W. Norton, 2001.

Fields, Armond. *Lillian Russell: A Biography of "America's Beauty."* Jefferson, North Carolina: McFarland, 2008.

Freedland, Michael. *Irving Berlin.* New York: Stein and Day, 1974.

Furia, Philip. *Irving Berlin: A Life in Song.* London: Music Sales Group, 1998.

Gilbert, Douglas. *American Vaudeville: Its Life and Times.* New York: Whittlesey House, 1940.

Hamm, Charles. *Irving Berlin: Songs from the Melting Pot: The Formative Years, 1907–1914.* New York: Oxford University Press, 1997.

Jablonski, Edward. *Irving Berlin: American Troubadour.* New York: Henry Holt, 1999.

Lahr, John. *Show and Tell: New Yorker Profiles.* Berkeley: University of California Press, 2000.

Morell, Parker. *Lillian Russell: The Era of Plush.* Whitefish, MT: Kessinger, 1940.

Morris, Lloyd. *Curtain Time: The Story of the American Theater.* New York: Oxford University Press, 1953.

Nye, Russel. *The Unembarrassed Muse: The Popular Arts in America.* New York: Dial Press, 1970.

Sanjek, Russell. *American Popular Music and Its Business: The First Four Hundred Years*, vol. III, *From 1900 to 1984.* New York: Oxford University Press, 1988.

Stein, Charles W., ed. *American Vaudeville as Seen by Its Contemporaries.* New York: Alfred A. Knopf, 1984.

FOUR

The Cinematic Artist and the Literary Lion

D.W. GRIFFITH AND ERNEST HEMINGWAY

In the first decades of the twentieth century, visual images, literally or figuratively drawn, transformed American culture. Technological advances, coupled with greater affluence, enabled the motion picture industry to emerge in the United States. Drawing on photographic representations, scientific acumen, and the commercial genius of individuals like Thomas Alva Edison, American cinema began to flourish. Edison initially called on the Kinetoscope, which provided peep shows in amusement arcades, but soon turned to the Vitascope, capable of projecting images on large theater screens. Nickelodeons served as viewing sites for early film in this country, proving affordable to both native-stock Americans and immigrants. Vaudeville houses, dance halls, and penny arcades all offered films, which experienced a breakthrough in 1903 with the release of Edwin S. Porter's narratives, *Life of an American Fireman* and *The Great Train Robbery*. One-reel films remained standard, often being seen in the ever-growing number of nickelodeons. The young director D.W. Griffith signed a contract with Biograph Studios in 1908 to produce *The Adventures of Dollie*, the initial film of a legendary cinematic career. Griffith offered two-reel films by 1911, including *His Trust* and *His Trust Fulfilled*, but he left for Mutual Studios two years later, having produced 500 short films. Griffith's masterpiece, *The Birth of a Nation*, appeared in 1915, proving enormously controversial because of its racially rooted presentation of the Civil War and Reconstruction. By the end of the decade, Griffith joined with other top film artists Charlie Chaplin, Mary Pickford, and Douglas Fairbanks to create United Artists. While Griffith continued to produce films, including a pair of talkies, his later efforts were far less successful than his earliest work. Nevertheless, he maintained a reputation as a cinematic innovator who transformed American film, uniquely recognizing its artistic and commercial potential. Lillian Gish termed him "the father of film" and stated he "was the movie industry. It had been born in his head." Charlie Chaplin considered Griffith "the teacher of us all." Cecil B. DeMille declared that Griffith "taught us how to photograph thought," while Orson Welles praised Griffith as "the premier genius of our medium."

As American cinema flourished in the early twentieth century, its pace, style, and tenor increasingly influenced other popular cultural venues, including literature. The director of *The Birth of a Nation* offered techniques that authors soon emphasized, including fade-ins, fade-outs, close-ups, and flashbacks, all of which, of course, were not entirely new literary devices. Nevertheless, by the 1920s, even before the advent of talking motion pictures, such devices transformed American literature in the very period when it experienced something of a renaissance. Using modernist techniques, such as stream of consciousness, and provocative imagery, modern novels featured alienated individuals seeking to make their way in the midst of fragmentation and chaos. As a young writer who had experienced the horrors of World War I, Ernest Hemingway honed his own literary skill, aspiring to a clean, minimalist, cinematic-like approach, but one that included complex psychological analyses befitting an age when psychoanalysis was increasingly in vogue. In the 1920s alone, Hemingway produced *In Our Time*, *The Sun Also Rises*, and *A Farewell to Arms*, presenting tales of the American heartland, innocence lost, battles fought in the cauldron called the Great War, and resulting disillusionment and withdrawal. He became associated with the so-called Lost Generation of young American writers and artists that included F. Scott Fitzgerald, Sherwood Anderson, John Dos Passos, and Hemingway himself, who resided in Paris and other European cities after the war. These disillusioned intellectuals rejected the staid Victorianism of prewar America and demonstrated their dismay over U.S. involvement in the conflict, as their own country experienced a cultural clash of considerable proportions. Hemingway's 1920s novels, his posthumously released *A Moveable Feast*, Fitzgerald's *The Great Gatsby*, and portions of Dos Passos's *USA* trilogy perhaps best captured that youthful angst, which appeared to dissipate only with the advent of the Great Depression and a turn toward more collective solutions.

D.W. Griffith

On January 22, 1875, David Wark Griffith was born in Crestwood, Kentucky, the fourth son of Mary Perkins Oglesby Griffith and Jacob Wark Griffith, a former colonel in the Confederate army. Jacob practiced medicine, fought in the Mexican War, joined the Kentucky legislature, and became a hero to Confederate forces. Following the war, the Griffiths, who had been prosperous slaveholders, experienced financial difficulties that only heightened after

Jacob's death in 1882. Poverty eventually led Mary to take her five youngest children to reside in Louisville, where the simply "impractical" Griffith, tall, lanky, and angular, worked for dry-goods stores and a bookstore, served as a salesman for a Baptist publisher, and became a reporter for the *Louisville Courier-Journal*. Griffith failed to complete high school but had been introduced to Shakespeare at an early age by his father and to literature and history thanks to an older sister, Mattie, a schoolteacher. Hoping to become a writer, Griffith tracked the police beat for the *Courier-Journal*, but seeing a performance of *Romola* inspired him to become an actor. Griffith first appeared in *Trilby*, for which he received eight dollars a week in salary. He toured with a number of different companies including Nance O'Neill's Touring Stock Company, receiving favorable reviews in places like Boston and Los Angeles. On May 14, 1906, Griffith married the actress Linda Arvidson Johnson from San Francisco. He completed his own play, *The Fool and the Girl*, obtaining a $700 advance, but once in production in 1907 it acquired poor reviews and sparse audiences. The Griffiths moved to New York City, where he hoped to obtain an acting job.

In 1908 the financially desperate Griffith received word that new motion picture companies in the city would purchase stories for five or ten dollars apiece. Griffith summoned up his courage to visit Edwin Porter, who had directed *The Life of an American Fireman* and *The Great Train Robbery*, an early American film classic, albeit a mere twelve minutes in length. American cinema remained in its infancy, largely unformed and lacking artistry. Yet, great potential existed along with commercial possibilities of virtually unlimited sorts, given silent film's ability to reach out to the growing American populace, which boasted native-stock individuals and growing numbers of immigrants, including many from southern and eastern Europe. Porter agreed to hire Griffith as an actor but not as a writer. Griffith did sell several stories to Biograph Studio, which was located in a brownstone at 11 East Fourteenth Street, and acted in two films based on his work for a daily wage of five dollars. By June 1908 the astonishingly energetic Griffith began directing films for Biograph, producing 450 short films over the next five years, including melodramas and historical treatments, with a pair of films touching on the Civil War. His initial films led to a contract that paid a minimum of fifty dollars weekly while his final contract, signed in 1911, effectively guaranteed four times that amount.

Drawing on Porter's techniques, Griffith began to refine American cinema, assisted by cameraman G.W. Bitzer. Following the lead of Porter, notwithstanding claims to the contrary, the director began offering close-ups, camera movements, switchbacks (later called flashbacks), and fade-outs, while presenting a smooth, extended story line. Social messages crept into several of his films in keeping with the era's progressive movement, which sought to address some of the worst injustices associated with industrial capitalism. Griffith offered films like *A Corner in Wheat*, which, drawing from Frank Norris's novel *The Pit*, dealt with class divisions in American society, and *The Musketeers of Pig Alley*, an examination of the Lower East Side. He also directed films such as *The Redman and the Child* and *The Battle at Elderbush Gulch* that cast Native Americans in a favorable light. But those films were the exception, as Robert Sklar notes, with other Griffith works celebrating the rich and vilifying Indians. Lillian Griffith, Blanche Sweet, Lionel Barrymore, Robert Harron, and Henry B. Walthall appeared in his Biograph films, along with the previously undiscovered Mary Pickford, Lillian Gish, and Dorothy Gish. While Griffith employed a star system, Biograph proved unwilling to feature those performers or the director himself, to his mounting dismay. Partially shot in Biograph's new studio on 175th Street in the Bronx, *Judith of Bethulia*, Griffith's final film for the motion picture company, starred Sweet, Lillian Gish, and 2,000 actors or extras, and required four reels.

Biograph's longtime resistance to publicizing its director, along with the inflated costs of *Judith*, led Griffith, whose marriage had dissolved, to leave the company that had given him his start in the film industry. So did the decision of Jeremiah J. Kennedy, president of Biograph Studios, to skip over Griffith as he planned to produce lengthier films. Kennedy reportedly informed Griffith:

> The time has come for the production of big fifty thousand dollar pictures. You are the man to make them. But Biograph is not ready to go into that line of production. If you stay with Biograph it will be to make the same kind of short pictures that you have in the past. You will not do that. You've got the hundred thousand dollar idea in the back of your head.

In departing from the company, Griffith told the *Dramatic Mirror* that he had crafted "all great Biograph successes, revolutionizing Motion Picture drama and founding the modern technique of the art." Others referred to Griffith as an artist who was, as early film critic Louis Reeves Harrison claimed, "hindered by the traditions of the studio."

Attractive offers soon came Griffith's way. Adolph Zukor offered to hire him at a salary of $50,000 a year, but too many strings appeared to be attached. In December 1913, Harry Aitken, who headed Mutual Films, agreed to partner with Griffith, who spirited his cameraman, Billy Bitzer, and several of his top actors, including Lillian Gish, Dorothy Gish, Blanche Sweet, Robert Harron, and Henry B. Walthall, away from Biograph. Griffith was sure that they could produce "the greatest pictures ever, make a million dollars and retire." Relocating in Hollywood, a still sleepy community outside of Los Angeles, where he had begun seasonal filming three years earlier, Griffith directed a series of films. They included the psychological drama *The Avenging Conscience*, while Biograph refused to release *Judith* in an obvious effort to damage Griffith's reputation.

All the while Griffith was envisioning a new film that would transform American cinema by its scope, grandeur, and ability to appeal to Americans of all classes. The storyline hearkened back to the Civil War and Reconstruction, times of glory and ruin for the Griffith family. In conjunction with childhood memories of stories spun by his father, Griffith drew on a pair of novels by the Reverend Thomas E. Dixon from North Carolina, which focused on those traumatic developments. The books, *The Clansman* and *The Leopard's Spots*, afforded Griffith the plot line for his projected film, which was obviously intended as an affirmation of his father's life and beliefs. Although Mutual appeared unlikely to provide the $50,000 financing Griffith considered necessary, Aitken guaranteed that level of support for the director's newly formed Epoch Film Corporation. Griffith's new film, featuring Henry B. Walthall, Lillian Gish, George Siegmann, and seemingly innumerable extras and horses, cost over $100,000 and netted $5 million in profits. One-quarter of the actors were African-Americans, and Griffith, employing "military discipline," set up "a camp for the whites and a camp for the black," along with a pair of commissaries.

Requiring twelve reels and running for an unprecedented two and a half hours, *The Clansman* opened in Los Angeles on February 8, 1915. Appearing in New York at the Rose Garden, located on Fifty-third Street, it soon boasted a new title, *The Birth of a Nation*. The ticket price was two dollars, the cost of admission to many Broadway shows. After the film opened at the Liberty in early March, the *New York Times* called Griffith's effort "elaborate" and "ambitious," offering "an impressive new illustration of the scope of the motion picture camera." Griffith employed many of his now standard techniques, including crosscutting, flashbacks, close-ups, and fade-outs, but the film itself was a standard melodrama, complete with blackface. Reflecting on film as a whole following the completion of his latest masterwork, Griffith believed "there are no limits to its possibilities in artistic work. This is only child's play." Purportedly drawn from interviews with Civil War historians, the narrative centers on the trials endured by a Southern family and a Northern family as the nation divided. Griffith strove for authenticity in producing battle scenes, employing artillery, cavalry, and foot soldiers, and he erected a handful of Southern communities. The director presented burning towns, dying soldiers, mobs, and the assassination of President Abraham Lincoln. Much of the film highlights cross-sectional romances that suffered when the war broke out, while the conclusion resulted in the unfortunate developments associated with Reconstruction, as presented by Griffith. The *New York Times* review bemoaned the film's inclusion of "inflammatory material" from Dixon's novel and "the sorry story rendered by its plucking at old wounds." Stock figures were aplenty, including uppity blacks, conniving carpetbaggers from the North, and Southern scalawags ready to sell out their home region. All but inevitably, innocent white womanhood in the film became imperiled, with rape looming, while determined Southerners began to fight back, led by the noble figures that joined the Ku Klux Klan. Writing in *The New Republic*, Harold Stearns discussed the film's denouement when silhouetted Klansmen galloped on horseback. As that scene appeared on screen, "every audience spontaneously applauds." After President Woodrow Wilson watched a special screening of *The Birth of a Nation* at the White House, he allegedly exclaimed, "It is like writing history with lightning, and my only regret is that it is all so terribly true." Thomas Dixon, a classmate of Wilson's at Princeton, acknowledged that his purpose in supporting the film adaptation of his novel "was to revolutionize Northern audiences . . . [to] transform every man into a Southern partisan for life."

The highly favorable treatment of the Klan, the denigrating depiction of African-Americans, and the casting of wooden images of the Reconstruction South enraged many, leading to riots in Boston and Philadelphia among other locales. Public officials in New York City insisted that various controversial scenes be removed. Jane Addams of Hull House fame proved "painfully exercised over the exhibition." *The Nation*'s Oswald Garrison Villard decried the film's "deliberate attempt to humiliate 10,000,000 American citizens and portray them as nothing but beasts." The Illinois state legislature considered a measure to ban artwork that "tends to incite race riot, or race hatred." The recently established National Association for the Advancement of Colored People sought injunctions to prevent the showing of *The Birth of a Nation*, which the organization decried as "vicious." The Boston chapter of the National Association for the Advancement of Colored People (NAACP) put out a lengthy pamphlet, *Fighting a Vicious Film: Protest Against The Birth of a Nation*, condemning "the foul and loathsome misrepresentations of colored people and the glorification of the hideous and murderous band of the Ku Klux Klan." The pamphlet underscored Thomas Dixon's admission that he had hoped "to create a feeling of abhorrence in white people, especially white women, against colored men" and "to have all Negroes removed from the United States." When asked if complaints might lead to the film's suppression, Griffith responded, "I hope to God they stop it! Then you won't be able to keep audiences away with clubs!"

Griffith, who believed his presentation of *The Birth of a Nation* was "the truth," was beset by considerable anxiety, $300,000 in legal fees, and numerous attacks on his reputation. He insisted that the film's true villains were the carpetbaggers, not blacks, and pointed to the fact that he had grown up with African-Americans and been "nursed by a Negro mammy." Griffith defended his movie during interviews, insisting that it offered a historical lesson. Then in a pamphlet, *The Rise and Fall of Free Speech in America*, he blasted calls for censorship, which confronted cinema in the United States from the outset. Institutions of higher learning opened their doors to only "the limited few," Griffith wrote. Motion pictures by contrast could impart lessons about "mistakes of the past . . . to the entire world" at little cost while entertaining the masses. Consequently, efforts to censor cinema were wrongheaded, in addition to violating First Amendment rights regarding freedom of speech and the press. Censorship, that "malignant pygmy," endangered "the growth of the art." This had occurred although film afforded "a medium of expression as clean and decent as any mankind has ever discovered," Griffith wrote.

Responding to continued criticisms that came his way, Griffith abandoned his original intention to produce a film about labor relations and chose to make another epic that he called *Intolerance*. Determined to present a panoramic look at bigotry and prejudice over the generations, Griffith initially intended this to be his final motion picture. He worried that "the story for Truth . . . has become barred from" movies, in contrast to the theater, where "freedom of expression" might still be found. Griffith maintained sixteen- to twenty-hour workdays in making *Intolerance*. Many critics thought he succeeded spectacularly with his latest offering. *Current Opinion* indicated that "the superman of the American movies" had pulled off his "greatest achievement." Writing in *Life*, James S. Metcalfe claimed, "He has carried the picture play to the limit of its possibilities so far as doing everything that can be done with the motion picture." *Film Daily* affirmed that "as a spectacle *Intolerance* is the greatest offering ever staged." In viewing the three-hour-long epic—which demanded the construction of elaborate sets, featured thousands of extras along with stars Lillian Gish, Mae Marsh, and Robert Harron, required thirteen reels, and cost $1.9 million—critics appeared particularly taken with Griffith's depiction of ancient Babylon. They were somewhat less impressed with his presentation of the life and death of Jesus and the massacre of French Huguenots on St. Bartholomew's Eve, which occurred late in the sixteenth century. The film opened at the Liberty Theatre in Manhattan on September 5, 1916, and led to a decidedly mixed review from the *New York Times*. The paper termed Griffith "a real wizard of lens and screen" but pointed to his latest film's "utter incoherence, the questionable taste of some of its scenes, and the cheap banalities into which it sometimes lapses." The *Times* did applaud "the stupendousness of its panoramas, the grouping and handling of its great masses of players," which "make it an impressive spectacle." Audiences responded in an equally ambivalent fashion to *Intolerance*, undoubtedly wowed by its glorious sweep but confused by the separate episodes, which hardly presented a seamless thread. The scenes of nudity or near-nudity, along with the condemnations of both battlefields and prisons, proved disturbing to many viewers. Despite experiencing early record attendance figures, the film soon bottomed out, to Griffith's chagrin. The result was a commercial failure that subsumed even the large profits earned by *The Birth of a Nation*. It also led to the dissolving of his business relationship with Aitken and Griffith's moving over to Artcraft Pictures (later, Paramount Studios).

Hoping that *Intolerance* would receive a better reception abroad, Griffith sailed to London in mid-March 1917 as the third full year of hostilities in Europe approached. Griffith also was responding to a request that he produce a propaganda film for the British government. On the very day *Intolerance* premiered in London, Griffith received word that the United States had entered the war. He proceeded to offer a showing of *Intolerance* for the royal family and met Prime Minister Lloyd George, who repeated the call for Griffith to deliver a film for propaganda purposes. In preparation for his latest work, the director toured battlefields in France where he witnessed actual combat for the first time. Griffith later revealed that he experienced "something of the stir and thrill of the movie battle. Artillery is in motion, ambulances come tearing down the roads with the dying screaming as they take their last ride. Streams of prisoners are marching in tatters and dejection back to the bases; wounded soldiers are making their own way. Motor-cyclists are speeding to and fro." At the same time he realized that the trenches contained "nothing but filth and dirt and the most soul-sickening smells. The soldiers are sometimes almost up to their hips in ice-cold mud. The dash and thrill of wars of other days are no longer there." The returning soldiers would recall trenches, replete with lice and "reeking vile odors . . . horrible with filth and mud," Griffith predicted. First appearing in New York on April 4, 1918, *Hearts of the World* starred Lillian Gish, Dorothy Gish, Robert Harron, and Erich von Stroheim. The *New York Times* indicated that the film—three-quarters of which was shot back in Hollywood—strove "to make the war a big reality" and apparently succeeded in that regard, as evidenced by the audience reaction. The *Times* declared, "Sometimes one does not know whether what he is seeing is a real war or screen make-believe" thanks to "the pictures of hand to hand fighting in the trenches, the bursting of shells from big guns, and demolition of buildings, the scouting trips and raids into enemy trenches." Elected to head the Motion Picture War Service Association, Griffith also called for the purchase of Liberty bonds to support the Allied cause.

Griffith presented a series of films in 1918 and 1919, including *The Great Love*, *The Greatest Thing in Life*, *A Romance of Happy Valley*, *The Girl Who*

Stayed at Home, *True Heart Susie*, *Scarlet Days*, *Broken Blossoms*, and *The Greatest Question*. Particularly celebrated was *Broken Blossoms*, the first Griffith film to appear under the auspices of United Artists. A relatively low-budget affair costing less than $90,000, *Broken Blossoms* presents the story of a Chinese Buddhist who in the midst of World War I ventures to London to foster support for nonviolence. Played by Richard Barthelmess, Cheng Huan falls in love with the Lillian Gish character, Lucy Burrows, who has been abused by her father. The film's dark quality turned off Adolph Zukor of Artcraft. After viewing *Broken Blossoms*, Zukor exploded: "You bring me a picture like this and want money for it? You may as well put your hand in my pocket and steal it. Everybody in it dies. It isn't commercial." Zukor proved wrongheaded about that. He allowed Griffith to purchase the film back from Artcraft for $250,000, and eventually *Broken Blossoms* resulted in profits of $700,000 for United Artists. It also received glowing reviews, with *Film Daily* offering, "This film is a poetic tragedy given a masterly production; it is a masterpiece of its kind."

His battles with movie moguls convinced Griffith of the need for greater artistic freedom, which he believed required commercial independence. That sensibility had led Griffith to join with three of the greatest stars in Hollywood's early days—Charlie Chaplin, Mary Pickford, and Douglas Fairbanks—in creating their own production company: United Artists. Demanding still more autonomy, Griffith left Hollywood for Mamaroneck, New York, where he set up his new studio. There he completed *The Idol Dancer* and *The Love Flower*, in addition to filming *Way Down East*, which came out in 1920, cost just over $1 million, and proved highly profitable. Again starring Barthelmess and Lillian Gish, the melodramatic *Way Down East* features an ill-treated young woman who gives birth to an illegitimate child who dies. Played by Gish, Anna meets a stolid farmer who loves her and saves her from an ice storm.

Griffith had received international acclaim in the period since the release of *The Birth of a Nation*. Erich von Stroheim, Raoul Walsh, and Sergei M. Einstein were among the many filmmakers who drew from his work. The April 1921 issue of *The American Magazine* delivered a lengthy article titled "The Greatest Moving Picture Producer in the World," in which the master director indicated that "making a moving picture is like *painting* with *lights*." He remained a workaholic, even toiling around the clock on occasion. In *The Mentor*, Griffith wrote a piece called "Motion Pictures: The Miracle of Modern Photography," recalling that he had directed 500 pictures during a thirteen-year period. He indicated that "great motion pictures" required "good audiences, too."

Griffith followed up *Way Down East* with the well-liked *Orphans of the*

Storm (1921), *One Exciting Night* (1922), *The White Rose* (1923), *America* (1924), the acclaimed *Isn't Life Wonderful* (1924), and *The Joyless Street* (1925), the last film that he produced independently. Over the course of the next several years, Griffith made a series of motion pictures for United Artists but had seemingly lost his touch. Still, according to an article in the May 1928 issue of *Overland*, Griffith's associates considered him "their 'Master,'" one who possessed "almost hypnotic power." In 1930 Griffith sought to produce another epic, *Abraham Lincoln*, a talkie starring Walter Huston. The reviews by critics proved mixed, at best, and audiences also responded tepidly. A harsher fate still awaited his final film, *The Struggle*, which came out in 1931. Griffith was soon reduced to a weekly radio program that lasted less than a year. The Academy of Motion Picture Arts and Sciences delivered an honorary Oscar to Griffith in 1936, with the citation stating, "For his distinguished creative achievements as director and producer and his invaluable initiative and lasting contributions to the progress of the motion picture arts." That same year he showed up at the set where his former assistant W.S. Van Dyke was shooting in San Francisco. Van Dyke asserted, "All I know I learned from you, Mr. Griffith." In 1936 Griffith married Evelyn Baldwin, a young woman who had appeared in his movie *The Struggle*, although that marriage also would end in divorce. In 1938 he became an Honorary Life Member of the Directors Guild of America (DGA). He spent much of his time at the Knickerbocker Hotel in Hollywood. The Museum of Modern Art published *D.W. Griffith: American Film Master* in 1940; the volume proclaimed Griffith "one of the greatest and most original artists of our time."

Notwithstanding some aborted efforts, Griffith's name never again appeared on the silver screen as director of a motion picture. On July 23, 1948, the day after suffering a massive cerebral hemorrhage, he died. Actor Lionel Barrymore referred to Griffith as "Hollywood's greatest," while others bemoaned the fact that the film industry had closed its doors to him. Griffith received accolades from James Agee, the author, screenwriter, and film critic who wrote, "He achieved what no other known man has ever achieved. To watch his work is like being witness to the beginning of melody or the first conscious use of the lever or the wheel, the emergence, coordination, and first eloquence of language, the birth of an art: and to realize that this is all the work of one man." The French film director Rene Clair asserted, "Nothing essential has been added to the art of the motion picture since Griffith." The famed Austrian director and actor Erich von Stroheim claimed that Griffith "fully realized the education values of the film and felt personally responsible for the authenticity of everything in them." In addition "it was Griffith who . . . put the motion picture on the same level with the best productions of the legitimate stage." Von Stroheim termed Griffith "the greatest man the cinema had, or will ever have," praised his generosity, and deemed him "the master." Five years after Griffith's death, the Directors Guild of America established the D.W. Griffith Award, its most prestigious honor. Honorees included Cecil B. DeMille, John Huston, John Ford, and Stanley Kubrick. In late 1999 the DGA discarded Griffith's name, with its president explaining, "There is no question that D.W. Griffith was a brilliant pioneer filmmaker whose innovations as a visionary film artist led the way for generations of directors. However, it is also true that he helped foster intolerable racial stereotypes."

ERNEST HEMINGWAY

On July 21, 1899, Ernest Hemingway was born in Oak Park, Illinois, the second of the six children of Clarence Edmonds and Grace Hall Hemingway. His upbringing was financially comfortable with the Hemingways residing in a sprawling Victorian house and possessing stature in the Protestant, middle-class Chicago suburb. Oak Park retained a village feel although many graduates of the local high schools went on to attend elite universities. The Hemingway family included realtors, a medical missionary, and professionals like Doctor Ed, Ernest's father. All was hardly tranquil, however; Ed suffered from depression and the domineering Grace was disappointed that she had not had twins. While clearly adopting something of his mother's interest in music, Hemingway also was drawn to the hunting and fishing expeditions that his father conducted in northern Michigan. At Oak Park and River Forest High School, Hemingway thrived in the classroom, in athletic competition, and in school plays. He particularly excelled in English classes, becoming editor of his school newspaper and literary magazine. Initially intending to study journalism at the University of Illinois, the handsome young man graduated from high school in June 1917, two months after the United States entered World War I.

His eventual involvement in that conflagration altered Hemingway's future prospects and the state of American literature. Ed opposed the idea of Ernest's enlisting in the U.S. military but agreed on his son's move to Kansas City, where Ed's younger brother Tyler resided, as did a good friend of the family, Carl Edgar. A well-regarded businessman, Tyler helped Hemingway obtain a position at the *Kansas City Star*, which Ernest considered to be "the best paper in the U.S." Paid sixty dollars a month, cub reporter Hemingway adopted the *Star* method of writing in terse but strong and precise sentences. He also followed the lead of Lionel Calhoun Moise, a seasoned and well-read journalist who insisted on objective writing that avoided "tricks" of all kinds. Equally helpful was Pete Wellington, who carefully edited the *Star* articles, demanding "simplicity through brevity." Another friend at the *Star*, Ted Brumback, who returned from service as an ambulance driver in France, also influenced Hemingway. The two resigned from the *Star* in April 1918, soon accepting positions as honorary lieutenants with the Red Cross ambulance corps in Italy. Hemingway apparently had been turned down for service in the U.S. military because of problems with his vision. President Woodrow Wilson and his wife reviewed Hemingway and Brumback's unit as it marched in a parade down Fifth Avenue in New York City.

Hemingway and Brumback arrived in Paris as the city experienced shelling from the Germans. Determined to reach the front, Hemingway soon reported back to Kansas City that he was stationed a mere "40 yards from the Austrian lines," listening to shells explode. Writing on his nineteenth birthday, he informed his family that he was the first American to be shot in Italy, having his fingers, knees, legs, and right foot riddled with shrapnel or machine gun fire at Fossalta. According to his surgeon, Hemingway suffered 227 wounds. His injuries had been received two weeks earlier, but had not precluded an act of heroism when he carried a wounded soldier to safety. A month later, again writing home, Hemingway admitted that "there isn't anything funny about this war. . . . I wouldn't say it was hell. . . . but there have been about 8 times when I would have welcomed Hell. Just on a chance it couldn't come up to the phase of war I was experiencing." During his convalescence in a hospital in Milan, Hemingway had an affair with a nurse, Agnes von Kurowsky, after whom he later patterned one of the great literary heroines. Following his recuperation Hemingway joined the Italian infantry, serving there during the last several weeks of the war and subsequently receiving a silver medal for valor. Hemingway wrote in mid-October 1918 that he was unable to return to the States while he could remain "of service over here." He wanted to see his family. "But I can't until after the war is finished," he insisted. He acknowledged "an awfully satisfactory feeling to be wounded" for "it's getting beaten up in a good cause." Hemingway suggestively asserted, "There are no heroes in this war. . . . All the heroes are dead." He departed from the Red Cross in early January and soon set sail for New York. There the *Sun* suggested he possessed "probably more scars than any other man, in or out of uniform, who defied the shrapnel of the Central Powers."

Returning to Oak Park proved disconcerting with another knee operation impending. His friend Carl Edgar later recalled, "He came back figuratively as well as literally shot to pieces." Moreover, "he seemed to have a tremendous need to express the things that he had felt and seen." His family wanted him to return to school, but Hemingway hoped to make a living from writing, particularly fiction. During the summer of 1919 he received word from Agnes von Kurowsky that her latest love affair had ended badly. As he informed a friend, "Poor damned kid. I'm sorry as hell for her. But there's nothing I can do. I loved her once and then she gypped me. And I don't blame her. But I set out to cauterize out her memory and then I burnt it out with a course of booze and other women and now it's gone." During the fall of 1919 the broad-shouldered, six-foot-tall, dark-haired Hemingway resided at the home of Ralph Connable, a leading Canadian merchant and good friend of Doc Hemingway, who introduced Ernest to Arthur Donaldson, publisher of the *Toronto Star Weekly*. The *Star Weekly*'s editor, J. Herbert Cranston, featured human-interest stories and first presented a satirical story of Hemingway's without attribution on February 14, 1920. Hemingway received his initial byline within three weeks. His third offering for the *Star*, "How to Be Popular in Peace Though a Slacker in War," condemned Canadians who had evaded the draft. His next article focused on soldiers who had managed to avoid combat.

Beginning in late 1920 Hemingway became associated with the *Co-operative Commonwealth*, headed by Harrison Parker of Chicago, who sought "to cut the cost of living through the elimination of profiteering on the necessities of life." That short-lived endeavor soon ended but a fifty-dollar-a-week salary from the magazine helped sustain Hemingway for a while. He continued honing his craft, submitting articles and stories to magazine editors who invariably rejected his work. In 1921 the *Star Weekly* published several of Hemingway's articles, which began appearing in his own column and featured reflections on subjects ranging from organized crime to major league baseball. That September he married Hadley Richardson and the two sailed for Europe at the end of the year. Hemingway was named the *Star*'s "roving correspondent" to be based in Paris. After skirting along the Spanish coast, the Hemingways arrived in the French capital where Ernest began "earning . . . daily bread on this write machine." With a letter in hand from Sherwood Anderson—who referred to Hemingway as "an American writer instinctively in touch with everything worth-while going on here"—he settled in the Latin Quarter and met Gertrude Stein, who introduced him to a group of expatriates. In March 1922 Hemingway indicated that he had encountered James Joyce's "wonderful" new book, *Ulysses*, and had six of his own poems sent by Ezra Pound to *The Dial* magazine, a leading forum for cutting-edge writers. Scofield Thayer, editor of *The Dial*, rejected "the things" as he referred to Hemingway's poems. In the March 25 edition of the *Toronto Star*, Hemingway wrote about "American Bohemians in Paris," referring to "the scum of Greenwich Village" as "a strange-acting and strange-looking breed" that "have all striven so hard for a careless individuality of clothing that they have a sort of uniformity of eccentricity." He dismissed most other American expatriates as "nearly all loafers expending the energy that an artist puts into his creative work in talking about what they are going to do and condemning the work of all artists who have gained any degree of recognition." He attended the Genoa Economic Conference in the spring of 1922 and wrote about fascists, whom he recognized as intolerant of their opponents, "firmly convinced that they are in the right." Ernest and Hadley traveled to Milan and Venice, engaging in mountain climbing along the way, before returning to Paris in mid-June. Hemingway traveled to Lausanne later that year to track the peace conference ending the Greco-Turkish War. He spent a good deal of time there with Lincoln Steffens, the legendary muckraker.

The following year found the Hemingways in Spain, where they attended bullfights and resided at a bullfighters' pension in Madrid. In a letter to a former Chicago roommate, Hemingway referred to bullfighting as "a great tragedy—and the most beautiful thing I've ever seen"; it "takes more guts and skill and guts again than anything possibly could." During one amateur bullfight that Hemingway, John Dos Passos, and Don Stewart participated in, Ernest got gored, accepting the injury as a badge of honor. Hemingway considered Spain "the only country left that hasn't been shot to pieces" and bemoaned the fact that the "fascisti, bad food and hysterics" had taken over Italy. On a happier note, Margaret Anderson's small magazine *The Little Review* published a series of Hemingway's writings. In July Robert McAlmon put out Hemingway's first book, *Three Stories & Ten Poems*, a number of which had already appeared in *Poetry*. Returning briefly to Toronto, Ernest and Hadley had their only child, John Hadley Nicanor, and Hemingway again wrote for the *Star* before resigning at the start of the New Year. In a note to Ezra Pound, he expressed dismay regarding developments in the United States. He wrote, "But for Christ sake if anybody pulls any more of that stuff about America, Tom Mix, Home and Adventure in search of beauty refer them to me." Back in Paris early in the year, Hemingway determined to produce serious literature. In the midst of an argument with Gertrude Stein, she criticized Hemingway and his compatriots: "That's what you all are. All of you young people who served in the war. You are a lost generation." Hemingway's volume, *In Our Time*, came out in the springtime and reviews of his works began to appear. Edmund Wilson reviewed Hemingway's first two books in the October 1924 issue of *The Dial*, dismissing the poetry but declaring the prose to be "of the first distinction." Wilson indicated that Hemingway had joined with Stein and Sherwood Anderson "to form a school by themselves," employing brevity of language and "a distinctively American development in prose." Still Hemingway was "rather strikingly original" and had "almost invented a form of his own" through his vignettes, Wilson noted. Moreover, Hemingway had proven "remarkably successful in suggesting moral values" through "simple statements." *In Our Time* was the "more important" work, exhibiting "a harrowing record of barbarities," ranging from political executions to police assassinations to war's "cruelties and enormities." Wilson likened Hemingway's spare language to "the dry sharpness and elegance of the bull-fight lithographs of Goya." The result was a small book possessing "more artistic dignity" than any other American work about World War I.

Horace Liveright published a series of Hemingway's short stories in 1925 in a revised version of the volume that Wilson had heralded. Liveright printed only 1,100 copies. *In Our Time*, with its tales of a young Nick Adams, a Hemingway-like character raised in northern Michigan, garnered reviews in both *The New Republic* and *The Nation*, at the time the top left-liberal publications. The music and art critic Paul Rosenfeld asserted that Hemingway's tales "belong with cubist painting, 'Le Sacre du Printemps' and other recent work bringing a feeling of positive forces through primitive modern idiom." Hemingway's prose, Rosenfeld wrote, exhibited "lyricism, aliveness and energy tremendously held in check." Referring to the "many beauties" of Hemingway's book, Rosenfeld stated that it contained "his epoch's feeling of a harsh impersonal force in the universe." The American writer Allen Tate pointed to Hemingway's "facile accumulation of *petites sensations*," his "infallible deftness at projecting personality by isolating into typical significance some trivial accident of conduct." Tate praised the writer's "passionate accuracy of particular observation, the intense monosyllabic diction, the fidelity to the internal demands of the subject" that "fuse in the most completely realized naturalistic fiction of the age." Hemingway's friend F. Scott Fitzgerald delivered his own review in *Bookman*, declaring that few contemporary short tales by American writers matched the best in *In Our Time*.

Hemingway and Fitzgerald had met during the summer of 1925 shortly after the publication of F. Scott's novel *The Great Gatsby*, which captured the zeitgeist involving Jazz Age participants. Encouraged by Fitzgerald, Hemingway terminated his professional relationship with Liveright after the latter refused to publish *The Torrents of Spring*, an obvious attack on Sherwood Anderson, one of Liveright's leading authors. Hemingway proceeded to sign a contract with Charles Scribner, who published both *Torrents* and *The Sun Also Rises* in 1926; the latter appeared shortly after Ernest and Hadley separated and had been completed during a furious spate of six weeks of writing at La Closerie des Lilas, a restaurant in Montparnasse that Hemingway favored. Allen Tate reviewed *Torrents*, deeming it "a small masterpiece of American fiction." However, it was *The Sun Also Rises* that made Hemingway a major force in American literature. Like *The Great Gatsby*, the novel presents a telling examination of the disillusioned young people who wandered aimlessly after World War I, forming something of the Lost Generation Gertrude Stein had pinpointed. The protagonist, Jake Barnes, is another Hemingway-like figure who has been wounded by both the guns of war and a love affair gone sour.

He has been reduced to impotency, unable to consummate his relationship with the lovely but sterile Brett Ashley, who represents the New Woman of the 1920s and is at the same time something of a castrator. Jake, Brett, and various friends move from spot to spot in postwar Europe while most determined to hang out in Paris or run with the bulls in Pamplona. Early in the novel, Jake repeats Hemingway's earlier pronouncement that "nobody ever lives their life all the way up except bull-fighters." During the same conversation, Jake warns, "You can't get away from yourself by moving from one place to another," something he has obviously attempted. A later conversation finds another friend delivering a damning indictment of the Lost Generation:

> You're an expatriate. You've lost touch with the soil. You get precious. Fake European standards have ruined you. You drink yourself to death. You become obsessed by sex. You spend all your time talking, not working. You are an expatriate, see? You hang about cafes.

The novel fittingly concludes with an exchange between the two lead characters in which Brett declares, "Oh, Jake, we could have had such a damned good time together." He responds, "Yes. Isn't it pretty to think so?"

A series of glowing reviews soon poured forth. Conrad Aiken in the *New York Herald Tribune* referred to Hemingway as "a writer with very unusual gifts" who "is in many respects the most exciting of contemporary American writers of fiction." Most significant to Aiken was Hemingway's "extraordinary individuality of style," the product of his understated approach that resulted in a "quite extraordinary effect of honesty and reality." Aiken particularly pointed to the use of dialogue that he considered "brilliant." Aiken wrote, "If there is better dialogue being written today I do not know where to find it." Allen Tate suggested that Hemingway's first novel "supports the recent prophecy that he will be the 'big man in American letters.'" The *New York Times* declared that "no amount of analysis can convey the quality of *The Sun Also Rises*. It is a truly gripping story, told in a lean, hard, athletic narrative prose that puts more literary English to shame."

The next year, 1927, found Hemingway married to Pauline Pfeiffer. The two had initiated an affair when Ernest was still married to Hadley. Substantial wedding gifts followed while Pauline's uncle helped the two cover the rent on an apartment in Paris. That year also witnessed the publication of *Men without Women*, another collection of short stories that included "The Undefeated," "The Killers," and "Hills Like White Elephants." Hemingway's growing celebrity was demonstrated by reviews of his new book by Virginia Woolf, Dorothy Parker, Cyril Connolly, Edmund Wilson, and H.L. Mencken, among others. In a lengthy write-up in the *New York Herald Tribune Books*,

Woolf described Hemingway's latest book as "bare, abrupt, outspoken" and the author as "conscientious," "courageous . . . candid . . . highly skilled," able to plant "words precisely where he wishes." In the *New Yorker*, Parker considered the "stripped to its firm young bones" prose in *Men without Women* "far more effective, far more moving," than in Hemingway's novel. She exclaimed, "He is, to me, the greatest living writer of short stories" and the author of "a truly magnificent" new work. In the *New Republic*, Wilson pointed to Hemingway's "masterly relevance in apparent indirection" and noted that the writer was "primarily preoccupied with these problems of suffering and cruelty."

In 1928 Hemingway began spending time in both Cuba and Key West, Florida, writing during the mornings and drinking heavily in the evenings. *Scribner's Magazine* promised to pay $10,000 for the serialized version of the new novel that he would eventually name *A Farewell to Arms*. After returning to Oak Park late in the year, he received word that his father, afflicted with diabetes and financial worries, had committed suicide. Hemingway revealed in a brief note to Fitzgerald, "I was fond as hell of my father and feel too punk—also sick etc.—to write a letter." He acknowledged to Max Perkins, his editor at Charles Scribner's Sons, "What makes me feel the worst is my father is the one I cared about." Hemingway soon returned to completing his novel, which he did in late January 1929. He was wrestling with Perkins about proposed edits by early June. He confessed that he too did "not want trouble—But want everything that can be had without trouble." Hemingway again corresponded with Perkins later that month, indicating that he had just spoken with the writer Owen Wister, who advised, "Don't touch a thing!" *A Farewell to Arms* became a best seller in the United States and again led to sparkling reviews for its author. In the *New York Herald Tribune*, Malcolm Cowley suggested that Hemingway's reputation "may partly be attributed to his living away from New York and its literary jealousies, to his ability to surround himself with a legend, to the pride which has kept him from commercializing his work, and also in some degree to his use of rather sensational material." Still Cowley admitted, "One is forced to conclude that the principal explanation lies in his having expressed, better than any other writer, the limited viewpoint of his contemporaries, of the generation which was formed by the war and which is still incompletely demobilized." Dorothy Parker noted, "People so much wanted him to be a figure out of a saga that they went to the length of providing the saga themselves." Writing in the *New Masses*, John Dos Passos exclaimed that Hemingway's latest novel was "the best written book that has seen the light in America for many a long day." It was "a magnificent novel because the writer felt every minute the satisfaction of working ably with his material and his tools and continually pushing the work to the limits of his effort." Along with Erich Maria Remarque's recently released war novel *All Quiet on the Western Front*, Hemingway's book, Dos Passos stated, would help young people get "the dope straight." H.L. Mencken asserted that the "virtue" of *A Farewell to Arms* "lies in its brilliant evocation of the horrible squalor and confusion of war." The screen rights to *A Farewell to Arms*, the film version of which starred Gary Cooper and Helen Hayes, went for $80,000, although Hemingway received only $24,000.

Hemingway's financial status nevertheless was increasingly secured thanks to the continued generosity of Augustus Pfeiffer, who purchased a home for Ernest and Pauline in Key West and paid for an African safari. Hemingway himself garnered considerable income from magazines, the sale of his books, and payments received from both film and television producers. Indeed, he was on his way to becoming probably the most commercially successful American writer, at least of serious note, by mid-century. Along the way he produced a series of nonfiction works and novels, volumes of short stories, and a play. After *A Farewell to Arms*, he produced no additional novel until 1937 when *To Have and Have Not* was published, about a skipper for hire by the name of Harry Morgan, based in Key West, but *Death in the Afternoon* and *Green Hills of Africa* appeared in 1932 and 1935, respectively, extolling bullfighting, big-game hunting, and other contests of will. In between Hemingway published another short story collection, *Winner Take Nothing*, with a look at an older Nick Adams in the tale "Fathers and Sons." *First Forty-Nine Stories* came out in 1938, containing "The Killers," "The Undefeated," "The Snows of Kilimanjaro," and "The Short Happy Life of Francis Macomber," among other works. That same year Hemingway published *The Fifth Column and Four Stories of the Spanish Civil War.*

In the *New Yorker*, Robert Coates contended that *Winner Take Nothing* contained "some of the most honest and some of the best writing" Hemingway had produced, but Max Eastman, despite acknowledging the presence of "gorgeous pages" in the new book, insisted that it contained "bull . . . juvenile romantic gushing and sentimentalizing of simple facts." In discussing the book in *The Nation*, William Troy noted that Hemingway's fans were worried "that the champion is losing," a notion the reviewer reinforced by claiming the author had produced "the poorest and least interesting writing he has ever placed on public view." Bernard De Voto, editor of the *Saturday Review of Literature*, stated that *Green Hills of Africa* "is not exactly a poor book, but it is certainly far from a good one," containing lengthy dull portions, "a new experience for readers and reviewers" of Hemingway. In *The New Republic*, Edmund Wilson termed it "a great disappointment," "certainly far and away" Hemingway's "weakest book." *To Have and Have Not* also received mixed reviews, with Alfred Kazin stating in the *New York Herald Tribune* that "the

Hemingway legend has lost its luster." Nevertheless, Kazin called Hemingway "a genuine artist who has worked his way out of a cult of tiresome defeatism." Kazin termed the play *The Fifth Column* "an interesting Hemingway period piece" while declaring the new tales in *The First Forty-Nine Stories* "simply terrific." By contrast, Edmund Wilson damned the play, along with Hemingway's fellow traveling, but acknowledged that the latest short story collection represented "one of the most considerable achievements of the American writing of our time."

Hemingway delivered his greatest work, *For Whom the Bell Tolls*, in 1940. This novel about the Spanish Civil War resulted from Hemingway's and the American intelligentsia's fascination with Spain, one of the first staging grounds for World War II. Francisco Franco initiated a military campaign in 1936, supported by reactionary elements in the Roman Catholic Church, large landowners, and the military, to oust the democratically elected Spanish government, which was composed of left-of-center forces. Spain became a cause célèbre for numerous writers and political activists throughout the world, with a couple of thousand joining the communist-dominated Abraham Lincoln Brigade, which fought on behalf of the Spanish government. The English socialist George Orwell, himself already an acclaimed author, fought in Spain. Hemingway and Dos Passos were two of the leading writers who traveled to the battlefront. Different lessons were learned with Hemingway producing his sympathetic but critical treatment of the Spanish Loyalists and Dos Passos returning, disillusioned with the sectarianism and communist machinations. In a note to the writer Harry Sylvester, dated February 5, 1937, Hemingway admitted that "the Spanish war is a bad war . . . and nobody is right." However, he wrote, it's

> not very catholic or christian to kill the wounded in the hospital in Toledo with hand grenades or to bomb the working quarter of Madrid for no military reason except to kill poor people; whose politics are only the politics of desperation. I know they've shot priests and bishops but why was the church in politics on the side of the oppressors instead of for the people. . . . It's none of my business . . . but my sympathies are always for exploited working people against absentee landlords even if I drink around with the landlords and shoot pigeons with them.

The Hemingway-Dos Passos friendship disintegrated as a consequence, but Ernest went on to produce one of the great war novels of the twentieth century. His protagonist, Robert Jordan, is a college English instructor who chooses to fight and die in Spain in an effort to stave off an advance by the fascist-backed Falangists and General Franco. In the middle of the novel,

Hemingway expressed his perspective regarding such engagement: "You learned the dry-mouthed, fear-purged, purging ecstasy of battle and you fought that summer and that fall for all the poor in the world, against all tyranny, for all the things that you believed and for the new world you had been educated into." Although accused by some of being apologetic for communist actions in Spain, Hemingway offered a nuanced analysis, as when one Russian commissar in the novel acknowledges, "We do not admit to acts of terrorism by individuals. Not of course by criminal terrorist and counter-revolutionary organizations." That commissar acknowledges, "But I still believe that political assassinations can be said to be practiced very extensively." As a war veteran himself, Hemingway hardly viewed bloodletting lightly. Jordan reflects, "So you fought, he thought. And in the fighting soon there was no purity of feeling for those who survived the fighting and were good at it. Not after the first six months." Still, he believes, "If we do not win this war there will be no revolution nor any Republic nor any thou nor any me nor anything but the most grand *carajo [shit]*." He reasons that "as long as we can hold them here we keep the fascists tied up." He further reflects near the close of the novel, "I have fought for what I believed in for a year now. If we win here we will win everywhere."

While in Spain, Hemingway maintained an affair with the journalist Martha Gellhorn. Notwithstanding the birth of two sons, his marriage to Pauline disintegrated. More happily, Edmund Wilson penned a rave review of *For Whom the Bell Tolls* in *The New Republic*. Wilson suggested that readers who were not enamored with Hemingway's last several books would savor the newest one: "The big game hunter, the waterside superman, the Hotel Florida Stalinist" had disappeared, replaced by "Hemingway the artist." The love story in *For Whom the Bell Tolls* cried out for Hollywood. As the novel won rave reviews, Paramount Pictures offered $100,000 for the film rights to Hemingway, who was in the process of divorcing Pauline so that he could marry Gellhorn. A film version of *For Whom the Bell Tolls*, starring Gary Cooper and Ingrid Bergman, appeared in 1943; one of *To Have and Have Not*, with Humphrey Bogart and Lauren Bacall, came out the next year. Hemingway served as an overseas correspondent during World War II, reporting on D-day, traveling with George Patton's Third Army, heading into Paris during the liberation, and joining in the fierce fighting along the German-Belgian border.

Following the war he divorced Martha Gellhorn, soon marrying Mary Welsh Monks. He spent a considerable amount of time in Cuba, hunting around Ketchum, Idaho, dwelling in northern Italy, and residing in Paris once again. Hemingway's later books included *Across the River and into the Trees* (1950) and *The Old Man and the Sea* (1952), which ensured receipt of both a Pulitzer Prize and the Nobel Prize for Literature, with the latter said to result from "his powerful, style-forming mastery of the art of modern narration." The December 13, 1954, cover of *Time* featured a sketch of Hemingway accompanied by a lengthy article that began with a stanza by Archibald MacLeish: "Veteran out of the wars before he was twenty: Famous at twenty-five; thirty a master/Whittled a style for his time from a walnut stick/In a carpenter's loft in a street of that April city." *Time* declared that "as an artist," Hemingway "broke the bounds of American writing, enriched U.S. literature with the century's hardest-hitting prose, and showed new ways to new generations of writers." All the while manic depression and high blood pressure continued to beset Hemingway. Following his death at his own hands in 1961—the same fate his father had suffered—a number of posthumous books such as *A Moveable Feast* appeared about his involvement with the Lost Generation.

Bibliography

Barry, Iris. *D.W. Griffith: American Film Master.* New York: Doubleday, 1940.

Bowser, Eileen. *The Transformation of Cinema 1907–1915.* Berkeley: University of California Press, 1990.

Croy, Homer. *Star Maker: The Story of D.W. Griffith.* New York: Duell, Sloan and Pearce, 1959.

Donaldson, Scott. *By Force of Will: The Life and Art of Ernest Hemingway.* New York: Viking, 1977.

Fenton, Charles A. *The Apprenticeship of Ernest Hemingway: The Early Years.* New York: Farrar, Strauss and Young, 1954.

Geduld, Harry M., ed. *Focus on D.W. Griffith.* Upper Saddle River, NJ: Prentice Hall, 1971.

Hemingway, Ernest. *Ernest Hemingway: Selected Letters 1917–1961*, ed. Carlos Baker. New York: Scribner, 1981.

Joost, Nicholas. *Ernest Hemingway and the Little Magazines: The Paris Years.* Barre, MA: Barre Publishers, 1968.

Koszarski, Richard. *An Evening's Entertainment: The Age of the Silent Feature Picture 1915–1928.* Berkeley: University of California Press, 1990.

Leff, Leonard J. *Hemingway and His Conspirators: Hollywood, Scribner's, and the Making of American Celebrity Culture.* Lanham, MD: Rowman & Littlefield, 1997.

Meyers, Jeffrey, ed. *Hemingway: The Critical Heritage.* New York: Routledge, 1982.

Nelson, Gerald B., and Glory Jones. *Hemingway: Life and Works.* New York: Facts on File, 1984.

Ramsaye, Terry. *A Million and One Nights: A History of the Motion Picture through 1925.* New York: Simon & Schuster, 1964.

Schickel, David. *D.W. Griffith: An American Life.* Milwaukee, Wisconsin: Limelight Editions, 2004.

Shipman, David. *The Story of Cinema: A Complete Narrative History from the Beginnings to the Present.* New York: St. Martin's Press, 1982.

Sklar, Robert. *Movie-Made America: A Cultural History of American Movies.* New York: Vintage Books, 1994.

Stanton, Edward F. *Hemingway and Spain: A Pursuit.* Seattle: University of Washington Press, 1989.

Stokes, Melvyn. *D.W. Griffith's The Birth of a Nation: A History of "the Most Controversial Motion Picture of All Time."* New York: Oxford University Press, 2008.

Wagner-Martin, Linda. *A Historical Guide to Ernest Hemingway.* New York: Oxford University Press, 2000.

The "New Woman" and the "New Negro"

CLARA BOW AND BESSIE SMITH

The 1920s continue to captivate historians, filmmakers, writers, and sports aficionados. Chroniclers of the period wrestle with the complexities of a decade when decidedly conservative figures presided over the American government, purportedly resulting in a return to laissez-faire practices. The administrations of Presidents Warren G. Harding, Calvin Coolidge, and Herbert Hoover (at least initially) moved away from the progressivism of the early twentieth century, ushering in deregulation of business, reduced taxes on the wealthy, and an exalting of social Darwinism. Advertising executive and later congressman Bruce Barton produced a book, *The Man Nobody Knows*, which apparently captured the mindset of pro-business forces. In his best-selling work, Barton compared Jesus and his twelve disciples with modern business operatives. Advertising increased greatly during the decade as did both credit purchases and the nation's productivity. Ford Motor Company started its employees off at five dollars a day with the expectation that they too would participate in the culture of consumption that included ownership of an automobile, preferably Ford's own Model T. The *Ladies' Home Journal* extolled modern conveniences like vacuum cleaners and refrigerators that provided housewives with greater flexibility and more time to partake of the consumer culture. Suburban developments continued to expand the reach of American enterprise while altering the ethnic and racial makeup of urban centers. Technological advances allowed for a communication revolution that offered the possibility of bridging class and sectional divides.

Americans still continued to view themselves as apart from one another in numerous ways. Rural and city dwellers looked on each other with suspicion, as did many native-stock Americans and immigrants. Proponents of Prohibition battled with those opposed to efforts to legislate morality, while organized crime took advantage of the discomfiture caused by the Eighteenth Amendment. Fundamentalist religious believers viewed the teaching of evolution in public schools with trepidation, while proponents of that type of pedagogy castigated their foes as ignorant, misguided buffoons. Fearful of supposedly foreign-sounding ideologies, the champions of 100 percent Americanism continued their prewar and wartime efforts to extinguish radicalism in the United States. Four or 5 million people purportedly joined the ranks of the Ku Klux Klan (KKK), while immigrant, Catholic, Jewish, and liberal forces contested its campaign to stand as the moral guardian of conservative, white, Protestant, American values. Harding, Coolidge, Secretary of the Treasury Andrew Mellon, and Secretary of Commerce Hoover, who became president at the end of the decade, certainly championed pro-business policies. But figures like Wisconsin senator Robert La Follette and Socialist Party leader Eugene Debs, before their deaths in the mid-1920s, along with Roger Nash Baldwin of the American Civil Liberties Union, Norman Thomas of the Socialist Party, and attorney Clarence Darrow continued to expound progressive and even radical nostrums. Evangelist Billy Sunday orated in his fire-and-brimstone manner against liberalism, evolution, and alcohol. At the same time, backers of the Social Gospel like Thomas and pacifist A.J. Muste, both former Protestant ministers, continued to call for the church to seek "the salvation of humankind" by fostering "social righteousness" and the "exhibition of the Kingdom of Heaven to the world."

All the while progressives and conservatives battled for political, cultural, and religious supremacy, popular culture continued to exemplify changes occurring in the American psyche. Following U.S. participation in World War I, both American women and blacks underwent transformations that led some to herald the appearance of the "New Woman" and the "New Negro." During the nineteen months that the United States acted as a belligerent, industrial plants opened their doors to women, white and black, and to African-American men. Those job opportunities threatened to disappear shortly after the Armistice, given the expected return of millions of men who had served in the U.S. armed forces, which had remained segregated in training camps at home and in combat units overseas. A cult of domesticity reemerged but many women determinedly remained on the job, enjoying the pay, sense of accomplishment, and social freedom some experienced. The popular media demonstrated the ambivalent attitude of the American populace regarding gender roles. Publications like the *Ladies' Home Journal* and *Good Housekeeping* hardly proved immune to talk of a New Woman more liberated and sexually emancipated than many of her sisters. Sometimes side by side with the New Woman, much to the chagrin of conservatives and fundamentalists, the New Negro cropped up in magazines, books, and various sectors of the American nation, challenging long-standing racial stereotypes.

The silent film actress Clara Bow and blues singer Bessie Smith exemplified those images in their own fashion. Born into poverty, Bow and Smith each achieved stardom in her field while serving as an icon of the Roaring Twenties. Fair, sleekly attired, and sporting bobbed hair, Bow became the "It" girl, starring in the movie of the same name that appeared in the middle of the decade. Bow represented the feisty, controversial aspects of the New Woman, exuding the sexuality so displeasing to many who held onto Victorian tenets but exalted by others enamored of Freudian concepts, at least superficially. Equally sexy but far earthier, Bessie Smith too sometimes wore the form-fitting outfits of the flappers as she belted out blues hits on stage or in recordings. Smith was her own kind of New Woman, but also the embodiment of the New Negro, troubling to many whites who felt more comfortable with existing discriminatory race relations. Bow and Smith experienced meteoric ascendancies to stardom during the Jazz Age, but burned out shortly after the crash of the American economy terminated the 1920s and seemingly the mindset that accompanied it.

CLARA BOW

Clara Bow was born on July 29, 1905, in a rough tenement in Brooklyn, New York, the child of Sara and Robert Bow. Mental illness ran in Sara's family, afflicting her as well, and was undoubtedly hardly relieved by an unhappy marriage to the womanizing, alcoholic, physically abusive Robert, who worked as busboy, carpenter, and handyman, and frequently abandoned his wife and daughter. At those times the epileptic Sara resorted to prostitution to provide for herself and Clara. The poorly clad child remained stowed in a closet during visits by Sara's patrons. Sexually abused as a child, Bow later acknowledged, "Even now I can't trust life. It did too many awful things t'me as a kid." She reported, "I have known hunger, believe me." She also grieved for the death of her best friend, a young boy by the name of Johnny, who died in a tenement fire that the nine-year-old Bow failed to extinguish. Fantasizing about escaping from that kind of existence, Bow became enamored of motion pictures. Like millions of other Americans, she went to see films by many of the greatest stars of the silent film era, including Mary Pickford, her particular favorite, Lillian Gish, Norman Talmadge, and Wallace Reid.

The ivory-skinned, dark-eyed, red-haired Bow won the 1921 Fame and Fortune Contest run by Brewster Publications, which published *Motion Picture* magazine, her favorite. In announcing Bow's triumph, *Motion Picture* revealed:

She is very young, only 16. But she is full of confidence, determination and ambition. She is endowed with a mentality far beyond her years. She has a genuine spark of the divine fire. The five different screen tests she had, showed this very plainly, her emotional range of expression providing a fine enthusiasm from every contest judge who saw the tests. She screens perfectly. Her personal appearance is almost enough to carry her to success without the aid of the brains she indubitably possesses.

Notwithstanding the opposition of her mother, who referred to movie actors as "hoors," Bow desperately wanted to become an actress. Handed a minor role in *Beyond the Rainbow*, which appeared in 1922, Bow was crushed when her scene was cut. Nevertheless, she was approached by a representative from Preferred Pictures who offered to send her to Hollywood for a screen test. While the poorly attired Bow hardly impressed producer B.P. Schulberg during their first meeting, her screen test floored him. He signed her to an initial three-month contract that paid fifty dollars a week. Director Elmer Clifton hired Bow for a part in his film *Down to the Sea in Ships*, and she appeared as an extra in *Enemies of Women*. Her role as "a little roughneck and a tomboy" in *Grit*, a 1924 release, led Frank Tuttle to record, "This dynamic and erratic whirlwind was a joy to her director." *Variety* praised Bow for the way she "lingers in the eye after the picture has gone." Bow appeared on the cover of the December 1924 issue of *Moving Picture Stories*. A brief article referred to her as "the talented little player" who was considered an "extraordinary talent" and "a potential star." The next June found Bow on the cover of *Motion Picture Classic* with an accompanying observation that she "shows alarming symptoms of becoming the sensation of the year in Hollywood. There is something vital and compelling in her presence. She is the spirit of youth. She is Young America rampant, the symbol of flapperdom."

Still little more than a bit player, the five-foot-three, 110-pound Bow was about to achieve stardom as she was cast in a number of roles as a flapper, that iconic representation of the New Woman of the 1920s. The popular British author Elinor Glyn came across Bow on a screen set. "That girl has It," she reported. Asked what she meant, Glyn replied, "You either have It or you don't." Explaining more fully, the writer declared, "There are few people in the world who possess It. The only ones in Hollywood who do are Rex the wild stallion, actor Tony Moreno, the Ambassador Hotel doorman, and Clara Bow." Her role as a flapper in *The Plastic Age* changed Bow's life, enabling her to become Preferred Pictures' most prominent star and introducing her to actor Gilbert Roland, whom she dated. Fellow actor David Butler indicated that those who watched the shooting of *The Plastic Age* were taken with Bow: "They all bristled up when she walked on the set. She was a very sexy-looking girl." Helpful too was Bow's refusal to put on airs in dealing with actors and technicians alike. The reviewer in the *New York Times* recounted that the movie offered "an interesting afternoon's entertainment largely because of Clara Bow. She has . . . the lissomeness . . . and eyes that would drag any youngster away from his books, and she knows how to use eyes, shoulders, and all the rest of her tiny self in the most effective manner. She radiates an elfin sensuousness." *Screenland* indicated that Bow "is the jazz-mad, sex-mad girl" who in the film led a "nice boy" astray. A review of *Dancing Mothers*, produced by Paramount Pictures, that appeared in the February 17, 1926, issue of *Variety* referred to Bow's character as "the flapper daughter" and credited her fine performance to her director, Herbert Brenon. *Moving Picture World* declared that Bow, with her "rampant exuberance . . . overplays, sometimes far too much, but she comes soundly through the big scene. She does surprisingly well in the dramatic moment, but as the flapper she flaps too much."

Bow made an even larger splash with the 1926 production of *Mantrap*, adapted from the Sinclair Lewis novel of the same title. She played a young, fast-talking manicurist from Minneapolis who marries a middle-aged store-owner from a small community in Canada, but absconds with a big-city divorce attorney. *Photoplay* noted, "As a wife who can't make her eyes behave, she runs away with everything. She is personality and sex appeal plus." *Variety* concluded in its issue of July 14, "Clara Bow! And how! What a 'Mantrap' she is! And how this picture is going to make. . . . this corking little ingenue. . . . Miss Bow just walks away with the picture from the moment she steps into camera range. Every minute that she is in it, she steals it." *The New York Times* declared, "She could flirt with a grizzly bear." Referring to Bow's performance, film historian Jeannine Basinger states, "She's shown in close-up after close-up, and allowed to dance, wiggle, and jump into the laps of unsuspecting—but delighted—men. She's outrageously flirtatious and highly aware of what she's doing. . . . She's the prize to be won, and the primary plot motivation. After *Mantrap*, she is a star."

In 1927 Bow starred in *It*, directed by her latest lover, Victor Fleming, and adapted from a novel by Elinor Glyn, who again discussed sex appeal in presenting the story of Betty Lou Spence, a young flapper. As Glyn noted, "To have 'It,' the fortunate possessor must have that strange magnetism which attracts both sexes. 'It' is a purely virile quality, belonging to a strong character. He or she must be entirely unself-conscious and full of self-confidence, indifferent to the effect he or she is producing, and uninfluenced by others." In the movie, Bow's character works at a counter at Waltham Department Store, where she soon catches the eye of the storeowner's dapper son. Unable to afford the kinds of clothes that flappers wear, she cuts up her dress in order to appear stylish. Studio boss B.P. Schulberg referred to Bow as the "It" girl.

Shortly after the film appeared, F. Scott Fitzgerald exclaimed that Bow "was the girl of the year, the 'It' girl, the girl for whose services every studio was in violent competition. This girl was the real thing, someone to stir every pulse in the nation." Bow was "the quintessence of what the term 'flapper' signifies as a definite description: pretty, impudent, superbly assured, as worldly-wise, briefly-clad and 'hard-berled' as possible. There were hundreds of them, her prototypes. Now, completing the circle, there are thousands more, patterning themselves after her." When asked what "It" was, Bow responded, "I ain't real sure."

It "did much to establish Bow as a popular icon, and the film itself was an exemplary showcase for the basic Clara Bow movie persona—cheerful impudence and free-spirited sexiness transcending the barriers of class and Victorian inhibition," scholar Peter Hogue contends. Decades after release of the movie, *Time* magazine indicated that *It* ensured Bow's status as "the ultimate flapper" for cinematic viewers during the 1920s as her sex appeal surpassed that of Theda Bara and Pola Negri, two early cinema sexpots. She appeared "as fresh and authentic as the girl next door, only more so" in contrast to the exaggerated imagery associated with those actresses. *Time* wrote, "She had enormous saucer eyes, dimpled knees, bee-stung lips, and a natural boop-poop-a-doop style. She was the cat's pajama, the gnat's knee, and the U.S.'s favorite celluloid love goddess." Film historian David Thompson affirms that *It* made Bow "the first mass-market sex symbol." Other stars like Pearl White and Theda Bara, respectively, grappling with *The Perils of Pauline* or appearing as "The Vamp," achieved stardom by relying on physical beauty and sexuality. However, by the time Bow became a big Hollywood star, American cinema's reach was far greater, a fact that reinforces Thompson's analysis. The Sears and Roebuck winter catalog featured a Clara Bow hat line. She became one of Hollywood's leading box-office draws, pulling in $5,000 a week, yet lived in a relatively modest house in Beverly Hills while also retaining a small house along the beach in Malibu. The same year that *It* was released saw *Wings* appear, the $2 million film directed by William Wellman. Starring Charles "Buddy" Rogers, Richard Arlen, and Bow in a girl-next-door role as a Red Cross nurse, *Wings* captured the first Best Picture Oscar for its depiction of the horrors of World War I. She was Paramount's biggest film star.

Bow soon returned to type in a series of films, such as *Red Hair* and *Three Week Ends*. Richard Watts Jr. of the *New York Herald Tribune* analyzed Bow as a symbol of her age:

> Because this delectable young star happens to be an alluring, dashing little flapper, whose exuberant charms demonstrate the happiest features of the highly publicized jazz spirit, all her vehicles must overrun with self-

consciously youthful gaiety. . . . Because she has had the misfortune to be labeled the It Girl, she must turn out to be a sort of Northwest Mounted Policeman of sex, who gets her man if she has to bludgeon him.

As talkies became the rage of the motion picture industry, Bow and several other silent film stars attempted to make the transition. The twenty-four-year-old Bow appeared in *The Wild Party*, the tale of a flirtatious college coed, but the film hardly succeeded as Bow had envisioned. At the time she was the top movie star in the land, receiving 45,000 fan letters monthly. Bow later admitted she felt "constant fear" as the film was being shot. She reportedly cried on hearing a recording of her voice with its hard-edged, nasal Brooklyn accent. *Film Daily* acknowledged, "Clara Bow speaks just as you'd expect she would. Her voice is hard and metallic, but she does her usual wild stuff in a way to satisfy her fans." Harry Lang far less generously mocked Bow in "The Microphone—The Terror of the Studios," which appeared in the December 1929 issue of *Photoplay*:

Miss Humpty-Dumpty sat on a wall;
Miss Humpty-Dumpty had a great fall—
For all her 'S.A.' [sex appeal] and all of her 'It'
Just couldn't make her in talkies a hit!

In its review of *Dangerous Curves*, also appearing in 1929, *Film Daily* proved dismayed with the recasting of Bow away from her usual flapper persona: "If there is one thing Clara can't do it is trying to be coy. She's just a red hot flaming little baby with a sex appeal all her own, and why they can't be satisfied to let her ride that way is more than we can understand." *Film Daily* continued, "She's not enough of an actress to ever be anything. Just a flaming personality—that's all. But that's enough."

The September 1930 issue of *Motion Picture* contained a surprisingly revealing "interview-story" by Elisabeth Goldbeck, titled "The Real Clara Bow: She Is a Girl You Have Never Seen Before." Goldbeck noted that "you couldn't find a more genuine or a more honest person than Clara," who remained, when allowed to, "that crazy kid from Brooklyn. Sweet, generous, simple-hearted." Having endured a tough childhood, Bow still struggled "with the life she has to lead." Seven years in Hollywood had failed to change her temperament, and one "can almost see on her face that constant battle that is raging. One minute, brooding and bitter. The next, radiant and child-like." All in all, Bow was "confused," with the many criticisms she had endured wearing on her "instinctively friendly and trusting" nature, and dampening "her natural sweetness." Notwithstanding her "sensational" personality and successes, Bow "has been persecuted more than any other individual in pictures. Everything she does is seized upon and exaggerated." Bow therefore resorted to "shutting out the world . . . trying to shield herself from the constant barbs." Signs read "Invited Guests Only" around her beach house, screened by a high wall along the beachfront. "Prying eyes" still hounded Bow. She remained "a prisoner to her own longing for privacy." Reviled by movie critics, she shunned reviews whether favorable or not. Goldbeck suggested that depression afflicted Bow, who "even turns night into day in her effort to escape from the world," sleeping until the late afternoon. Bow seemed contented while with friends, "but when she's alone with her thoughts, life is pretty black." Reflecting on her situation, Bow complained about the cost of movie stardom, including youth and energy. "When you get it, you find you don't want it. It not only doesn't bring you happiness, but you find it has robbed you of all the other things that might have given you happiness." She bemoaned the constant scrutiny by the movie studio, which afforded her no time of her own, and she condemned New York "newspaper people" who had been "terribly mean" in misquoting and lying about her. Admitting to her uneasiness with talkies, Bow declared, "I'm really not the girl I play. I wish I were. She's much happier than I am." Bow pointed to one explanation about why she had best represented the flapper. Amid all her frivolity, the flapper possessed an aura "of tragedy underneath," a state of perpetual unhappiness and disillusionment.

Leonard Hall, writing in the October 1930 issue of *Photoplay*, warned that Bow "faces a crisis" in having passed her "schoolgirl" days. "She can't continue to gallop off the reservation, and continue to delight us too . . . she must develop resources within herself, a spiritual fortress that can defend her against all the varied and cruel assaults of life and destiny." Adela Rogers St. Johns, in the December 1930 issue of *The New Movie Magazine*, suggested that Bow "could be the greatest dramatic actress if Paramount would . . . give her stories worthy of her genius." To St. Johns, Bow possessed "more than a touch of mad, Byronic young genius." In the fashion of her generation, Bow refused to consider the future but also determined not to look back. Still, St. Johns emphasized, "I believe her capable of reaching heights as an actress not yet reached by anyone in pictures."

The public relations offensive Bow undertook at this point hardly served her well, at least from a professional vantage point. Then there was the constant talk about her relationships with various lovers, including Victor Fleming, Bela Lugosi, Gary Cooper, John Gilbert, and singer-nightclub operator Harry Richman. Little helpful too was a scandal involving a former secretary, Daisy DeVoe, whom Bow accused of embezzlement. DeVoe struck back, talking about Bow's sex life, fondness for gambling, and addiction to alcohol. By

1931 Bow's stardom seemingly dimmed as she departed from Paramount. Other studios soon clamored to sign her, however, with Fox agreeing to pay $250,000 for her to star in two films. The 1932 release *Call Her Savage*, featuring Bow as the troubled heiress Nasa Springer, proved a box office smash despite decidedly mixed reviews. In telling dialogue, Springer states, "Nobody is good or bad. People are what they have to be, that's all. Something inside makes them. Nobody ever likes any of the things I do—but I've got to do them." Bow's last film, *Hoopla*, appeared in 1933, when she was only twenty-eight years old. She refused Fox's solicitations for additional films, reasoning, "I've had enough. . . . I don't wanna be remembered as somebody who couldn't do nothin' but take her clothes off." Other silent film stars like Mary Pickford and Colleen Moore also began to depart the silver screen. In retirement, Bow resided with her husband, Rex Bell, a cowboy star and future lieutenant governor of the state of Nevada, and their two sons on a 350,000-acre ranch outside Searchlight, Nevada. Mental illness, involving schizophrenia and substance abuse, afflicted her, and she spent considerable time in sanatoriums over the next three decades. When informed in 1962 of the death of Marilyn Monroe—considered a genuine successor by Bow—she said, "A sex symbol is a heavy load to carry when one is tired, hurt and bewildered." That same year witnessed the death of Bow's estranged husband, who had been running for governor of Nevada.

Bow suffered a fatal heart attack in 1965. The *New York Times* delivered its obituary: "More than any other woman entertainer of her time, Clara Bow perhaps best personified the giddier aspects of an unreal era, the 'Roaring Twenties.'" The story knocked two years off her age while relating the "pretty bitter" thoughts of a woman who was "supposed to have everything." Reflecting on the actress, David Robinson wrote:

> Bow fitted perfectly a character which is recurrent in the films of the later Twenties—the flapper, the wild party girl, the inheritor of post-war woman's emancipation, an emancipation which was not simply political but involved equally liberation from demanding Victorian domestic habits and from Victorian moral restraints. The character and the films reveal a touching determination to vindicate the new girl and her new, liberated morality. . . . She seems not to care what she says or where she goes or what she does or with whom she does it. But when put to the ultimate test, the Modern Girl reveals resources of honesty and strength and decency and a capacity for self-sacrifice and courage quite unknown to her meeker sisters.

Nearly a quarter-century after her death and following scurrilous rumors spun by writers like Kenneth Anger in his *Hollywood Babylon*, Bow returned to the public limelight in a more positive fashion with the publication in 1988 of David Stenn's sympathetic biography, *Clara Bow: Runnin' Wild.* Stenn declared, "Bow was sexually aggressive and confident—a real role model." He continued, "Marilyn Monroe sort of took that back because she was sort of a Barbie doll. Clara Bow was in charge. She domesticated the men. She taught men to come to her. She never gave up her autonomy or her independence." At the same time, she lacked confidence in "herself as being someone who was creative and gifted." Still, Bow "overturned the whole manner of courtship in this country." In reviewing Stenn's book, Dominick Dunne wrote, Bow "was Marilyn Monroe decades before Marilyn." Elizabeth Kendall's 1990 book, *The Runaway Bride: Hollywood Romantic Comedy of the 1930s*, declared that although Bow had been depicted as a "semi pornographic flapper and Cinderella," her talent was considerable and she recast "female screen acting in America. Bow not only summed up the techniques of her predecessors Mary Pickford, Lillian Gish, and Mae Marsh . . . she suggested those of her 'descendants.'" Bow "brought to the screen an openness that hadn't been seen before, and elemental good nature, a wish to please that read as a healthy sexuality, and an unstudied naturalness about the extremes of grief and joy." Moreover, she did all this on her own with no coaching from directors, producers, or screenwriters. Altogether "this most exploited of actresses haunts the genre. Her trustingness lives in its heroines; her magnificent vulnerability prepared the way for them." Hugh Hefner, publisher of *Playboy* magazine, provided the funding for a 1999 documentary, *Clara Bow: Discovering the It Girl.* Referring to Bow, Hefner reported, "She had her moment in the sun. But even at the height of her popularity, she was an outsider." A number of Bow's films were subsequently shown at movie revivals or restored thanks to the National Film Preservation Foundation.

BESSIE SMITH

Bessie Smith too endured early, bitter poverty. Born on April 15, 1894 (or possibly somewhat later, as some biographers suggest), in Chattanooga, Tennessee, she was the eighth child of William and Laura Smith, who got by on his income as a laborer and sometime Baptist preacher. They lived in "a little ramshackle cabin." Tragedy struck the family early with two children dying in infancy and Bessie losing both her parents before she was ten years old. The oldest Smith child, Viola, was left to take care of Bessie and her four siblings. To help out, Bessie, accompanied by her younger brother Andrew, who carried a guitar, took to singing, dancing, and offering jokes on street corners of Chattanooga to garner small tips. Having joined a traveling show, her older brother Clarence obtained an audition for Bessie with the Moses Stokes Theatre Company in 1912. Smith initially performed as a dancer for the troupe, which featured Gertrude "Ma" Rainey, who became known as the "Mother of the Blues."

Rainey was clearly fond of Bessie, who performed in the chorus. A tour operator considered Smith "a natural singer" but lacking the kind of beauty he considered essential. She was seen, as her biographer Chris Albertson notes, as "too black." Smith left the Rainey tour within a year, appearing instead in a series of black theaters throughout the South. The Theater Owners Booking Association (TOBA—referred to as "Tough on Black Asses" by African-American artists) orchestrated these vaudeville performances. Smith began to acquire a following of her own as when she sang at the 91 Theatre in Atlanta. She became particularly noted for her rendition of "Weary Blues." The ever-competitive Smith complained about "these Northern bitches" when a crowd called for Ethel Waters to sing at the club. She soon informed Waters, "Come here, long goody. You ain't so bad. It's only that I never dreamed that anyone would be able to do this to me in my own territory and with my own people. And you damn well know you can't sing worth a fuck." In the fashion of her mentor Ma Rainey and other vaudeville performers, Smith presented her own bawdy brand of song, dance, and comedy. All the while she demonstrated a fondness for alcohol, partying, and sex.

In 1920, at the start of the Jazz Age, Smith moved to Philadelphia and soon appeared in clubs and theaters along the East Coast. She spent a good deal of time in Harlem, which was experiencing something of a rebirth. Based in this enclave of New York City, black politicians, artists, writers, and musicians expressed themselves through oratory, creative offerings, live performances, recordings, and verse. Similar developments occurred in other pockets around the country, but Harlem took the lead in this political, cultural, literary, and musical flowering, also known as the New Negro Movement. The assertion of black pride characterized this phenomenon, coming on the heels of migration out of the American South, black participation in World War I, both at home and on the bloody fields of Western Europe, and race riots following the conflict. W.E.B. Du Bois, the editor of *Crisis* magazine, put out by the National Association for the Advancement of Colored People, had his offices in Harlem. The Savoy, the Apollo, and the Cotton Club opened their doors to black performers, although the Cotton Club welcomed only whites to attend shows. The dancer Florence Mills, the actors Charles Gilpin and Paul Robeson, and the sculptor Aaron Douglas could be spotted in Harlem. Former heavyweight boxing champion Jack Johnson ran a nightclub there for several years. Present too were Marcus Garvey, with his black nationalist Back to Africa campaign, and A. Philip Randolph, the socialist editor of

The Messenger and the head of the influential Brotherhood of Sleeping Car Porters. Writers as skilled as James Weldon Johnson, Zora Neale Hurston, Countee Cullen, Langston Hughes, and Claude McKay filtered in and out of Harlem, along with less-well-known authors who aspired to achieve the status that V.F. Calverton heralded. In his own publication, *The Modern Monthly*, Calverton asserted that to be a writer in Harlem during the 1920s was to be "a literary son of God." Wafting throughout the district, in the sleek clubs, gin joints, and parlor houses, ragtime, blues, and jazz captured the spirit of the era. A young Louis "Satchmo" Armstrong, Duke Ellington, Ella Fitzgerald, and Mamie Smith were among the popular musicians who spent considerable time in Harlem during the heyday of the Harlem Renaissance.

So too did the six-foot-tall, 200-pound Bessie Smith, who was about to acquire a loftier status of her own. In the process she came to represent both the New Negro and the New Woman, somewhat uniquely. Jazz drummer Arthur "Zutty" Singleton referred to Smith as "a big woman, with that beautiful bronze colour and stern features, stately, just like a queen." Like other blues and jazz musicians, Smith benefited from changes in the recording industry, changes that helped to spread the gospel of the Jazz Age. Ragtime and jazz records by white musicians did well commercially before the decade began, but many black performers had little success in obtaining recording contracts, notwithstanding the artistry displayed by W.C. Handy, Scott Joplin, and other brilliant musicians. By 1920, Perry Bradford, one of the early black record producers, gauged the potential audience for such records: "There's 14 million Negroes in our great country and they will buy records if recorded by one of their own because we are the only folks that can sing and interpret hot jazz songs just off the griddle." Finally, record companies such as Black Swan, Okeh, Paramount, and Columbia began issuing "race records" targeted for black audiences. Mamie Smith recorded "Crazy Blues" and "It's Right Here For You, If You Don't Get It, 'Tain't No Fault of Mine," for Okeh Records in August 1920, the initial recordings of vocal blues by a black musician. Mamie Smith's first recording quickly sold over 1 million copies and later sold twice that number, with many of the buyers being working-class blacks.

Variety stated that "only a Negro can do justice to the native indigo ditties." As record companies began seeking out female blues singers, Bessie Smith's former mentor, Ma Rainey, signed her first recording contract in 1923 with Paramount, producing 100 songs during a five-year span with accompaniment by the likes of Louis Armstrong and Fletcher Henderson. The decade saw numerous black women singers signing record contracts, including Ida Cox, Clara Smith, Ethel Waters, and Alberta Hunter. Artists at first received only twenty-five to fifty dollars for each record they made. Black publishing and recording companies, such as Black Patti and Black Swan, became important venues for leading African-American singers. Black Swan typically promoted its recordings as "The Only Genuine Colored Record. Others Are Only Passing for Colored."

Ma Rainey and Bessie Smith proved to be the best-known vaudeville blues singers, who along with other blues divas helped to birth modern jazz. Starting in 1923, Rainey and Smith became top recording artists as well. Rainey particularly appealed to southern blacks, while Bessie's attraction proved greater still, coursing as she did through black America from the Deep South up north and out west. Smith also resonated in her own fashion with white southerners, northern audiences, and intellectuals. She generally played the part expected of her, while being treated well by white southern theater operators. As another entertainer recalled, "She went along with the game—unless somebody gave her trouble. Then, it didn't make any difference whether they were white, black, Southern or Northern, she'd give them a tongue-beating or she'd beat up on them with her fists." Smith's niece Ruby Walker later acknowledged, "She would tell anybody to kiss her ass. Nobody messed with Bessie, black or white, it didn't make no difference." Interestingly, both Okeh and Black Swan declined to offer Smith a recording contract. They considered her singing "too rough, too 'Negro,'" historian Ann Douglas reports.

Columbia Records signed Smith to a contract in 1923. On February 16 of that year, at Columbus Circle, situated at Fifty-ninth Street in Manhattan, she recorded "Downhearted Blues" and "Gulf Coast Blues," with accompaniment by pianist Clarence Williams. In her haunting version of "Downhearted Blues," Smith sang out, "Trouble, trouble, I've had it all my days/It seems like trouble's going to follow me to my grave." These two recordings were the first of 160 songs that Smith delivered during a ten-year period. Columbia initially publicized Smith as "Queen of the Blues." "Downhearted Blues" soon sold nearly 800,000 copies at seventy-five cents apiece, ensuring the stardom of the woman who acquired another title: "the Empress of the Blues." Smith's recording sold 2 million copies within a year of its release. The black-owned *Chicago Defender* indicated that she was "known from coast to coast as a singer of blues that are really blue." Her newfound celebrity resulted in Smith's inclusion on the TOBA theater circuit, enabling her to tour throughout the American Midwest and South. Large crowds flocked to hear her sing, and she performed for both segregated and mixed audiences. She also recorded with leading jazz musicians, including Fletcher Henderson, James P. Johnson, and Coleman Hawkins. One of her less successful sessions involved a recording of "St. Louis Blues" with Louis Armstrong. Nevertheless, Armstrong indicated, "She used to thrill me at all times, the way she would phrase a note with a certain something in her voice no other blues singer could get. She had music in her soul and felt everything she did. Her sincerity with her music was an inspiration." Most of Smith's recordings proved more fruitful and, along with record sales and tours, enabled her to purchase expensive clothing and jewelry. They also allowed her new husband, Jack Gee, to leave his job as a night watchman and join her on tour. The two had a tempestuous relationship that sometimes erupted in violence. Smith conducted affairs with other men and with women too, further enraging her husband. The marriage withered and eventually ended, although Smith chose to adopt a six-year-girl. All the while she regularly frequented private homes and clubs where freewheeling sex took place.

Meanwhile Smith's record sales surpassed those of any other black artist of the period. Her songs sometimes provided insights, whether intended or not, into her relationships with Gee and other lovers. Another of her early recordings, "Aggravatin' Papa," spoke of the two-timing "Triflin' Sam," who was warned not to "stay out with a high-brown baby" or else suffer the possible consequences of "a darn forty-four." Smith's version of "Beale Street Mama," recorded on March 15, 1923, asked her man why he failed to "come back home," promised that she had never gone out on him, but warned that she could get "plenty of petting" and her "sweet cookies constantly," although admittedly "not the kind you serve to me." The riveting "Baby Won't You Please Come Home," delivered on April 11, referred to the blues that resulted when the storyteller's man was away from home. Smith implored her man, "Baby won't you please come home/'Cause your mama's all alone," with a broken heart and rent to pay. Recorded in mid-October 1923, "Any Woman's Blues" bemoaned the fact that the singer's "man ain't acting right, he stays out late at night" and was obviously messing around with another woman.

Reviewing Smith's performance in Nashville in 1923, a reporter from the *Chicago Defender* exclaimed, "She played a special show for white[s] only and knocked all the tin off the roof of the theater. Trouble was had in getting the people to leave the theater as they cried for more." The Memphis *Commercial Appeal* praised Smith in 1924: "Bessie has a voice that will never be mistaken for another's. She is in a class by herself in the field of 'blues.'" The *Pittsburgh Courier* reported on another performance by Smith at a whites-only event and quoted a white music dealer who acknowledged that her records "actually outsell everything else in the catalog." The *Courier* celebrated Smith, declaring she was "known from the Atlantic to the Pacific and from the Gulf of Mexico to the Hudson Bay as one who really sings the 'blues' as they should be sung. She is the girl who put the blue in 'blues.'" Now recording with Fletcher Henderson's band, Smith sang songs of love and despair. On July 19, 1924, the *Chicago Defender* contained an advertisement exclaiming:

> Wow—but Bessie Smith spills fire and fury in *Hateful Blues* on Columbia Record 14023D. Talk about hymns of hate—Bessie sure is a him-hater on this record. The way she tells what she is going to do with her 'butcher' will make trifling fellows catch express trains going at sixty miles an hour. The music is full of hate too. You can almost see hate drip from the piano keys. Fury flies off the violin strings. Every note is a half-note. No quarter for anyone.

Pairing *Hateful Blues* with *Frankie Blues*, Columbia indicated that "this scorching record" would help listeners appreciate why Smith was referred to as "The Empress of Blues Singers." John Hammond, still a teenager at time, went to a Smith performance in Harlem because he saw her as "the greatest blues singer I had ever heard." As her fame mounted, Smith traveled in her own railroad car, which was yellow, seventy-eight feet long, two stories high, and contained a series of luxurious staterooms.

In May 1925 Smith put out "Cake Walking Babies," the first record to be electronically recorded. By the middle of the 1920s, African-American musicians were selling 5 or 6 million records annually. During the next couple of years, those sales possibly doubled before declining by the end of the decade. The last half of the 1920s witnessed the peak of Smith's career as she led her own tour, for which she received as much as $2,000 weekly. Smith undoubtedly wrote or coauthored many of her 160 recorded songs, but, as Buzzy Jackson indicates, she failed to receive credit for many of her original works.

In the March 1926 issue of *Vanity Fair*, Carl Van Vechten wrote about three "Negro 'Blues' Singers": Ethel Waters, Clara Smith, and Bessie Smith. He recalled heading to Newark to hear Bessie Smith perform at the Orpheum Theatre late one evening. The sale of her records compared with the circulation figures of the *Saturday Evening Post*, Van Vechten noted. Bessie's extended tours of the American South enabled "her rich voice" to reach "the ears of the race from which she sprang." Now she was appearing close to New York City for the first time in over a year. Van Vechten's white taxicab driver asked, "Going to hear Bessie Smith? . . . No good trying. You can't get in. They've been hanging on the chandeliers all the week." At the theater, Van Vechten witnessed "a vast sea of happy black faces." Unlike in Harlem, where "Negroes are many colors . . . these were all chocolate browns and 'blues.'"

Van Vechten saw "a great brown woman" come on stage, attired "in a rose satin dress, spangled with sequins, which swept from her trim ankles." Her face appeared "beautiful," boasting "the rich, ripe beauty of southern darkness, a deep bronze brown, like her bare arms." She began singing to jazz music with an "African" drumbeat. To Van Vechten, Smith suggested "strange rites in a voice full of shoutin' and moanin' and prayin' and sufferin,' a wild, rough Ethiopian voice, harsh and volcanic, released between rouged lips and the whitest of teeth." Smith swayed to the music as she sang, "Yo' treated me wrong/I treated yo' right/I wo'k fo' yo' full day an' night/Yo' brag to women/I was yo' fool/So den I go dose sobbin' . . . Blues."

The writer was moved "by the power and magnetic personality" of Smith and her "African voice, quivering with pain and passion" that recalled "the sources of the Nile." The audience exploded "into hysterical shrieks of sorrow and lamentation" with "amens" abundant. When Smith chimed in with, "It's true I loves yo' but I won't take mistreatments any mo,'" a woman exclaimed, "Dat's right." Leaving the stage at the close of her first song, Smith reappeared in "a clinging garment fashioned of beads of silver steel," looking "more than ever . . . like an African empress, more than ever like a conjure woman." Smith moaned, "Everybody's cryin' de wo'khouse Blues all days/ All 'long'/All 'long,'" causing the crowd to sigh deeply. For Van Vechten, Smith cast a spell, complete with "African voodoo, the fragrance of chinaberry blossoms, the glimmer of the silver fleece of the cotton field under the full moon." In the air too was "the spell of sorrow: misery, poverty, and the horror of jail." Smith exuded what was "crude and primitive" to Van Vechten, but also she represented "the true folk-spirit of the race. She sings Blues as they are understood and admired by the coloured masses." Van Vechten wrote, "It would seem incredible to me that anybody with any feeling—musical or otherwise—could listen to Bessie Smith's recording of 'The Weeping Willow Blues' . . . without becoming a convert."

Accounts of other events reinforced Smith's reputation as a passionate woman, little disposed to suffer indignities of the kind that so many African Americans endured during the period. One summer evening in 1927, she confronted a band of Ku Klux Klansmen who intended to bring down the tent where her band was performing. "What the fuck you think you're doin'?," she demanded. "I'll get the whole damn tent out here. You just pick up them sheets and run," Smith warned. After the members of the KKK scurried away, she went back to the stage and reported that the hooligans were "nothin' but a bunch of sissies." That same year, while attending a party in Chattanooga, Smith was stabbed in the chest by a man who had been harassing a group of chorus girls. Smith reportedly ran after the man before finally urging a young woman, "Baby, take this thing out of me." After the man was released from jail, a group of her fans got hold of him and pummeled him to death, while Smith was back on stage the day after she was attacked.

One evening in 1928 Van Vechten and his wife Fania Marinoff, a former ballerina, welcomed Smith to a party at their swank mid-Manhattan apartment on Fifth-fifth Street, also attended by George Gershwin, Broadway dancer Adele Astaire, and opera performer Marguerite d'Alvarez. When Van Vechten asked, "How about a lovely, lovely dry martini?" Smith, beautifully dressed and sporting a white ermine wrap, responded, "Shiit! . . . Ain't you got some whiskey, man? That'll be the only way I'll touch it. I don't know about no dry martinis, nor wet ones, either." Her singing proved exquisite, with Van Vechten declaring, "She got down to the blues, really down to 'em. . . . It was the real thing, a woman cutting her heart open with a knife until it was exposed for us all to see, so that we suffered as she suffered." Smith continued drinking between songs until she was completely inebriated. Friends sought to convince her to leave, with one warning, "Let's get her out of here quick, before she shows her ass." Marinoff declared when they reached the door, "Miss Smith, you're *not* leaving without kissing me goodbye." Smith bellowed, "Get the fuck away from me! I ain't never heard of such shit!" and knocked over the hostess. Van Vechten assured Smith as he guided her to the elevator, "It's all right, Miss Smith. You were magnificent tonight." Tales of the evening swept through Harlem. Smith evidently enjoyed telling anyone who would listen, "Shiit. You should have seen them ofays lookin' at me like I was some kind of singin' monkey."

In August 1928 Smith released "Poor Man's Blues," perhaps her best record, or so biographer Chris Albertson claims. The socially conscious song rang out, "Mister rich man, rich man, open up your heart and mind/Mister rich man, rich man, open up your heart and mind/Give the poor man a chance, help stop these hard, hard time." Smith sang that the war was over so the "poor man must live the same you" and asked, "If it wasn't for the poor man, mister rich man, what would you do?" Solicited by W.C. Handy, Smith appeared in a seventeen-minute long movie, *St. Louis Blues*, which appeared in 1929 when she was still at her peak. Her fame at least equaled that of the greatest African-American artists of the period, although hard times lay ahead. Nevertheless, after the white jazz pianist Art Hode saw Smith for the first time and listened to her sing, he indicated, "I'm hearing the best and I'm seeing her, too . . . she completely dominates the stage and the whole house." With her rendition of "Yellow Dog Blues," Smith "just reaches out and grabs and holds me," Hode continued. She "sings from the heart. She never lets me get away from her once." Hode considered Smith "resplendent": she "ain't beautiful" in the eyes of most observers but she was to him.

The advent of the Great Depression crippled the recording industry; Columbia went bankrupt. Smith's fondness for alcohol hardly helped her career, and her soulful brand of blues appeared to be little favored during a period of such distress. TOBA folded in 1930, closing off many theatrical venues, but Smith toured in the Deep South with her *Broadway Revue*. Columbia terminated its contract with Smith in 1931. Thanks to John Hammond, she completed a recording session for Okeh—which had been taken over by her former company—two years later. Recognizing that "she was a star," Hammond approached the drunken Smith, then toiling as a hostess at a Philadelphia speakeasy. Although Smith agreed to record for Hammond, she stated, "Nobody wants to hear blues no more. Times is hard. They want to hear novelty songs." Smith went to New York City for the recording session, along with her bootlegger boyfriend from Chicago, Richard Morgan. Smith recorded "Do Your Duty," "Take Me For a Buggy Ride," "I'm Down in the Dumps," and "Gimme a Pigfoot and a Bottle of Beer," which included a couple of notes by Benny Goodman and contained the verses, "Gimme a pigfoot and bottle of beer," "Gimme a reefer and gang of gin." Hammond could pay only $37.50 for each of the recordings. She appeared in New York on several occasions from 1933 onward, performing at the Apollo Theatre in Harlem and the Newark Opera House, among other venues. An advertisement for the Harlem Opera House heralded her as "Queen of All Torch Singers," while also highlighting Clara Bow's appearance in *Hoopla.* In mid-1935 her appearance at the Apollo led the *New York Age* to declare that Smith "is one blues singer who has ever been a pleasure to hear, and the fact that she has kept step with the times has been all to her credit." The March 28, 1936, edition of the *Chicago Defender* contained a brief biography of Smith, who was said to have "rhythm in her soul." During her last years, Smith returned to the South to deliver a series of one-night performances. She tempered her consumption of alcohol and began favoring jazz, Broadway, and pop songs in the period when swing prevailed. In February 1936 Smith wowed audiences at Connie's Inn in Harlem, leading to discussion of possible movie roles and a recording contract with Columbia.

On September 26, 1937, while driving along Highway 61 to Clarksdale, Mississippi, with Morgan, following a late evening performance in Memphis, Smith suffered a fatal accident. Despite charges that a white hospital refused to admit her (John Hammond's article in *Downbeat* offered the headline, "Did Bessie Smith Bleed to Death While Waiting for Medical Aid?"), Smith evidently died at the black hospital in Clarksdale where she was driven. Some 7,000 people paid their respects at her funeral, but she ended up in an unmarked grave. The *New York Times* reported Smith's death and the fact that "show folk on Beale Street" were in mourning, with a headline reading, "'Blues Singers' Queen' Dead."

The great jazz singer Billie Holiday frequently expressed her indebtedness to Bessie, while blues singer Son House acknowledged the influence of both Rainey and Smith, asserting the latter "had the best voice." The musician

Danny Barker recalled, "She dominated the stage. You didn't turn your head when she went on. . . . You just watched Bessie. . . . She could bring about mass hypnotism." Playwright Edward Albee wrote *The Death of Bessie Smith*, a drama that premiered in New York City in 1960 and repeated the earlier accusation that the dying singer had been denied admission to a white hospital. A 1961 interview with James Baldwin resulted in the black writer's acknowledgement that "I had never listened to Bessie Smith in America . . . but in Europe she helped me to reconcile myself to being a 'nigger' and to accepting the fact that life is very difficult." Baldwin continued, "People cannot be free until they recognize this. Bessie Smith was much freer—onerous and terrible as this may sound—much freer than the people who murdered her or let her die. . . . That's what the Blues and Spirituals are all about." Janis Joplin later indicated, "When I first started singing I was copping Bessie Smith records. I used to sing exactly like Bessie Smith, and when I started singing with Big Brother that was the only thing I knew how to do." Joplin joined with John Hammond and Juanita Green, a registered nurse from Bessie's adopted town of Philadelphia, in paying for a gravestone for Smith in Sharon Hill, Pennsylvania. It reads, "The Greatest Blues Singer in the World Will Never Stop Singing—Bessie Smith—1895–1937." Guided by Hammond, Columbia Records put out five double albums in 1971, covering the body of Smith's recorded work. Hammond asserted, "What Bessie sang in the twenties and thirties *is* the blues of today." The Band, the brilliant rock group, recorded "Bessie Smith" in 1975, singing, "Bessie was more than just a friend of mine/ We shared the good times with the bad."

Bibliography

Albertson, Chris. *Bessie.* New Haven, CT: Yale University Press, 1972.

Basinger, Jeanine. *Silent Stars.* Middletown, CT: Wesleyan University Press, 1999.

Douglas, Ann. *Terrible Honesty: Mongrel Manhattan in the 1920s.* New York: Farrar, Straus and Giroux, 1996.

Feinstein, Elaine. *Bessie Smith.* New York: Viking, 1985.

Jackson, Buzzy. *A Bad Woman Feeling Good: Blues and the Women Who Sing Them.* New York: W.W. Norton, 2005.

Kendall, Elizabeth. *The Runaway Bride: Hollywood Romantic Comedy of the 1930s.* New York: Alfred A. Knopf, 1990.

Oakley, Giles. *The Devil's Music: A History of the Blues.* New York: Da Capo Press, 1976.

Stenn, David. *Clara Bow: Runnin' Wild.* New York: Doubleday, 2000.

Zierold, Norman. *Sex Goddesses of the Silent Screen.* Chicago: H. Regnery, 1973.

Voices of Radical Culture

MARGARET BOURKE-WHITE AND WOODY GUTHRIE

The stock market crash in October 1929 heralded the economic debacle that wracked America throughout the following decade. Although hardly the only factor spurring the collapse of the American economy, the plummeting of stocks served as a fitting close to the Roaring Twenties, at least its hedonistic ways as well as the extolling of laissez-faire and social Darwinism that accompanied marked productivity and industrial growth. In reality, the American economy, notwithstanding a 40 percent rise in the gross domestic product (GDP), experienced both surges and dips throughout the 1920s. While Republican nominee Herbert Hoover, one of the architects of the economic policies of the Harding and Coolidge administrations, promised "two chickens in every pot and a car in every garage" during the 1928 presidential campaign, signs already existed of approaching hard times. During the same period that F. Scott Fitzgerald's Armory Blaine left Princeton and his Jay Gatsby built a financial fortune seemingly out of nothing, maldistribution of income and wealth heightened, a worrisome sign for an increasingly consumer-oriented economy. As the GDP mushroomed, wages for average workers hardly did likewise. While some people were able to dance until dawn and live in the fashion of old European aristocrats or nouveau riche Americans, women and people of color on average received far less than white male workers did for their labor. Although cities appeared to be bustling and readily flaunted Prohibition, rural pockets already experienced tough economic circumstances. Various sectors of the economy were noticeably slowing down by the mid-1920s, including construction and real estate, at least in areas, such as southern California and Florida, where growth had been explosive. Led by Secretary of the Treasury Andrew Mellon and Secretary of Commerce Hoover, Republican administrations and a Republican-led Congress supported tax polices that benefited the rich, tariff rates that hardly favored the free flow of commerce, and regulatory moves that gutted efforts to halt corporate abuses.

The American economy undertook a slide beginning in late 1929 that continued for the next thirty-three months. By the end of that period, at least one-quarter of the American workforce lacked jobs. One million or more people simply milled about or rode the rails from town to town, looking for work. Shantytowns—soon derisively called Hoovervilles after the despised occupant of the Oval Office—appeared in every major city. Foreclosures of homes and farms swept across the national landscape. Long lines of individuals, some shabbily dressed, some not, cropped up in city after city, spurred by faltering hopes of getting food or jobs from soup kitchens, charitable organizations, and badly overstretched municipal governments. Banks shut their doors, refusing to release the money millions had amassed in savings accounts, that money forever lost to depositors. With no federal welfare aid available and state and local governments lacking funds for relief efforts, desperation and eventually anger mounted. Initially, many of the jobless blamed themselves as befitting the American ethos of individualism. As time passed and circumstances became more dire, as malnutrition soared and even starvation occurred in the world's richest land, so did frustration increase and a greater willingness to strike out and attach blame to something or somebody else. Many Americans cast aspersions on the Hoover administration, condemning the president's apparent inflexibility and unwillingness to provide relief to individuals notwithstanding his readiness to provide assistance for major corporations. Hoover did so through the newly formed Reconstruction Finance Corporation, which offered aid to large financial, industrial, and agricultural concerns. The president continued to draw an ideological line in the sand, however, insisting that federal help to individuals would erode capitalism.

Others failed to understand the distinction Hoover made or looked expectantly to capitalism's death throes. Both the American Socialist Party and the Communist Party of the United States experienced rebirth of a kind during the early years of the Great Depression. Helpful was the willingness of party comrades to subject themselves to criminal prosecution, police actions, or vigilantism as they championed the causes of workers and farmers alike. Unemployed councils sprang up, demanding work relief. Farmers, sometimes armed with pitchforks and shotguns, congregated at foreclosures to prevent farms from being pirated away from neighbors and friends. Progressives in both the Republican and Democratic parties demanded action too, in some cases even supporting ideas and programs viewed by many as antithetical to capitalism. In 1932 New York's Democratic governor, Franklin Delano Roosevelt, a member of the landed elite in the Hudson Valley, campaigned for the presidency demanding that government own up to its responsibility to attend to economic distress and promising—however vaguely—a "new deal" for America. The continued slackening of the American economy and the Bonus Army fiasco during the summer of 1932, when Hoover allowed military forces to roust World War I veterans encamped in the nation's capital, ensured a landslide victory for the Democrats in November. With the economy at rock bottom in March 1933, Roosevelt delivered his inaugural address, again promising to act and indicating that "the only thing we have to fear is fear itself," thus demonstrating a far more positive attitude than his sour, dour predecessor. The president spoke reassuringly to the American people in a series of "fireside chats," describing the steps that the federal government was undertaking to right the economy. Those steps included the beginning of the New Deal, with its package of relief, recovery, and reform for the unemployed, the dispossessed, businesses, and farms, or at least portions of those.

The economy would improve with the infusion of federal spending and the American spirit would seemingly lift, thanks to the charismatic Roosevelt's contagious enthusiasm. That process remained uneven and incomplete, however, and forces on both the right and the left demonstrated disapproval of the new national administration. Roosevelt proved generally dismissive of the criticism from the right, particularly condemnations of himself and his activist wife, Eleanor, as "traitors" to their class. The opposition from the left or at least from populist figures struck home more readily. Individuals like Louisiana senator Huey Long, Long Beach dentist Francis Townsend, Socialist Party head Norman Thomas, and even Communist Party chieftain Earl Browder thundered about the need to care for the millions who remained "ill-housed, ill-clad, and ill-fed," a dilemma Roosevelt acknowledged in his second inaugural address. A second and possibly a third New Deal would ensue, leading to the creation of the Social Security program, unemployment compensation, a federal minimum wage standard, prohibition of the use of child labor, and Aid to Families with Dependent Children. Taxes on the wealthy increased, the federal government sought to ensure the right of labor to bargain collectively, and the New Dealers even initiated a small number of planned communities.

The Roosevelt administration and its response to the Great Depression grabbed the attention of radicals in the United States, a fair amount of it disproving or at best critically sympathetic; many of the same radicals regarded the Soviet Union as an experiment in socialism but others considered Joseph Stalin's rule as amounting to a totalitarian dictatorship. Although relatively few in number, they possessed some influence in various sectors, including the film industry, journalism, literature, education, government, the arts, and music. Various critics, in the manner of Eugene Lyons, consequently referred to the period as "the Red Decade." They pointed to the inordinate influence of the Soviet Union at least in the hearts and minds of many intellectuals and political activists. That influence revolved around proposed solutions to the Great Depression and the threat of fascist aggression emanating from Italy and Germany. The crushing of democracy in Germany, with the corresponding creation of concentration camps for political dissidents, labor activists, out-of-favor Catholics, Jews, homosexuals, and gypsies, troubled many American radicals and intellectuals. So too did the encroachments on Austrian autonomy by Germany, which began to rearm, thereby violating international prohibitions devised after World War I, and the push by Japanese militarists into Manchuria and China. The Italian fascists' assault on the eastern African state of Ethiopia was troubling, too. The outbreak of civil war in Spain, in which right-wing forces led by General Francisco Franco battled against the democratically elected government, particularly drew the attention of many on the left, serving as the first staging ground for another worldwide conflagration. These were the big issues—capitalism versus communism and the fascist march, as encapsulated in Spain—that American radicals fixated on during the Depression decade. Indeed, support for the Spanish Republic seemed to unite most progressive Americans, particularly those who had come to accept the need for a Popular Front made up of left-of-center individuals and organizations that viewed socialism sympathetically and disdained fascism altogether.

A number of writers and artists shifted leftward during the period. Ernest Hemingway and John Dos Passos headed off to Spain to report on the war there. Bands of Americans, including the screenwriter Alvah Bessie, joined the Abraham Lincoln Brigade, volunteering to fight for the Spanish Republic, as did the British socialist George Orwell. The League of American Writers backed the Republican cause, led by such authors as Van Wyck Brooks, Erskine Caldwell, Malcolm Cowley, Upton Sinclair, and Hemingway. Other creative artists, including photographers and musicians, supported the Loyalists in Spain while also championing civil rights and economic equality at home. The photojournalist Margaret Bourke-White and the folk singer Woody Guthrie were two of the most important artists who stood as progressives of different stripes during the 1930s and beyond. Through their artistry—hers displayed through photographic stills, his by way of folk songs and literary treatments—Bourke-White and Guthrie demonstrated how the events of the troublesome era influenced American popular culture. Strands of radical culture took hold, shaped by events overseas and in the United States, where visions of economic democracy and heightened political engagement by the citizenry, along with a determination that the fascist advance be halted, guided many on the left side of the ideological spectrum. Sometimes those very visions, however generously inclined, resulted in shaded perspectives with a red-hewn or rose-colored cast.

MARGARET BOURKE-WHITE

On June 14, 1906, Margaret Bourke-White was born in the Bronx, New York City's northernmost borough, to Minnie Bourke, a publisher of English-Irish descent, and Joseph White, an engineer designer of Polish-Jewish descent. The family moved to Bound Brook, New Jersey, where Margaret spent most of her childhood, reading widely, exploring the nearby woods and "hilly ranges" with her "absent-minded" father, and joining with her parents on bird walks in New York City's Central Park. After attending Columbia University during her freshman year, Bourke-White enrolled at the University of Michigan, where she almost immediately fell in love with Everett Chapman, a graduate student in electrical engineering. In June 1925 the nineteen-year-old Bourke-White married "Chappie" and the two soon moved to West Lafayette, Indiana, where he taught and she studied at Purdue University, but the relationship quickly fell apart. Having studied herpetology and paleontology, Bourke-White attended night school at Western Reserve while working at the Cleveland Natural History Museum. Moving to Ithaca, New York, Bourke-White enrolled at bucolic Cornell, eventually turning to her camera in a desperate attempt to meet expenses. She shot photographs of the lovely campus vistas, selling them outside a campus dining hall. Receiving requests to produce covers for the *Cornell Alumni News*, she began considering photography as a career.

Returning to Cleveland, Bourke-White obtained a divorce and planned to become an architectural photographer to finance her experiments with industrial photography. Professor Roy Stryker, an economist at Columbia, soon requested the use of her photographs for *Trade Winds*, a magazine sponsored by the United Trust Company, declaring, "They are without doubt the finest set of industrial pictures I have ever seen and . . . wish to commend you upon your ability to capture the artistic in the factory." Bourke-White began producing covers for *Trade Winds*, an assignment that paid fifty dollars a month. She headed into the mills at Otis Steel, photographing mammoth smokestacks, a terminal tower, and a giant ladle, which won the Cleveland Art Museum award. For the Ford Motor Company, Bourke-White shot "Ford Motor: Open Hearth Mill," which presented a worker, cast in shadows, seemingly worshipping at the altar of industrial machinery.

During the spring of 1929, Henry Luce, the editor of *Time* magazine, fired off a telegram to Bourke-White: "Have just seen your steel photographs. Can you come to New York within week at our expense?" Although little inclined to accept the offer, she decided to take advantage of a free trip to Manhattan, intending to visit large architectural firms there. On her arrival at the *Time* office building on Forty-second Street, Luce and editor Parker Lloyd-Smith informed Bourke-White that they were establishing a new magazine through which the camera would serve "as interpreter," providing a record of "modern industrial civilization." Agreeing to work part-time for the still unnamed publication—she held corporate commissions amounting to $25,000 annually—Bourke-White wrote to her mother, "I feel as if the world has been opened up and I hold all the keys." By July 1929, Bourke-White carried out her initial assignment for *Fortune*, as Luce's new magazine was called, to photograph a shoemaking enterprise in Lynn, Massachusetts. A soon-to-be socially conscious young writer, Dwight MacDonald, joined Bourke-White for her next task, photographing glassmaking in Corning, New York. Archibald MacLeish, a Harvard Law School graduate and poet recently returned from a period alongside fellow expatriates Ernest Hemingway, F. Scott Fitzgerald, and John Dos Passos in Paris, was another of her work companions during this early period. She shot paper mills along Lake St. John, Canada; a coal rig on Lake Superior; and the George Washington Bridge in New York City. Afforded considerable latitude by Luce, Bourke-White found herself "among the cranes, ladles, and blast furnaces." In the midst of the economically faltering winter of 1929–1930, perched on a tower on the sixty-first floor, 800 feet above ground, the bob-haired Bourke-White photographed the still incomplete Chrysler Building. When the building was completed, Bourke-White occupied a studio there designed by her friend John Vassos.

Significantly, the previous decade had witnessed the extolling of technology in the art world and the cult of the machine, a so-called Machine Aesthetic that built on the earlier fascination with industrial developments associated with aviation and automobiles. Charles Lindbergh's solo flight across the Atlantic in his *Spirit of St. Louis*, a single-engine plane; Henry Ford's Model-T and then his Model-A; talking motion pictures, introduced in 1927 with *The Jazz Singer*; and radio networks, including the National Broadcasting Corporation and the Columbia Broadcasting System, symbolized the changes ushered in during the 1920s. In 1930 Bourke-White participated in the "Men and Machine" exhibition in New York City. She offered, "Any important art coming out of the industrial age will draw inspiration from industry, because industry is alive and vital," its beauty residing "in its truth and simplicity." Few artists were more attuned to the Machine Aesthetic than Bourke-White, who became a valuable contributor to Henry Luce's publishing empire, which extolled the virtues of industrial capitalism.

In 1930 the still politically unformed Bourke-White traveled to Germany abroad the SS *Bremen* and then to the Soviet Union, becoming the first photographer in the West admitted into the communist state. As she related, "With my enthusiasm for the machine as an object of beauty, I felt the story of a nation trying to industrialize almost overnight was just cut out for me." In this first of three trips she would undertake to Russia during the early part of the decade, Bourke-White was struck by the ever-present "machine worship" she encountered and the belief that capitalism was collapsing. Bourke-White returned to the communist heartland in 1931, providing material for a series of articles, including "Silk Stockings in the Five-Year Plan" and "A Day's Work for the Five-Year Plan," published in the *New York Times* Sunday Magazine. She again visited Russia in the summer of 1932, shooting documentary footage that later appeared in two short films, *Eyes on Russia*, also the title of her first book, and *Red Republic*. Bourke-White's visits took place during the period of Stalin's first Five-Year Plan and as economic woes worsened in the United States, resulting in more Americans, albeit relatively few, becoming attracted to communism. As the 1932 presidential campaign wound on, scores of leading intellectuals, including Malcolm Cowley, Matthew Josephson, Edmund Wilson, and John Dos Passos, supported Communist Party candidate William Z. Foster, to demonstrate their belief that capitalism required wholesale alterations. Bourke-White's Russian photographs cast a romantic glow, but then so did her pictures of American corporations. Still, her visits to Russia hardly resulted in a critical reading of the Soviet state, which actually was experiencing a terribly bloody assault on supposedly wealthy peasants, derisively known as "kulaks." That campaign was part of a concerted effort to build up Soviet heavy industry and collectivize agriculture, which resulted in great resistance among peasants and mass starvation costing millions of lives. Many radical American intellectuals and political activists failed or refused to acknowledge the horrific price being paid to usher in Stalin's plan to transform the Soviet Union as rapidly as possible.

Back home, Roosevelt's New Deal resulted in improved financial conditions and an elevating of spirits for many. However, both American industry and agriculture continued to lag behind pre-1930 standards and millions remained mired in dire economic circumstances. As drought, soil erosion, and plunging prices ravaged the American heartland, Bourke-White, like other top photojournalists during the period, began to provide a photographic record of the Great Depression's continuing impact. Dorothea Lange's photograph "Migrant Mother" became perhaps the most iconic image of the era, but Bourke-White presented similarly gripping photographs of the Dust Bowl for *Fortune* and other publications. She thereby followed a tradition established by Mathew Brady during the Civil War and by Jacob Riis and Lewis Hine as rapid modernization transformed American work and cities during the latter stages of the nineteenth century and the first part of the twentieth. By 1902, Alfred Stieglitz, along with Edward Steichen and Clarence H. White, initiated a campaign for photography to be viewed "as a distinct medium of individual expression." During the same period Frances Benjamin Johnston continued helping to pioneer documentary photography. By the 1920s Samuel Brody had singled out Ralph Steiner as "the healthiest and most sincere artist in the 'avant-garde' of the bourgeois cinema and photo." Bourke-White's contemporaries during the ensuing decade included Paul Strand, Alfred Eisenstaedt, and Ansel Adams, during a golden age of American photojournalism.

Fortune's editors, appreciating the enormity of the situation, assigned Bourke-White to photograph the Dust Bowl in 1934. Flying aboard a two-seater, Bourke-White soon discovered that the extent of damage in the cornbelt was far greater than she had anticipated. In her autobiography, *Portrait of Myself*, she revealed:

> I had never seen landscapes like those through which we flew. Blinding sun beating down on the withered land. Below us the ghostly patchwork of half-buried corn, and the rivers of sand which should have been free-running streams. Sinister spouts of sand wisping up, and then the sudden yellow gloom of curtains of fine-blown soil rising up and trembling in the air. Endless dun-colored acres, which should have been green with crops, carved into dry ripples by the aimless winds.

The people she encountered appeared equally bleak. They seemed "caught helpless . . . in total tragedy," lacking any defense or plan, "numbed like their own dumb animals," which were "choking and dying in drifting soil." *Fortune* presented Bourke-White's pictorial images along with commentary by James Agee. Although moved by the plight of the farmers, Bourke-White was not averse to taking on more corporate clients, including RCA, Goodyear, the William Wrigley Jr. Company, Trans World Airlines, Pan-American Airways, and Eastern Airlines.

In a series of articles for *The Nation*, Bourke-White discussed both the Great Depression and international events. Reviewing a book by the journalist Louis Fischer, *Soviet Journey*, in the magazine's April 17, 1935, issue, she donned similar rose-colored lenses in referring to the Russian people as "warm . . . lovable . . . childlike, progressive, eager" as they moved from toiling on blast furnaces to discussing "Marxian dialectics." The former palaces of aristocrats now stood as rest homes, hospitals, and museums, frequented by factory workers. Fischer's Bolsheviks supposedly studied painting, attended the opera, and "read books by the millions." Strikingly, "ruddy" women labored in Russian industry. For Bourke-White, Fischer captured the Russian "spirit of endless change" as he chronicled the Bolsheviks' campaign "to change the core of life itself."

Bourke-White returned to the Dust Bowl phenomenon the following month, warning that "this year there is an atmosphere of utter hopelessness" with "nothing to do," no reason to prevent the dust from sweeping into houses or to stave off foreclosures. Numerous farm families joined in a mass migration out of farm counties. Along with her pilot, Bourke-White witnessed families loading all their goods, along with their children, onto wagons or trucks and setting out on this odyssey. Reports intensified of children and adults being lost in dust storms. The dust that "coats the lungs and threatens death to cattle and men alike, that ruins the stock of the storekeeper lying unsold on his shelves, that creeps into the gear shifts of automobiles, that sifts through the refrigerator into the butter, that makes housekeeping, and gradually life itself, unbearable," transformed rural America.

In the summer of 1935, Bourke-White reviewed a new book by M. Lincoln Schuster, *Eyes on the World*, which offered a synthesis of recent photographs along with an analysis of international events. She referred to striking workers dying, the homeless, and the shooting of cattle in a drought-afflicted America, but also to the German Nazis, the Italian fascists, Oswald Mosley's black-shirted British Union of Fascists, fascist eruptions in France and Austria, student unrest in Spain, and Japanese militarists. Once again, Bourke-White, like Schuster, portrayed the Soviet Union in a glorified light, depicting "the war against illiteracy," babies in nurseries, young beachgoers, and even Stalin himself conversing "good-humoredly" with Maxim Gorky about literature. For Bourke-White, Schuster's volume demonstrated a metamorphosis that photography was experiencing, including a greater emphasis on "the candid-camera" approach. Various photographs underscored the fact "that dynamic composition can exist with" the instantaneous new focus. Bourke-White tellingly quoted from Schuster, who declared, "Honest pictures can give us an impact, a startled awareness, a deep flooding illumination which even honest words cannot always attain. In the right hands, an artist's lens is an instrument of truth, a probing and searching instrument." Bourke-White acknowledged in a letter that while industrial photographs remained "very important . . . it is becoming more and more important to reflect the life that goes on behind these photographs." In "Photographing This World" the following February, she wondered whether photographers were "aware of the social scene and how significantly are their photographs portraying it." She compared the photographer to the painter. Each sought "a wide world, one in which his desire for self-realization is not achieved at the cost of his integrity." Bourke-White referred to the first American Artists' Congress, supported by over 300 artists, including Rockwell Kent, Edward Steichen, Paul Strand, Art Young, and herself, all sympathetic to the Popular Front. Those artists urged that freedom of expression be safeguarded and that war and fascism be thwarted.

A number of socially committed photographers worked for the Farm Security Administration under the stewardship of Roy E. Stryker, while others operated under the Federal Arts Project, a subsidiary to the Works

Progress Administration (WPA). Operating on behalf of the federal government, brilliant photographers like Dorothea Lange, Walker Evans, and
Ben Shahn captured poignant scenes of the suffering and dislocations
associated with the Great Depression. Increasingly determined to do likewise, Bourke-White heard that Georgia native Erskine Caldwell, author
of *Tobacco Road* and *God's Little Acre*, was seeking a photographer for a
book he was intending to publish. For eighteen months, beginning in June
1936, the famed photographer and the best-selling author passed through
some of the bleakest spots in the land while falling in love. Caldwell taught
Bourke-White a new approach to her craft, one that allowed the subject,
not the artist, to reveal itself.

Caldwell and Bourke-White crafted a book, *You Have Seen Their Faces*, a
"photographic documentary text" like the ones Jacob Riis and Lewis Hine had
earlier produced. The short but powerful volume opened with a photograph
of a young lad from Elbow Creek, Arkansas, and a caption indicating that
he and his brother had left school to work on their father's farm. A second
photograph displayed a black man lying next to tobacco leaves with the
explanation that "the auction-boss talks so fast a colored man can't hardly
ever tell how much his tobacco crop sells for." A scene of a family with three
children, pulling a carriage in Ringgold, Georgia, was described as "those poor
people walking all the way from Florida looking for a job, and hungry every
step." Bourke-White captured a young woman sitting with her daughter on her
lap at an old plantation in Clinton, Louisiana, where "a lot of families" now
dwelled, some paying, as she did, five dollars a month for a pair of rooms. A
photograph of a white man from Fairhope, Louisiana, possessed the caption,
"Folks here wouldn't give a dime a dozen for white tenants. They can get
twice as much work out of the blacks. But they need to be trained. Beat a dog
and he'll obey you. They say it's the same way with the blacks." *You Have
Seen Their Faces* offered a picture of a black man from Porter, Arkansas, and
the statement that blacks received "seventy-five cents a day in the cottonfield
last year, and a whipping if we didn't stay and work." Another photograph
presented a young, worn-looking woman with her infant child sitting on a
dilapidated mattress in a cabin with a copy of *Revival Joy* on the bed and a
caption reading, "Sometimes I tell my husband we couldn't be worse off if
we tried." Writing in *The New Republic*, Malcolm Cowley declared that "the
photographs themselves are almost beyond praise. They belong to a new
art, one that has to be judged by different standards from those applying to
painting or sculpture." The *World-Telegram* claimed that "the pictures have
the quality of the very finest portraits. They depict man and the intention of
his soul." Critics would later compare *You Have Seen Their Faces* with the
classic work by James Agee and Walker Evans, *Let Us Now Praise Famous*

Men, whose publication was delayed for five years because of Bourke-White and Caldwell's book.

During the period when Bourke-White and Caldwell engaged in their odyssey in the American South, she became one of four photojournalists—the only woman among them—hired for Luce's newest publication, a revised version of *Life*. Luce indicated that his magazine intended "to see Life; see the world," and he sent photographers around the world to capture the events of the day, many of epochal importance but not all. Bourke-White provided the initial cover for *Life* on November 23, 1936, a black-and-white photograph of Fort Peck Dam in Montana, devised by the Public Works Administration, and other photos of life out west, including the Bar X in New Deal, Montana, with a baby perched on the counter. The magazine's editors stated that these were shots "as only Bourke-White can take them," providing "a human document of American frontier life" that amounted to "a revelation." The first printing of 200,000 copies of *Life* sold out quickly and nearly 500,000 eventually were produced. Bourke-White loved working for *Life*, recognizing the "enormous amount of freedom of choice" its editors afforded her, including the ability to produce photographic essays. The photo- or picture-essay increasingly came into vogue during this period, initiated by German journalists. Bourke-White became one of the leading practitioners of this new art form, and *Life* gave her a venue to explore the human condition in far-flung locales. Shortly before the magazine's first issue appeared, Archibald MacLeish wrote to Luce, contending that "the camera no longer illustrates. The camera tells. The camera shall take its place as the greatest and by all measurements the most convincing reporter of contemporary life."

The Museum of Modern Art in mid-Manhattan featured an exhibition of Bourke-White's photographs in 1937. Early that year she began residing with Caldwell at the Mayflower Hotel in New York City. She took a photograph of black men, women, and children standing in a bread line in Louisville, Kentucky, next to a giant billboard paid for by the National Association of Manufacturers that read, "World's Highest Standard of Living" and "There's no way like the American Way." *You Have Seen Their Faces* appeared in November. The following spring as war threatened, Bourke-White and Caldwell collaborated again while traveling through Czechoslovakia and Hungary. She shot photographs of life in the Czech countryside and also scenes of a Nazi rally, a munitions factory, and a training class for young Nazi storm troopers. Back home, she purchased a house in Darien, Connecticut, with Caldwell, and Bourke-White and Caldwell married in February 1939.

Bourke-White soon asserted in a radio interview, "It is my firm belief that democracy will not lose hold as long as people really know what is going on and the photographer has a very valuable part to do in showing what is going on." That fall after the German invasion of Poland and Great Britain's declaration of war, Luce sent Bourke-White to London. In the spring she photographed Winston Churchill, then serving as First Lord of the Admiralty but only weeks away from becoming prime minister. During that same period she also worked for the newly formed *PM*, a left-liberal publication and an experiment in adless journalism. The staff of the consciously anti-isolationist *PM* included I.F. Stone; Theodor Seuss Geisel, better known as Dr. Seuss; Max Lerner; and James Wechsler. During the spring of 1941, Bourke-White and Caldwell, on assignment for *Life*, passed through China into the Soviet Union and were in Moscow when German soldiers attacked the Soviet capital in July. Summoned to the American embassy, they met with Ambassador Laurence Steinhardt, who offered them train passage to Vladivostok but also expressed a willingness to provide assistance if they chose to remain. The only foreign photographer present, Bourke-White delivered gripping images of Moscow under siege. German flares ironically enabled her to offer stunning vistas, including Moscow at night during a major bombing raid. She also interviewed Joseph Stalin thanks to U.S. presidential assistant Harry Hopkins, who carried her film out of the country. Bourke-White and Caldwell left Moscow after two trying months.

During the spring, Bourke-White, the first female war correspondent accredited by the American military, returned to England in uniform to track B-17s arriving from the United States. She again photographed Churchill, now serving as British prime minister, and also Haile Selassie, the emperor of Ethiopia. With Caldwell having filed for divorce in November, she went on to North Africa in late December, but her convoy was torpedoed, leaving her and the other passengers stranded in lifeboats for several hours. In January Air Force general James Doolittle allowed her to go along on a bombing raid of a German airbase at El Aouina outside Tunis. He asked her, "Maggie, do you still want to go on a bombing mission?" She replied, "Oh, you know I do. I had given up asking, because I didn't want to make a nuisance of myself all the time." The general retorted, "Well, you've been torpedoed. You might as well go through everything." In the summer of 1943, she accompanied the Army Supply Services in Italy moving through the Cassino Valley, where war raged fiercely, returning home in the fall. Many of her most moving photographs of the Italian campaign, however, disappeared when a package of film was lost.

She returned to the battlefront during the fall of 1944, shooting scenes of Rome, now in Allied hands, and the fighting near Bologna. In early 1945 she flew from Paris into Germany, where she joined the Third Army, headed by General George Patton. In April Bourke-White began taking photographs at the Nazi concentration camp in Buchenwald. As she reported, "I saw and photographed the piles of naked, lifeless bodies, the human skeletons in furnaces, the living skeletons who would die the next day because they had had to wait too long for deliverance, the pieces of tattooed skin for lampshades." She added, "Using a camera was almost a relief. It interposed a slight barrier between myself and the horror in front of me." Even worse were "the smaller, more intimate atrocity camps." Her scenes of "The Living Dead of Buchenwald"—including a former prisoner returning to a work camp, burned bodies in a slave labor camp in Leipzig-Mochau, and German civilians being forced to confront piles of slaughtered concentration camp victims—were stunning. Those photographs appeared in the May 7, 1945, issue of *Life*, which stated, "Dead men will have indeed died in vain if live men refuse to look at them."

Her fame at its greatest, Bourke-White went to India and Pakistan in early 1946, remaining there for several months, taking photographs of Mahatma Gandhi—who was in the midst of his campaign of nonviolent resistance against British rule—on a walk with two young relatives and others, and at his spinning wheel in Poona. That summer she went through Calcutta, where she photographed vultures picking at the bodies of Hindus and Muslims killed during an extended riot. In 1947 Bourke-White was in Bombay, New Delhi, and East Punjab in India and in Wagah, Pakistan. She delivered a photograph, titled "Misery of the Dispossessed," which captured refugees dwelling in a tent city. Another photograph, "The Emigrant Train," revealed only a portion of 45,000 Sikh refugees moving across the Punjab plains. She photographed Jawaharlal Nehru, leader of the Indian National Congress, and Mohammed Ali Jinnah, who initiated his own direct action campaign to emancipate Pakistan. She interviewed Gandhi, who said that "the world is not at peace. It is still more dreadful than before." Only hours later, an assassin murdered the Indian pacifist. She bemoaned the death of "one Christlike man giving his life to bring unity to his people."

Beginning in December 1949 Bourke-White spent several months in South Africa, where she took photographs of black miners, a three-year-old "Shantytown Dweller," the city of Johannesburg, and a camp for black squatters. In the spring of 1951, *Life* assigned her to take photographs of the Strategic Air Command, giving her access that columnist Westbrook Pegler, who accused her of communist sympathies, decried. Ignoring the attack, Henry Luce sent her to Asia in 1952, where she visited Japan and covered the Korean War, producing photographs of a smiling South Korean soldier standing next to the head of a guerrilla from the North, rural women grieving over a coffin, and a sobbing mother encountering the son she feared had been killed in the war. By the following year, however, Bourke-White began to experience a "mysterious malady" that turned out to be Parkinson's disease. She began writing her autobiography, *Portrait of Myself.* By 1957 her last feature for *Life* appeared and her career as a photojournalist ended. Her autobiography was published six years later and became a best seller, but Bourke-White's health continued to deteriorate. On August 27, 1971, she died in Darien, Connecticut.

WOODY GUTHRIE

Named after the recently chosen presidential nominee of the Democratic Party, Woodrow Wilson Guthrie was born on July 14, 1912, in newly incorporated Okemah, Oklahoma, to Charley and Nora Belle Guthrie. A land speculator, politician, ex-cowboy, and insurance agent, Charley experienced a financial roller coaster affected by oil booms and busts. In 1919 a fire caused the death of the Guthrie's fourteen-year-old daughter Clara, a crushing blow to seven-year-old Woody and his mother Nora, whose mental illness later became still more obvious. By the early 1920s Okemah witnessed both the growth of the Ku Klux Klan and a prolonged recession, which proved devastating to Charley, overextended through real estate operations. By 1924 the family was reduced to dwelling in "the rottenest and wormiest and the dirtiest, dustiest house in the whole town." Bantam-sized Woody plodded along in school and turned into something of an "alley rat." He was increasingly drawn to music, learning how to play a harmonica and becoming adept at performing in public. Another fire, which badly burned Charley, led to a lengthy hospitalization and Nora's eventual confinement at the Central State Hospital for the Insane in Norman (where she died in 1930). Now largely on his own, Woody took to the road, hitchhiking along Route 66 to Texas during the summer of 1928. He accepted whatever odd jobs were available and also sang for change wherever possible, including in whorehouses. Back in Okemah, he lived at the homes of friends, even attending school regularly for a time, but moved to Pampa after receiving a letter from Charley, who had settled there. The five-foot-five Woody, packing all of 120 pounds and sporting a full head of black, curly hair, hitchhiked to the Texas Panhandle. Woody helped his father run a flophouse there, worked as a soda jerk and sign painter, learned how to play the guitar, and again dropped out of school.

Guthrie joined a band, the Corncob Trio, which played old-time music at weekend barn dances. Country music had experienced a revival during the 1920s thanks to radio stations that featured programs such as Chicago's *Barn Dance* and Nashville's *Grand Ole Opry*, still in its infancy. Record companies pumped out songs by the likes of the Carter Family and Jimmie Rodgers, the greatest hillbilly star and the author of the famed "T for Texas," who became Guthrie's particular favorite. The Corncob Trio occasionally got on the airwaves, generally to pitch an upcoming dance. By the middle of the decade, Guthrie, now married to Mary Jennings, began shaping songs about the Great Depression, particularly the Dust Bowl and those affected by the hard times. Having purchased "the ricketiest of the oil town shacks," where he lived with Mary and the first of their three children, Guthrie felt no compunction about coming and going as he pleased. Grabbing his guitar, he departed from Pampa during the summer of 1936, jumping aboard freight train boxcars, often playing his own tunes for other men there. The refrain of one favorite song ran, "I'm goin' down the road feelin' bad, Lord God/And I ain't gonna be treated this a-way." He slept wherever he could, including in ramshackle hotels and even jails, after being arrested for vagrancy. Invariably he returned to Pampa and Mary before he got the itch to head back on the road again. In early 1937 he hitchhiked along Route 66 to California, following the path taken by many others who were still victimized by the Great Depression and the no longer fertile land that had once provided for them and their families. Processions of Okies, Arkies, Texans, Alabams, and Missous, among others, undertook that odyssey, elegantly portrayed in John Steinbeck's *The Grapes of Wrath*, the epic novel about dreams of California held by the impoverished Joad family. If Steinbeck was the finest novelistic chronicler of Depression-era America, then Guthrie became the most poignant recorder in verse of those displaced by the Dust Bowl: "This dusty old dust is a-getting' my home/And I've got to be drifting along."

Traveling through snow and dust, so hungry that he resorted to begging, Guthrie arrived in downtown Los Angeles and then visited his Aunt Laura in Turlock. Eventually, he returned to Los Angeles along with his cousin Jack, tall, handsome, and ambitious. This was the era of the singing cowboy when Gene Autry and Leonard Slye of the Sons of the Pioneers—Slye would soon be known as Roy Rogers—ruled that portion of the airwaves offering country or hillbilly music. Jack got a job at the Strand Theater in Long Beach with Woody as his comic sidekick before convincing the owner of radio station KFVD, J. Frank Burke, a populist Democrat, to air *The Oklahoma and Woody Show* for the first time on July 19, 1937. The audience response led Burke to feature the Guthrie cousins twice a day with their theme song, "I'm going down this road feelin' bad." Within a few weeks Woody invited a young friend, Maxine Crissman, to perform duets with him on the radio. After Jack departed, Woody and Maxine, now called Lefty Lou, discarded the cowboy songs Guthrie hardly favored, offering instead his own eclectic brand of hillbilly, folk, and country songs along with homespun philosophy. One of Guthrie's tunes, "Do-Re-Mi," became an anthem for the 1930s. Its lyrics spoke of Okies and other transplanted Americans who seemed to be "leavin' home every day" by "beatin' a hot and dusty way" as they headed "out of the old dust bowl" all the way "to the California line." The police at the border informed them, "You're number 14,000 for today!" and warned, "If you ain't got the do-re-mi, folks/If you ain't got the do-re-mi/Better hang on in beautiful Texas/Oklahoma, Kansas, Georgia, Tennessee." Shortly after Guthrie and Crissman received a year's contract from the Standard Broadcasting Company, Mary and their two daughters arrived in California. Guthrie remained an inattentive husband and father while the radio show, like Crissman, eventually flagged, ending on June 18, 1938.

Meanwhile, Burke, who headed the southern California effort by Culbert Olson, the liberal Democratic Party gubernatorial candidate, initiated a small newspaper, *The Light*, that championed progressive causes. At Burke's request, Guthrie took to the road again as *The Light*'s "hobo correspondent," riding in boxcars and landing in migrant camps where he was readily recognized. The mood appeared different now: desperately poor migrants exuded a simmering rage that threatened to erupt. Guthrie witnessed vigilantes lashing at striking cotton pickers and signs that read, "No Okies Allowed in Store." In response, he wrote "I Ain't Got No Home," about "a wandrin' worker" driven from his home by a "rich man" and thus forced to "go from town to town," encountering hostile police and seeing "my brothers and my sisters . . . stranded on the road." Guthrie more and more met up with radicals like Ed Robbin, a correspondent with the communist *People's World*, who invited Guthrie to sing at a rally honoring the jailed radical labor leader Tom Mooney that was sponsored by the Communist Party of the United States (CPUSA). Agreeing to perform, Guthrie explained, "Left wing, right wing, chicken wing—it's the same thing to me."

Undoubtedly influenced by his new acquaintances, Guthrie in March 1939 wrote "The Ballad of Pretty Boy Floyd," about the outlaw from Oklahoma who had carried out a series of bank robberies earlier in the decade, ended up on the FBI's public enemy list, and died at the hands of FBI director J. Edgar Hoover's G-men; with his flair for self-publicity, Hoover was himself something of a pop cultural icon. As Guthrie presented the story, Floyd and his wife rode into Shawnee, Oklahoma, only to encounter a deputy sheriff who treated him rudely. A fight ensued that resulted in the deputy's death and Floyd's escape, leading to "a life of shame" and "every crime in Oklahoma" being attributed to him. In Guthrie's telling, however, "many a starving farmer" told a different tale, speaking of "how the outlaw paid their mortgage and saved their little homes." Others remembered the stranger who begged for a meal before departing, leaving behind "a thousand dollar bill," or who delivered Christmas dinners "for the families on relief." Guthrie poignantly sang, "Yes, as through this world I've wandered/I've seen lots of funny men/Some will rob you with a six-gun/And some with a fountain pen." However, he concluded, "You won't never see an outlaw/ Drive a family from their home."

Beginning in May 1939, Guthrie contributed nearly 200 daily columns under the heading "Woody Sez" and over eighty cartoons to the *People's World*, the CPUSA's newspaper on the West Coast. Influenced by *The Grapes of Wrath*, published that year, Guthrie also produced "Vigilante Man," which referred to Jim Casey, John Steinbeck's Christ-like preacher. Guthrie wrote, "Preacher Casey was just a workin' man/And he said, 'Unite all you working men.'" Someone, possibly a vigilante, killed Casey. Guthrie wondered if a vigilante man would "shoot his brother and sister down." That summer Robbin introduced Guthrie to another party member, Will Geer, a veteran of Broadway and the Federal Theater Project, another New Deal program under the WPA, which hired several radical writers, actors, and directors. At a benefit in Los Angeles, Guthrie and Geer joined Burl Ives in providing entertainment for wounded Spanish Civil War veterans. Geer invited Guthrie to several Hollywood parties where he met the actor John Garfield and Steinbeck, among other luminaries.

During the fall Guthrie and Geer traveled with Steinbeck through California's Imperial Valley. Guthrie hardly appeared concerned about the nonaggression pact signed in late August by the foreign ministers of the Soviet Union and Nazi Germany, which led to numerous departures from the communist movement and the collapse of the Popular Front. By contrast, Guthrie became even more pro-communist in his *People's World* columns. J. Frank Burke and his son, who ran KFVD, became increasingly uncomfortable with Guthrie's political stance. In the *People's World*, Guthrie admitted that his songs "was (sic) so left wing, I had to . . . sing em with my left tonsil, an string my gittar up backwards to git any harmony." His "More War News" claimed that Stalin acted after Hitler invaded Poland to grab "a big strip of Poland and give/The farm lands back to the farmers." As for Estonia, Latvia, and Lithuania—all gobbled up by Russian forces—Guthrie sang out, "A lot of little countries to Russia ran/To get away from this Hitler man." After Guthrie defended Russia's assault on Finland, Burke terminated Woody's radio program. Then Geer left for a Broadway production and Guthrie dropped off Mary and their children—now numbering three—in Pampa before heading for New York City. Arriving in the midst of a bitter winter storm, Guthrie stayed with Will and Herta Geer at their apartment on West Fifty-sixth Street for about a week before taking a room at a seedy hotel located close to the New York Public Library on Fifth Avenue and Forty-second Street.

He began writing the song he became best known for: "This Land Is Your Land." He did so, at least initially, in response to Irving Berlin's "God Bless America," which seemed to be played everywhere when Guthrie undertook his trip up north. Considering Berlin's tune unbelievably saccharine, Guthrie responded with his own examination of his country. His initial version of the song, called "God Blessed America," was stark, containing the lines, "By the relief office I seen my people/As they stood hungry, I stood there wondering if/God blessed America for me." Guthrie soon added the lyrics that began with the stanza, "This land is your land, this land is my land/From California to Staten Island/From the redwood forest to the Gulf Stream waters/God blessed America for me." He further described "that golden valley," "the sparkling sands of her diamond deserts," and "the wheat fields waving."

Geer lined up performances for Guthrie, who wowed the crowd gathered at Mecca Temple on February 25, 1940, paying homage to Spanish Civil War refugees. Once more parroting the communist position, Guthrie sang "Why Do You Stand There in the Rain?," mocking President Roosevelt and referring to "the war lords" playing "the same old game again," butchering and murdering, as "Uncle Sam foots the bill/With his own dear children standing in the rain." The communist *Daily Worker* referred to Guthrie as a "real dust bowl refugee and discovery of Geer." Along with Alan and Bess Lomax, Aunt Molly Jackson, Huddie Ledbetter (better known as "Leadbelly"), and Geer, Guthrie played at a "Grapes of Wrath Evening" benefit held at the Forrest Theater on March 3 for the Steinbeck committee to assist farm workers. Particularly impressed by Guthrie was twenty-three-year-old Alan Lomax, assistant director of the Archive of Folk Song at the Library of Congress and the son of John Lomax, the well-known collector of western music. Viewing Guthrie as "a real ballad maker" and "a natural genius," Lomax invited him to record his songs for the Library of Congress collection.

For three days in late March, Lomax taped extended sessions with Guthrie in the basement of the Library of Congress, including interviews, extemporaneous reflections, and music, of course. With instrumental music from "Lost Train Blues" playing, Lomax introduced Guthrie, declaring he came from Okemah, Oklahoma. Indicating that Guthrie was about thirty years old, Lomax said, "He's seen more in those thirty years than most men see before they're seventy. He hasn't sat in a warm house or a warm office. He's interested in looking out. He's gone into the world and he's looked at the faces of hungry men and women. He's been in hobo jungles. He's performed on picket lines. He's sung his way through every bar and saloon between Oklahoma and California." Guthrie performed easily, offering his brand of homespun country philosophy while delivering forty songs, most his own compositions. Lomax would later say that Guthrie's voice "bit at the heart. A low, harsh voice with velvet at the edges, the syllables beautifully enunciated, the prose flowing with a professional writer's balance of sentence and the salt of a folk wit." Among the astonishing array of songs Guthrie sang for the Library of Congress recording were "So Long, It's Been Good to Know You," "Talking Dust Bowl Blues," "Do-Re-Mi," "Hard Times," "Pretty Boy Floyd," "They Laid Jesus Christ in His Grave," "I Ain't Got No Home," and "Goin' Down That Road Feeling Bad." In one of his most moving songs, "They Laid Jesus Christ in His Grave," Guthrie spoke of Jesus's catering to the sick, the poor, the hungry, and the infirm and his prophesying that "the poor would one day win the world." Consequently, "they killed Jesus Christ on the sly." In the same vein, Guthrie's column for the *Daily Worker*, dated April 11, 1940, claimed, "I'm a Proletarian and proud of it. I've met some dern good folks that worked right handed and thought left. I should of said they worked 2 handed and got left. Anyway, if you go right you get left, and if you go right you go wrong."

While in the nation's capital, Guthrie met Pete Seeger, a tall, lanky Harvard dropout who was working on Lomax's Archive of American Folk Song. The two hit it off and Seeger accompanied Guthrie on his return to New York City. They collaborated on a collection Guthrie was amassing, "Hard Hitting Songs for Hard-Hit People." Because of the collection's sprawling nature and Guthrie's inexperience in writing anything of great length, the project was put aside when Lomax contacted Woody about recording for RCA. On April 26 and May 3, 1940, Guthrie delivered thirteen songs for RCA, eleven of which appeared on two 78-rpm records. He fired off the $300 advance to Mary, who was still residing in Pampa. Released in early July, *Dust Bowl Ballads* included a booklet by Guthrie in which he referred to himself as "The Dustiest of the Dust Bowlers." The RCA songs included "Dust Bowl Blues," "Dust Bowl Refugees," and the powerful "Vigilante Man." The vigilante man, whose name was heard "all over the land," had "a gun and a club in his hand," "chased us out in the rain," killed Preacher Casey, would "shoot his brother and sister down," and "herded us around like a wild herd of cattle." In the *Daily Worker*, Guthrie wrote that his *Dust Bowl Ballads* "are as liberal as the dickens and as progressive as the angels. . . . They came out of the hearts and mouths of the Okies." He then acknowledged that if he were "most proud of anything . . . [it's] the fact that I seem to have been a shade pink."

By now Guthrie was making regular radio appearances, performed in saloons or at benefits, and became better acquainted with Huddie Ledbetter and Aunt Molly Jackson, among others. Then, in May 1940, Guthrie and Seeger headed for Oklahoma in Woody's year-old Plymouth. After a week visiting Mary and his children, along with other relatives, Guthrie and Seeger drove to Oklahoma City, where he met up with Bob Wood, a Communist Party congressional candidate, driving back with him to the organization's national convention in Madison Square Garden. RCA Victor Records released *Dust Bowl Ballads* that summer and Guthrie began appearing as a well-paid regular on Lomax's new radio program for CBS, *Back Where I Come From*. He was heard on other shows too, including the weekly folk music program *Adventures in Music* on public radio station WNYC. He played at the Sawdust Trail on Forty-second Street alongside Cisco Houston, a friend of Will Geer's. In the fall CBS offered Guthrie a spot as host of *Back Where I Come From*, and Guthrie wrote to Lomax, "They are giving me money so fast I'm using it to sleep under."

His newly arrived financial success, however, appeared threatened by the inevitable red-baiting that soon followed. A New York newspaper received letters accusing Guthrie of being a communist and a fifth columnist, or one who clandestinely or subversively undercut American strength. He felt compelled to write to Lomax about the charges, denying that he cared about such accusations. However, Guthrie wrote, "I aint a member of any earthly organization, my trouble is I really ought to go down in the morning and just join in everything." Guthrie also recognized that he had a chance to make things financially comfortable for his family. As his biographer Joe Klein notes, Guthrie stopped offering a column in the *Daily Worker*. Perhaps to assuage some guilt, he demanded a larger role for Leadbelly on his show. He also brought Mary and the kids to New York, setting them up in an apartment at 5 West 101st Street next to Central Park. However, shortly after beginning a new program, *Pipe Smoking Time*, with its theme song, "So Long, It's Been Good to Know You," Guthrie suddenly informed Mary, "Pack up the children. We're leaving." They moved to a hardscrabble house next to the home of his friend Ed Robbin in Los Angeles. Drinking heavily, Guthrie nevertheless worked hard on the autobiography Lomax had suggested he write. In May, having been recommended by Lomax, he received an offer from the Bonneville Power Administration to provide narration and music for a documentary on the Grand Coulee Damn, which the Department of the Interior was constructing on the Columbia River. Accepting the job, which paid $266 a month, he went to Portland and wrote twenty-six songs, including "The Grand Coulee Dam," in three weeks.

Returning alone to New York in June 1941 Guthrie intended to join Seeger, Millard Lampell, and Lee Hays, who had formed the Almanac Singers. This was the very period when the FBI initiated an internal security file on Guthrie, due to a confidential informant's report that he was a communist. On his way back to New York, Guthrie received word that German forces had attacked the Soviet Union. On greeting Seeger, Guthrie remarked, "Well, I guess we're not going to be singing any more of them peace songs," referring to the kind of music associated with the Almanac Singers. Shortly after the release of the group's first album in May, *Time* warned, "Honest isolationists . . . got some help from recorded music that they would rather have not received. . . . Professionally performed with new words to old folk tunes, *John Doe*'s singing scrupulously echoed the mendacious Moscow tune." The Almanacs' second album, *Songs for John Doe*, included the first recording of Guthrie's latest version of "Union Maid," whose protagonist remains true to her cause in spite of the National Guard, "company spies, and "the Legion boys."

Guthrie joined the Almanacs as they traveled out west, playing at union functions, before driving to Los Angeles without Hays, who had returned back east. They ran into the writer Theodore Dreiser, whom they had met earlier, the German writer Thomas Mann, and the German playwright Bertold Brecht, among others, before heading north along the Pacific Coast. In October 1941 they arrived back in New York City, settling into a Greenwich Village townhouse. There they encountered longtime figures from the communist movement, including Elizabeth Gurley Flynn and Mother Bloor, as well as musicians like Sonny Terry and Brownie McGhee. By November the Almanacs delivered their first pro-war song, Guthrie's "Reuben James," as befitting the Soviet Union's brutal fight against Nazi Germany and the United States' undeclared war in the Atlantic. After experiencing some financial bumps that resulted in their eviction from the Greenwich Village flat, the Almanacs appeared ready to thrive following their appearance on Norman Corwin's program, *This Is War*, which was transmitted by four networks to an audience of several million on February 14, 1942. Three days later, however, the *New York World-Telegram* charged, "Singers on New Morale Show Also Warbled for Communists," and the *New York Post* exclaimed, "Peace Choir Changes Tune." The Almanacs never fully rebounded as producers canceled scheduled performances or refused to schedule them.

Guthrie's attention was increasingly taken up with matters beyond the Almanacs, including a passionate love affair with Marjorie Marzia, a beautiful young performer with Margaret Graham's Dance Company. Guthrie agreed to narrate and provide music for a modern dance production, "Folksay," choreographed by Sophie Maslow and featuring Marzia. He signed a contract with William Doerflinger of E.P. Dutton to deliver an autobiography, which Alan Lomax encouraged. Doerflinger's wife, Joy, helped to make sense of Guthrie's sprawling, rambling manuscript, which he completed in the fall of 1942. He also joined with Leadbelly to form the Headline Singers and help sell war bonds while plastering a sign on his guitar that read, "This Machine Kills Fascists." Then, in March 1943, *Bound for Glory* was published, one month after Marzia gave birth to their daughter, Cathy. Clifton Fadiman of *The New Yorker* predicted that "someday people are going to wake up to the fact that Woody Guthrie and the ten thousand songs that leap and tumble off of the strings of his music box are a national possession, like Yellowstone and Yosemite." In May Guthrie received a Julius Rosenwald Fellowship for $1,800, having been nominated by Lomax, to enable him to "write books, ballads, songs, and novels that will help people to know each other's work better."

At the same time Guthrie remained eligible for the draft during a period when Uncle Sam took virtually any able-bodied man between the ages of eighteen and thirty-eight. Over the course of the next two-years he completed several tours with the Merchant Marine. Back home in March 1944, living with Marjorie and Cathy in a small apartment in New York City, he delivered "Hard, Ain't It Hard" and "More Pretty Gals Than One," the first of hundreds of recordings he would make over the next few years for Moe Asch, later founder of Folkways Records. That year, during an interview with a naval intelligence officer, Guthrie denied being a Communist Party member but also indicated he was not "ashamed to be described as a communist," Ed Cray notes. Notwithstanding an apparent blacklist, Guthrie was inducted into the army on May 7, 1945, the very day Germany surrendered. While on furlough in November he married Marjorie. He was released from the U.S. military on December 21, receiving an honorable discharge the following month.

Residing in a small house on Coney Island, Guthrie and Marjorie eventually had three more children. Cathy died in a fire at the age of four, an event that severely depressed him. On a happier note, he wrote and recorded children's songs for Asch. He also participated in Seeger's attempt to revive the cultural Popular Front through People's Songs, a musical collective. However, postwar America soon experienced a chill as relations with the Soviet Union dramatically worsened. The left, particularly the portion that remained attracted to communism, suffered accordingly, although there remained a few bright spots along the way. *Finian's Rainbow*, co-authored by an old Popular Fronter, E.Y. Harburg, opened on Broadway in 1947, condemning racism and economic policies that crippled the underclass. The character of Woody Mahoney, a merchant seaman obviously patterned after Guthrie, was "back from fighting fascism and fleas in the South Pacific and is no pushover for people who like to push other people around." However, Hollywood expressed no interest in Guthrie's own work, while fewer unions, many having adopted an anticommunist posture, welcomed him. In 1948 he crafted his final great song, "Plane Wreck at Los Gatos (Deportees)," which began elegantly, "The crops are all in and the peaches are rott'ning/The oranges are packed in their creosote dumps/ They're flying 'em back to the Mexico border/To take all their money to wade back again." Then, Guthrie sang the refrain, "Goodbye to my Juan, goodbye Rosalita/Adios mis amigos, Jesus & Maria/You won't have a name when you ride the big airplane/All they will call you will be 'deportees.'"

By the end of the decade Guthrie's life appeared to be in shambles as he became estranged from Marjorie and his children and engaged in a series of acts that brought into question his very sanity. He suffered a federal indictment after a young woman in California complained of having received obscene letters from him. Sentenced to 180 days in jail, he served little time before his release. Then, in the summer of 1950, Seeger convinced his new folk group, the Weavers, to record Guthrie's "So Long, It's Been Good to Know You," which became a smash hit. The sizable advance enabled the Guthries to relocate to a new apartment in Brighton Beach. His marriage remained volatile and Guthrie appeared more ready than ever to lash out, even violently. He also suffered an emergency appendectomy in early 1951. During his hospital stay he encountered a young would-be folk singer who came to be known as Ramblin' Jack Eliot. On January 7, 1952, Guthrie recorded his best-known version of "This Land Is Your Land" with the title replacing the earlier line, "God blessed America for me," in the refrain. However, he soon became another victim of the postwar red scare when Decca dropped both the Weavers and Woody shortly after "So Long" crested near the top of the hit parade. Guthrie's erratic behavior continued and he agreed to be committed to Bellevue in mid-1952. Other voluntary commitments would follow. Finally, on September 3, a physician diagnosed Guthrie as suffering from Huntington's chorea, a hereditary, degenerative disease of the nervous system that had no cure and obviously affected his behavior. Seeking a warmer climate, he moved to Topanga Canyon, California, where his friends Will and Herta Geer were now residing. He met a beautiful young woman, Anneke Van Kirk, who would become his third wife following his divorce from Marjorie in 1953. Anneke had a baby girl with Guthrie, but this tempestuous marriage lasted for only three years.

Concerned about Guthrie's continued difficulties, a group of his friends, including Seeger, established the Guthrie Children's Trust Fund in 1956 to oversee his estate. In March a benefit concert for the trust fund was held at Pythian Hall in New York City. Over a thousand people attended. The final song, "This Land Is Your Land," was interspersed with a standing ovation for Guthrie. Joe Klein suggests that this concert "was the beginning of Woody Guthrie's canonization." That occurred as Guthrie experienced an involuntary admission to Greystone Park in Morris Plains, New Jersey, and an eventual transfer to first Brooklyn State Hospital and later the Creedmoor Psychiatric Center in Queens, New York. Guthrie's legacy lived on, however, as a folk revival began in the late 1950s, with the Kingston Trio landing on the pop charts with songs like "Tom Dooley." A new crop of folksingers, many offering their own progressive slant on contemporary issues, appeared by the start of the 1960s, led by Joan Baez and Bob Dylan, another artist who considered Guthrie a mentor. In 1960 the *New York Times*'s Robert Shelton praised Guthrie as "a giant of a humanist, a hero of the American little man, a poet of major proportions and a singer and composer of some of our greatest songs." Lomax's recordings of Guthrie's music at the Library of Congress finally came out in 1964, three years before Woody died. Later he was posthumously inducted into both the Songwriters' Hall of Fame and the Rock and Roll Hall of Fame. The Smithsonian Institution offered a traveling exhibit from 1999–2002, *This Land Is Your Land: The Life and Legacy of Woody Guthrie*.

Bibliography

Bourke-White, Margaret. *Portrait of Myself.* New York: Simon & Schuster, 1963.

Callahan, Sean. *Margaret Bourke-White: Photographer.* Hinkley, IL: Little, Brown, 1998.

———, ed. *The Photographs of Margaret Bourke-White.* London: Secker and Warburg, 1973.

Cray, Ed. *Ramblin' Man: The Life and Times of Woody Guthrie.* New York: W.W. Norton, 2004.

Denning, Michael. *The Cultural Front: The Laboring of American Culture in the Twentieth Century.* New York: Verso, 1996.

Guthrie, Woody. *Bound for Glory.* New York: Penguin, 1943.

———. *Pastures of Plenty: A Self-Portrait.* New York: Harper Collins, 1990.

———. *Seeds of Man.* New York: Dutton, 1976.

Klein, Joe. *Woody Guthrie: A Life.* New York: Bantam Dell, 1982.

Ostman, Ronald E.; Harry Littell; and Margaret Bourke-White. *Margaret Bourke-White, the Early Work, 1922–1930.* Boston: David R. Godine, 2005.

Phillips, Stephen Bennett. *Margaret Bourke-White: The Photography of Design 1927–1936.* New York: Rizzoli, 2006.

Stomberg, John. *Power and Paper: Margaret Bourke-White, Modernity, and the Documentary Mode.* Seattle: University of Washington Press, 1998.

SEVEN

American Heroes

HANK GREENBERG AND EDWARD R. MURROW

From the inception of the United States, stories about heroes and heroines dominated the American cultural pantheon. Storytellers waxed eloquent about Founding Fathers and Founding Mothers, including the quintessential eighteenth-century American, Benjamin Franklin; the nation's first president, George Washington; the author of the Declaration of Independence, Thomas Jefferson; Abigail Adams with her admonitions to husband John; and Dolley Madison with her abundant personal charm and social graces. Frontiersmen such as Daniel Boone, Davy Crockett, and James Fenimore Cooper's literary creation, Leatherstocking, became iconic in their own fashion, setting the stage for the enormous popularity of Andrew Jackson. Abraham Lincoln's defense of the Union and emancipation of the slaves accorded him legendary status, while their prowess during the Civil War did the same for opposing commanding generals Robert E. Lee and Ulysses S. Grant. Contributions to the United States' ascension to industrial might turned John D. Rockefeller, Andrew Carnegie, and J. Pierpont Morgan into celebrities, however reluctant. Operating out of Hull House in Chicago, social workers Jane Addams and Florence Kelley, like Social Gospel ministers George Herron and Walter Rauschenbusch, strove to improve conditions for America's underclass during the period of rapid modernization, while acquiring considerable reputations as guardians of the American underclass. The Progressive movement spurred presidents Theodore Roosevelt and Woodrow Wilson, charismatic figures in their own right, to seek to ameliorate the worst aspects of industrial capitalism while striving to lead their nation to international prominence. Henry Ford and Charles Lindbergh, regardless of their actual familial origins, exemplified the self-made man as well as an apparent intertwining of human and machine. With the 1920s nearing a close the popular press depicted "the Great Engineer" Herbert Hoover, head of the American Relief Administration after World War I, secretary of commerce under presidents Warren G. Harding and Calvin Coolidge, and recently elected president of the United States, as an authentic American hero. Business leaders in general held great appeal during the 1920s, having apparently ushered in an era of prosperity if not for all then for those smart enough to take advantage of booming economic circumstances.

The image of the American hero altered as the Great Depression wound on while some who previously had been idealized fell from grace, in a manner of speaking. Henry Ford, Charles A. Lindbergh, and even New York Yankee home-run king Babe Ruth became diminished figures for various reasons. The auto tycoon's refusal to negotiate in good faith with organized labor, let alone his readiness to rely on company goons, infuriated many Americans. Lindy's anguish at the kidnapping and murder of his infant further elevated him as the embodiment of American heroism, but his flirtation with fascism, praise of Hitler's Germany, and isolationist stance before U.S. entrance into World War II lessened the goodwill Americans had felt for him. Ruth's fall from favor was different, of course, caused by the diminishing of his once matchless athletic skills, topped off by his inability to hit National League pitching after his trade to the Boston Braves in 1935. During the Depression decade other individuals acquired something of the celebrity and acclaim that business leaders such as Ford, self-reliant actors on the order of Lindbergh, and athletic giants like Ruth had previously possessed. In the manner of classic American heroes, Franklin Delano Roosevelt emerged, offering hope to a nation wracked by self-doubt and soaring numbers of destitute individuals and families. Both loved and reviled in the manner of the Founders, Jackson, Lincoln, corporate moguls, leading reformers, his distant cousin Teddy, Wilson, and Hoover, Roosevelt came across as a larger-than-life figure able to tackle both the Great Depression and the aggression of right-wing nations. Roosevelt's stature loomed so great that he became in effect the greatest representative of popular culture of his era, easily caricatured in *New Yorker* cartoons with his seemingly ever-present cigarette, rimless eyeglasses, jaunty smile, and aristocratic visage. He retained that preeminence for the full twelve years of his presidency, coming across first as "Dr. New Deal" and later just as gracefully affecting the image of "Dr. Win the War."

Two other handsome, dapper individuals, generally spanning the years of Roosevelt's three-plus terms in the Oval Office and some time beyond, made their own marks as genuine American heroes in a somewhat old-fashioned sense during a period when antiheroes were becoming more prominent. Hank Greenberg proved the great Jewish ballplayer major league managers and owners had long sought while standing as a refutation of the racist ideology associated with the Ku Klux Klan and the Silver Shirts at home and the Nazis in Europe. Appropriately enough, Greenberg also was the first big-league star to be drafted under the new Selective Service Act of 1940 and the first to be called back into service after the Japanese attack on Pearl Harbor. Serving in the States and overseas during the years that should have been the prime of his athletic career, he returned home in time to carry his Detroit Tigers to a World Series championship as the conflict ended. During stints overseas from the mid-1930s until the conclusion of World War II, Edward R. Murrow became America's top broadcast journalist, a reputation he retained throughout the early Cold War era. He delivered his *London After Dark* program during the Blitz and mentored a group of war correspondents, including Eric Sevareid and Charles Collingwood, for CBS News. After the war Murrow served as an executive for the network, but returned to broadcasting, eventually hosting both *See It Now* and *Person to Person*, which provided contrasting models for investigative and celebrity journalism. His eventual decision to challenge the red-baiting antics of Senator Joseph McCarthy helped to dampen the worst excesses of the domestic Cold War. Later he offered stunning documentaries, including *Harvest of Shame*, about migrant workers, and served in the Kennedy administration as director of the United States Information Agency (USIA).

Hank Greenberg

Henry Benjamin Greenberg was born in Greenwich Village on New Year's Day 1911, to David and Sarah Greenberg. Romanian-Jewish immigrants who maintained an Orthodox household, Yiddish-speaking David and Sarah initially raised their brood of four in an apartment house on Perry Street. Greenwich Village, with its lovely townhouses and wide streets, was something of an oasis in the lower sector of New York City, which contained large slum areas, many teeming with Jewish immigrants. By contrast, the Greenbergs lived comfortably thanks to David's work in the textile industry, where he became a respected clothier. Nevertheless, ethnic rivalries, pitting Irish and Italian kids against Jewish ones, rippled through the neighborhood. As Greenberg later reflected, "Kids down in the Village thought the national pastime was beating up kids of other nationalities." David's business prospered sufficiently to enable the family to relocate to a rambling, sixteen-room house in the East Tremont section on Crotona Park North at East 174th Street in the Bronx.

Known by his friends as Bruggy Greenberg, young Hank became hooked on baseball after his father took him to a Sunday doubleheader at the Polo Grounds, which housed both the New York Giants and the New York Yankees until the 1923 major league season. Tall and lanky—he was six-foot-three by the age of thirteen—the flat-footed Greenberg worked particularly hard at baseball, then viewed as America's national game. As he later acknowledged, "I didn't *play* ball when I was a kid, I *worked* at it." By 1928, Paul Krichell, a top scout with the Yankees, began to display interest in "the gangling Jewish kid with the powerful shoulders," and soon other teams followed his progress on the baseball diamond as well. An exception was John McGraw, the legendary skipper of the New York Giants, who, although he had long sought a Jewish star, showed no interest in signing Hank: one of McGraw's scouts had declared that Greenberg would "never make it." Many of Greenberg's neighbors agreed: as he later recalled, "Jewish women on my block . . . would point me out as a good-for-nothing, a loafer, and a bum who always wanted to play baseball rather than go to school. . . . I was Mrs. Greenberg's disgrace."

Hoping to attend Princeton University, the now six-foot-four Greenberg worked hard to maintain his grades, graduating from high school in February 1929. On the last day of the 1929 season, Krichell invited Greenberg to watch a game at Yankee Stadium. Referring to Lou Gehrig, Krichell indicated, "He's all washed up. In a few years you'll be the Yankees first baseman." But Greenberg proved overwhelmed by Gehrig. "His shoulders were a yard wide and his legs looked like mighty oak trees. I'd never seen such sheer brute strength. No way I'm going to sign with this team. Not with *him* playing first base," Greenberg told himself. He responded to Krichell, "That Lou Gehrig looks like he's got a lot of years left." Gehrig went on to play in every Yankee game for the next nine seasons before a fatal disease drove him from the game. Eventually Greenberg turned down the Yankees and several other teams, signing instead with the Detroit Tigers.

In early 1930 Greenberg headed down to Tampa for spring training with the major-league ball club. After he belted a homer in his first exhibition game, a Detroit newspaper reported, "Henry Greenberg, the prize rookie, stole the show. He made a couple of sensational plays at first base. . . . and his trip to the plate resulted in a home run and Babe Ruth never hit a ball harder." Although called "the greatest prospect in years," Greenberg soon proved overmatched by big-league pitchers and was sent down to Hartford, the Tigers' Class A franchise in the Eastern League. Despite smacking a homer in his final game there, the nineteen-year-old's struggles continued as he batted only .214 and soon dropped down to Raleigh in the Class C Piedmont League. After again flailing away at the plate, Greenberg rebounded by hitting .314 and knocking out nineteen homers. He also encountered something that would recur throughout his baseball career, expressions of amazement that a Jew was playing baseball. In this case, Greenberg asked a teammate who was gawking at him, "What're you looking at?" The teammate stated, "Nothing. I've never seen a Jew before. I'm just looking." Greenberg responded with, "See anything interesting?" The fellow admitted, "I don't understand it. You look just like anybody else." "Thanks," Greenberg countered and the conversation concluded. Near the close of his first season in organized baseball, Greenberg returned to the Tigers for the final few weeks of the major-league campaign. Getting into only one game, he managed to pop up to Yankee second baseman

Tony Lazzeri. At the tail end of the season, Tiger manager Bucky Harris, who had scarcely spoken to Greenberg, ordered him to play first base. An infuriated Greenberg blurted out "I ain't gonna play for this team" and headed for the clubhouse. The next season saw Greenberg play for Evansville in the 3-I League, where he batted .318 with fifteen homers and a league-leading forty-one doubles. He also committed a league-high twenty-five errors at first base before appearing as a pinch hitter in three games for Beaumont of the Texas League. He rejoined Beaumont in 1932, becoming the league's most valuable player (MVP) by hitting thirty-nine homers and driving in 131 runs.

During spring training in 1933, Harris informed Greenberg that he was going to be the Tigers' third baseman but he proved unable to play the position. Two months into the season, Greenberg finally replaced the slick-fielding, light-hitting Harry Davis at first base. Despite missing almost forty games, he ended the season with his first twelve major-league home runs and eighty-seven runs batted in (RBIs), while batting .301. He did so while proudly sporting his family surname, never considering the possibility of changing it as sportswriter Ford Frick suggested many other Jewish players had done. Frick had written back in 1925, "There must have been at least half a hundred Jews in the game but we'll never know their real names. During the early days of this century the Jewish boys had tough sledding in the majors and many of them changed their name."

Greenberg's second big-league campaign proved even better for both him and the Tigers, who had finished in fifth place in 1933. Detroit swept to the American League pennant, winning 101 games, ending up seven games in front of the runner-up New York Yankees. Appearing in all but one contest, Greenberg had his first great year in the major leagues, batting .339, the fifth best mark in the American League; scoring 118 runs; driving in 139, the third highest total; belting twenty-six homers; and leading the league with sixty-three doubles.

Capturing its first pennant in twenty-six years meant a great deal to Detroit, hit harder than any other major American city during the Great Depression. Like much of the United States, the city experienced a boom throughout most of the 1920s fueled by the automotive industry and exemplified by the construction of new General Motors and Fisher headquarters. In 1929 alone more than 5 million cars poured out of auto plants, but within a year that production level was down by 2 million. Unemployment soared. Licensed vendors sold apples on street corners for five cents apiece. Conditions deteriorated further by 1931: unemployed workers demonstrated in front of city hall, while auto production fell by another 2 million. The next year Detroit's Welfare Department ran out of funds that had been counted on to provide shelter for many homeless residents. In early March, 3,000 displaced autoworkers, family members, and political activists, including communists, joined the Ford Hunger March in nearby Dearborn. Their demands for union recognition, jobs, and a shorter workday resulted in a clash between demonstrators and the police. Battling tear gas, marchers hurled rocks and packed mud. Five marchers were killed and many others wounded. The situation in Detroit worsened by early 1933: unemployment approached 40 percent, while salaries of city workers were slashed and welfare was further reduced. A pair of the city's largest banks folded, and in April Detroit's public employees received scrip instead of paychecks. The introduction of Franklin D. Roosevelt's New Deal prevented the slide from worsening still more. Jobs programs along with the infusion of public spending began to improve economic conditions, however incompletely and inconsistently.

Although times remained difficult, sports heroes helped to lift the spirit of Detroit's inhabitants. A black high school student, Eddie Tolan, captured both the 100- and 200-meter dashes at the 1932 Olympic Games in Los Angeles. During the summer of 1934, as the Tigers marched to the pennant, a twenty-year-old African-American, Joe Louis, a two-time Golden Gloves champion, began his professional boxing career, delivering a first-round knockout. By late September Louis had won his first seven pro bouts, all but two by knocking out his opponent. But 1934 belonged to the Tigers, who attracted nearly 1 million fans to Navin Field. Led by playing manager and catcher Mickey Cochrane, the Tigers boasted other future Hall of Famers including the peerless second baseman Charles Gehringer and outfielder Goose Goslin, who along with Greenberg would be known as "The G-Men."

Toward the end of the season and with the pennant yet to be wrapped up, a controversy arose over whether Greenberg would play during the Jewish High Holidays. Earlier that year Greenberg had to contend with a teammate, pitcher Rip Sewell, who referred to him as "you big Jew bastard." Manager Cochrane sent Sewell down to the minors. The city of Detroit was hardly immune to anti-Semitism thanks to the continued influence of auto magnate Henry Ford, who had published anti-Semitic tracts in the 1920s, and Father Charles Coughlin, who regularly delivered diatribes against Jews on his syndicated radio program. In late September 1934, the *Detroit Free Press* sported a headline with Hebrew characters on its front page, wishing a Happy New Year to the Tigers' first baseman. One writer compared Greenberg's dilemma to "Jacob of old" who "spent the night wrestling with the angels," attempting to make up his mind. Now a rabbi apparently gave the nonobservant ballplayer permission, in a manner of speaking, to take the field during Rosh Hashanah, but Greenberg still proved to be "the last player to change into uniform, sitting in the locker room for some time debating with himself." He proceeded to belt a pair of homers, including one in the ninth inning, enabling the Tigers to defeat the Boston Red Sox 2–1. As Greenberg later related, "I caught hell from my fellow parishioners, I caught hell from some rabbis." Eventually he determined to sit out the game on Yom Kippur. When he walked into Shaarey Zedek Synagogue, Greenberg, towering over almost all the other congregants, received a standing ovation. The *Detroit Times'* Bud Shaver praised Greenberg, asserting that "his fine intelligence, independence of thought, courage and his driving ambition have won him the respect and admiration of his team-mates, baseball writers, and the fans at large. He feels and acknowledges his responsibility as a representative of the Jews in the field of a great national sport and the Jewish people could have no finer representative." The poet Edgar Guest responded to Greenberg's decision with a poem noting that the Irish had never imagined witnessing "a Jewish boy from Bronxville out where Casey used to be." However, those same fans "cheered like mad" when the movie-star-handsome Greenberg performed as he had on the Jewish New Year and made the decision he had about the Day of Atonement:

Come Yom Kippur—holy fast day world-wide over to the Jews—
And Hank Greenberg to his teaching and the old tradition true
Spent the day among his people and he didn't come to play.
Said Murphy to Mulrooney, "We shall lose the game today!
We shall miss him on the infield and shall miss him at the bat,
But he's true to his religion—and I honor him for that!"

The Tigers lost the 1934 World Series to the St. Louis Cardinals in seven hard-fought games. Greenberg batted .321 with one homer and seven RBIs, but he failed to deliver in the clutch in several instances. Consequently, he and the Tigers hoped for better results still in the upcoming season. After a slow start that found the Tigers in the cellar, Detroit repeated as American League title-holder, winning by three games over the Yankees. The G-Men all batted in over 100 RBIs with Greenberg driving in a league-best 170, along with smacking thirty-six homers, which tied Jimmy Foxx for most in the American League. Near the end of the regular season, Frederick G. Lieb penned an article in the *Sporting News*, "Oi, Oi, Oh, Boy! Hail That Long-Sought Hebrew Star," proclaiming Greenberg the game's "greatest Jewish player." The October 1935 issue of *Baseball Monthly* contained an article by F.C. Lane, "Baseball's New Sensation, 'Hank' Greenberg," referred to as "the outstanding player of the year." As Lane put it, Greenberg had accomplished more than simply guiding the Tigers. He had "led his ancestral race into a new promised land" and onto "a field where they have been comparative strangers." Lane considered this fitting as America was "the melting pot of all nations." In 1935 the Tigers went on to defeat the Chicago Cubs in six games to win their first World Series crown, while Greenberg was the unanimous selection as the MVP in the American League. Cubs bench jockeys railed at Greenberg, tossing out anti-Semitic slurs, with one player shouting, "Throw him a pork chop, he'll never hit it." In the second game, which Greenberg helped to win with a two run homer, he broke his wrist and missed the rest of the series. The year 1936 was virtually a lost one for the reigning World Series champs as Greenberg broke the same wrist after only twelve games and the Tigers finished nineteen and a half back of the resurgent Yankees, fueled by the sensational rookie outfielder Joe DiMaggio. The Tigers again finished second to New York in 1937, thirteen games behind despite winning eighty-nine contests. Wasted were brilliant years by both Gehringer, who won the batting title and was named league MVP, and Greenberg. Hank knocked out forty homers to finish second to DiMaggio but led the league in RBIs with 183, only one behind Gehrig's league record.

The Tigers again fell short in 1938, coming in fourth, although Greenberg had another sensational year. In fact, he flirted with the major-league home-run mark, staying close to the pace set by Babe Ruth eleven years earlier. With five games to go in the regular season, Greenberg stood at fifty-eight homers, two behind Ruth. Another controversy followed: some fans, players, and sportswriters claimed that pitchers simply refused to pitch to Greenberg, not wanting a Jew to possess the most fabled record in American sports. Greenberg denied this, stating that he simply was not up to the task. Having walked only four times in those last five games, Greenberg called the charges of anti-Semitism "pure baloney": "I didn't hit 60 or 61," he said, "because I ran out of gas." Nevertheless, Greenberg's fame in the sport was hardly unimportant given the fact that baseball was still considered the national pastime. Greenberg's stature held even greater importance for American Jews. While others referred to him as Hammerin' Hank and Hankus Pankus, Jews looked on Greenberg as "the baseball Moses," "a messiah," "a Jewish god." His stardom rose as abuse poured forth from the stands at opposing ballparks and from the dugouts of other American League squads. Harvard Law School professor Alan Dershowitz later reflected, "He defied every stereotype. He was They. He was what 'they' said we could never be. He defied Hitler's stereotype." Historian Peter Levine wrote, "Hank Greenberg was a tough Jew when tough Jews were important." The actor Walter Matthau noted, "You couldn't help but be exhilarated by the sight of one of our guys looking like Colossus." Other players must also have viewed Greenberg as a behemoth as indicated by an episode that took place in the middle of the 1938 season. During a contest with the Chicago White Sox, one of the opposing players called Greenberg "a yellow Jew son of a bitch." Greenberg tore into the White Sox clubhouse after the game and declared, "The guy that called me a yellow son of a bitch get on his feet and come up here and call it to my face." No one spoke up.

Bud Shaver underscored the symbolism of Greenberg's baseball feats in the late 1930s as Hitler's regime in Germany threatened other European states. As the Nazis goose-stepped, baseball fans in Detroit speculated about Greenberg's assault on Ruth's record: "Can he make it?" The *New York Post*'s Hugh Bradley similarly referred to Hitler's machinations, but then indicated that "in America the question is, 'Can Greenberg do it?'" Greenberg's fame carried greater weight as developments in Europe darkened. The Munich Pact allowed for the carving up of Czechoslovakia, and on the evening on November 9, 1938, Nazis engaging in a rampage against Jewish stores, homes, and individuals throughout Germany. Kristallnacht, the Night of Broken Glass, amounted to a massive pogrom that led to scores of unprovoked killings, the destruction of nearly 1,700 synagogues, and the herding of 30,000 Jews into concentration camps. Pro-Nazi forces in the United States, led by the German American Bund, championed the Hitler regime, with 20,000 people congregating in Madison Square Garden on February 19, 1939, to condemn President Roosevelt and his New Deal, cuttingly referred to as "Frank D. Rosenfeld" and the "Jew Deal."

As the 1939 season opened, Greenberg, major league baseball's greatest Jewish star, was also the highest-paid player in the game, with a $40,000 salary, but the season concluded with Detroit in fifth place, twenty-six and a half games behind the Yankees. Although Greenberg made the All-Star team once again and finished second in the league in homers with thirty-three, while batting .312 and knocking in 112, the year was clearly a disappointment: Hank was even benched at one point. Both Greenberg and the Tigers rebounded in 1940 as he topped the American League with forty-one homers, 150 RBIs, and a .670 slugging average, although he missed out on a Triple Crown despite hitting .340, as DiMaggio won the batting title with a mark of .352. Fred Haney, the manager of the St. Louis Browns, called Greenberg "the greatest competitor in the league." During the photo-finish pennant race, Greenberg went on a late-season tear as Detroit edged out Cleveland by one game and New York by two, ending the Yankees' four-year stretch of World Series titles. For the second time, Greenberg was the American League MVP, a feat that was still more noteworthy because he had agreed during spring training to move to left field so that Rudy York could play first base. Greenberg received a $10,000 bonus for successfully making the switch. *Baseball Monthly* suggested that "Greenberg won the pennant for the Tigers. He won it for a club which . . . could not possibly have finished in the first division without him. Not since the palmy days of Babe Ruth had there been so thorough a one-man job." During the World Series against Cincinnati, Greenberg hit .357 with one homer and six RBIs, but the Tigers dropped the final two games after taking three of the first five games and holding a 1–0 lead until the seventh inning of the deciding contest.

In May 1941, after playing in only nineteen games of the new season, during the last of which he belted two homers against the Yankees, the thirty-year-old Greenberg, having received induction orders, entered the U.S. Army. The military discharged the now Sergeant Greenberg on December 5 after a new draft provision excluded men over twenty-eight. Two days later the Japanese attacked the U.S. naval base in Pearl Harbor and he quickly reenlisted, becoming the first big-league star to do so. "We are in trouble and there is only one thing—return to service," Greenberg stated. Placed in the Army Air Forces, Greenberg entered Officer Candidate School, receiving a commission as a second lieutenant in August 1942. North Carolina senator Joshua Bailey lauded Hank "as an example of young men inducted into the Army who had made a 'real sacrifice'" and declared, "He's a bigger hero than when he was knocking home runs." Greenberg served in the military for four years and fifty-five days, one of the longest stretches for a major-league player. Becoming part of America's war culture in their own fashion, other star athletes appearing in uniform included Greenberg's fellow baseball stars Bob Feller, Ted Williams, Joe DiMaggio, and Stan Musial; former heavyweight boxing champions Gene Tunney and Jack Dempsey, along with the current titleholder, Joe Louis; golfer Bobby Jones; and college football player Tom Landry. The University of Iowa's Nile Kinnick, winner of the 1939 Heisman Trophy, awarded each year to the top football collegian, perished while training to be a fighter pilot. Greenberg's own military service attracted attention because of his accomplishments on the playing field and because he was the game's greatest Jewish player. World War II proved to be an ideological fight in which the United States and its allies, particularly Great Britain and the Soviet Union, battled against the Axis states: militarist Japan, fascist Italy, and Nazi Germany. While the Japanese posed a considerable threat in the Pacific, the Germans imperiled the European continent, the Middle East, and North Africa. Participating in the conflict that Studs Terkel would refer to as the Good Fight must have resonated with Greenberg as he and others became increasingly aware of the horrors that the Nazis were conducting, including a deliberate attempt to eradicate European Jewry. The U.S. Army itself was hardly immune to anti-Semitism, as Greenberg discovered. In one instance a drunken soldier aboard a ship Greenberg was shipping out on hollered, "Are there are Ginzbergs or Goldbergs here. Because if there are, I'm going to whip them." Standing up, Hank replied, "My name is Greenberg. What do you want to do about it?" The would-be combatant looked at Greenberg and responded, "I asked about Ginzbergs and Goldbergs, no problem with Greenbergs."

Unlike most ballplayers who served in the U.S. military during the war, Greenberg went into combat, an assignment he sought. Stationed in Fort Worth, Texas, along with the actor William Holden, Greenberg asked to be transferred. After heading to Washington, DC, he joined the first batch of B-29s sent overseas, spending six months in India and then passing through Burma into China. He flew on missions that passed over the Himalayas, the area known as the Hump. In mid-1944 Greenberg returned to the States, where he was assigned to a unit in New York City. Captain Greenberg traveled throughout New England, along with other combat officers, with the U.S. Army sending the famed ballplayer to speak to factory workers, including women, older men, and handicapped individuals to help sustain morale.

The still out-of-shape Greenberg, having only recently been discharged from the military, appeared at his home ballpark, Briggs Stadium, where a crowd of 47,729 gathered on July 1, 1945. He belted a home run in the eighth inning, and hit a dozen more the rest of the season while driving in sixty and batting .311 in only seventy-eight games. Herbert Simons in *Baseball Monthly* spoke of the significance of Greenberg's return to major-league baseball after a four-and-a-half-year absence. "Each blow broadcast to all players all over the world as they awaited V-J day and separation from the armed forces that they could come back successfully in their chosen profession, despite the inroads of the war and the millions of pessimistic words authored during the conflict on the improbability of baseball comebacks." Other top players returned that summer too, including Cleveland fireballer Bob Feller, Yankee outfielder Charley Keller, and White Sox shortstop Luke Appling. Detroit won the 1945 pennant, just nipping the Washington Senators, thanks appropriately enough to a ninth-inning grand slam by Greenberg in the final game of the regular season, notwithstanding "a charley horse, blistered hands, a sore arm and a sprained ankle." For Greenberg the happiest "part of that home run" occurred after hearing that Washington players wailed, "Goddamn that dirty Jew bastard, he beat us again." During the World Series, Greenberg hit a pair of homers, drove in seven, and batted .304, as the Tigers defeated the Chicago Cubs in seven games, to win their first World Series title in ten years. When asked what he planned to do next, Greenberg answered, "Collapse!"

The 1946 season started slowly for the now thirty-five-year-old Greenberg, who had lost several of his prime years during the war. A torrid September, in which he smacked sixteen homers, enabled him to win the home-run title with forty-four and the RBI crown with 127, although the Tigers came in second, a distant twelve games behind the Boston Red Sox. However, during the off-season Detroit sold Greenberg's contract to the Pittsburgh Pirates, who made him the first $100,000 player in the major leagues. Greenberg had his poorest season as a big-league ballplayer, hitting twenty-five homers but batting a mere .249. Yet the year proved memorable as he helped to tutor a still raw young player, Ralph Kiner, who became the National League's finest slugger, and certainly drew fans, resulting in the greatest attendance figures in the Pirates' history. Greenberg also played a role, however minor, in Jackie Robinson's integration of major-league baseball. The first black player in organized baseball in the twentieth century received vicious taunts from fans and competing players alike. Other teams threatened to refuse to take the field against Robinson's Brooklyn Dodgers. Even some of his own teammates demonstrated their displeasure about appearing on the same playing field with an African-American. Greenberg's last season in the major leagues, 1947, was Robinson's first and the two literally collided at first base during a game where Greenberg was covering the bag. When Robinson landed on first base again later in the same contest, Greenberg said, "I forgot to ask you if you were hurt in that play." When Robinson indicated that he was okay, Greenberg advised him, "Stick in there. You're doing fine. Keep your chin up." The *New York Times*, on May 18, 1947, offered a headline reading, "Hank Greenberg a Hero to Dodgers' Negro Star." The nation's foremost newspaper reported that Robinson happily received Greenberg's words of encouragement, especially given the severe jockeying he had encountered. Robinson said, "Class tells. It sticks out all over Mr. Greenberg." A former Tiger teammate, Birdie Tebbetts, later declared that only Robinson suffered more abuse from fellow ballplayers than Greenberg had.

After his playing career ended, Greenberg served as a top executive for both the Cleveland Indians and the Chicago White Sox. In 1956 he was inducted into the Hall of Fame, the first Jewish ballplayer so honored, declaring, "I guess this is what every ballplayer dreams about but never hopes to achieve." He later became a successful investment banker while rumors floated that he might be named baseball commissioner. As he grew older, Greenberg acknowledged, "When I was playing, I used to resent being singled out as a Jewish ballplayer. I wanted to be known as a great ballplayer, period. I'm not sure why or when I changed, because I'm still not a particularly religious person. Lately, though, I find myself wanting to be remembered not only as a great ballplayer, but even more as a great Jewish ballplayer." Retiring to Beverly Hills, California, Greenberg played tennis avidly, married the actress Mary Jo Tarola, and made a fortune in the stock market. His first marriage to the department store heiress Carol Gimbel had ended in divorce, with Greenberg and Gimbel sharing custody of their three children. Beset by cancer, Greenberg died on September 4, 1986, still viewed, along with Dodger pitcher Sandy Koufax, as the greatest of all Jewish ballplayers. The *Detroit News* praised another side of Greenberg: "He gave selflessly to any number of individuals and causes, without issuing self-aggrandizing press releases. If you don't believe that, just watch. Praise will flow from places you never considered: from entertainers, politicians, tennis players, celebrities, groundskeepers, restaurant owners, sportswriters, baseball fans."

Edward R. Murrow

The youngest of Roscoe Murrow and Ethel Lamb Murrow's three sons, Egbert Roscoe Murrow was born on April 25, 1908, in Polecat Creek, North Carolina. Hardworking Quaker farmers with decidedly Western European ancestry, Roscoe and Ethel initially lived with their children in a log cabin before moving to Blanchard, a small town in the northwest sector of Washington state. Roscoe became a brakeman and then a railroad engineer while Ethel served as treasurer of the local school board. Their boys attended the local, two-room school and worked on farms, at a sawmill, and at logging camps. Attending high school required taking a trolley or walking the five miles to Edison, where the hot-tempered, lanky Egbert, soon called Ed, played sports, joined the school orchestra and glee club, participated on the debate team, and became student body president. Along with his father, he worked with loggers at Beaver Camp, 100 miles west of Blanchard, for a year after finishing high school. In the fall of 1926, the six-foot-two Murrow enrolled at Washington State University in Pullman, where his brothers had gone to school. There he majored in speech, began to dress stylishly, performed in college plays, was the top Reserve Officer Training Corps (ROTC) cadet on campus, and served as class president. An address he delivered at Stanford University in late 1929 before the annual convention of the National Student Federation of America (NSFA) in which he exhorted fellow college students to focus less on "fraternities, football and fun" and take note of public affairs resulted in his election as president of the student organization, the nation's largest. Graduating the following June as the shadow of the Great Depression darkened over Washington state, Murrow boarded a train for New York City to head the NSFA for a weekly salary of $25. Within weeks Murrow participated in a gathering of the Confederation Internationale des Etudiants in Brussels, although he declined an offer to serve as the organization's president.

In mid-September 1930, Murrow made his initial appearance on CBS radio, talking on *The University of the Air*, a forum that he employed to solicit messages from international figures like Mahatma Gandhi, British prime minister Ramsay MacDonald, German president Paul von Hindenburg, and Albert Einstein. He rented a small, inexpensive apartment in Greenwich Village and traveled widely to campuses across the United States, again warning against "political apathy and complacency." Planning to enter Columbia Teachers

College, he chose instead to accept a position in the fall of 1932 as assistant to the director of the Institute of International Education, Stephen Pierce Duggan, a supporter of NSFA. On a train to New Orleans for the organization's annual convention that winter, he met a beautiful young campus activist from Mount Holyoke: Janet Brewster.

Following Duggan's lead, Murrow then served as secretary of the newly formed Emergency Committee in Aid of Displaced German Scholars, which helped to relocate scholars on the order of Paul Tillich, Martin Buber, Hans J. Morgenthau, and Herbert Marcuse after Adolf Hitler's ascendance to power. Now engaged to Janet, he criticized "an economic system that damns some of us before we are born" and worried that "we have no money, and I have no profession, and on top of that I'm at heart a bum and a vagabond and will always be that way." Notwithstanding such concerns, Murrow was already making $5,000 a year and had received an offer for a job in the Roosevelt administration that would have paid considerably more. Consequently, on October 27, 1934, he and Janet married and the newlyweds soon settled into an apartment in mid-Manhattan. Murrow corresponded with Albert Einstein, who had taken residence in Princeton, and Thomas Mann, among other luminaries, and he got involved in the CBS radio program, *School of the Air.*

In September 1935 Murrow went to work for CBS as director of Talks to Coordinate Broadcasts on Current Issues. By the mid-1930s, radio, like motion pictures and the print media, was helping to shape American society. Having become an influential force during the previous decade, radio, again like American cinema, experienced something of a golden age during the 1930s. NBC and CBS were the leading radio networks, offering President Roosevelt's fireside chats, the rants of Father Charles Coughlin, populist tirades by Louisiana senator Huey Long, and commercial broadcasts featuring variety programs, top actors, and the finest musicians. Guided by William S. Paley, CBS, with ninety-seven affiliates by 1935, presented performers such as Will Rogers, Kate Smith, Bing Crosby, and the comedy team of George Burns and Gracie Allen. As for the CBS news division, which remained largely limited to newscaster Bob Trout, Paley declared that his network would take no stand on public controversies; its broadcasting would necessarily "be wholly, honestly, and militantly non-partisan." Meanwhile, Murrow set up broadcasts at CBS for former cabinet members, European heads of states, and an American president seeking reelection. During a Christmas Eve party at CBS in 1936, Murrow grabbed the news script away from broadcaster Trout and delivered the report himself in "word perfect" fashion. He continued to present important commentaries from figures such as Gandhi, Bernard Shaw, Haile Selassie, Benito Mussolini, Leon Trotsky, Herbert Hoover, and John Maynard Keynes. Then, in February 1937, a top CBS news executive asked if

Murrow would care to become the network's European director. Ed and Janet next resided in a spacious apartment on London's Queen Anne Street where they socialized frequently and Murrow began sporting Savile Row attire.

Although still in its infancy, broadcast journalism soon underwent marked alterations, many of which Murrow helped to facilitate or originate, including the shortwave transmission of his network's broadcasts to England. Early during his stay overseas, Murrow delivered a series of public and private addresses in which he spoke of the "international aspects of broadcasting" and warned that broadcasting had failed "to accept its responsibilities, to seek for truth wherever it might be found and to disseminate that truth as widely as possible." Broadcast reporters, he contended, should employ "an honest mirror" to cover international events. The initial CBS broadcast from London of *The World Today*, the first news show delivered daily, occurred on March 13, 1938. Trout hosted the program in New York while William Shirer, the first of the Murrow Boys, a team of gifted correspondents Murrow began putting together, reported from London and other journalists spoke from Paris and Berlin. Coming on the air from Vienna, Murrow introduced himself before reporting that "many people . . . lift the right arm a little higher here than in Berlin and the 'Heil Hitler' is said a little more loudly." Murrow indicated two days later that not "everyone was out to greet Herr Hitler today. There is tragedy as well as rejoicing in this city tonight." Following announcement of the Anschluss, effectively giving Germany sovereignty over Austria, he spoke of the supposed "bloodless conquest" that had occurred: "But I'd like to be able to forget the haunted look on the faces of the long lines of people outside the banks and travel offices. People trying to get away. . . . I'd like to forget the sound of the smashing glass as the Jewish shop streets were raided; the hoots and jeers at those forced to scrub the sidewalk." One interviewer soon indicated that "great and grave responsibilities rest upon Murrow," who often extemporized freely rather than relying on fully drawn notes. Following Janet's suggestion, he also began opening his reports with the statement, "This is London," which came to be identified with its narrator. Robert Landry in *Scribner's Magazine* observed that Murrow possessed "more influence upon America's reaction to foreign news than a shipful of newspapermen." As Landry emphasized, "the influence is there, great and growing—and obvious to anyone who knows both radio and the press." Determined to reach out to that large audience, Murrow sought to offer broadcasts "down to earth, in the vernacular of the man on the street." It hardly hurt, as one colleague later recalled, that Murrow possessed "the best voice ever heard on the news. It sent a shiver through you."

Believing that a major war was impending, Murrow, along with his European staffers, determined that CBS radio field its own team of reporters.

Eventually he drew in cerebral types like Eric Sevareid, Winston Burdett, Charles Collingwood, Howard K. Smith, Richard C. Hottelet, and Marvin Breckinridge, among others, stationing them in London and across the continent. In the meantime, the Spanish Republic fell to General Francisco Franco, who was backed by Italy and Germany, and German soldiers occupied Prague, completing the dismemberment of Czechoslovakia. In late August 1939, the German and Russian foreign ministers signed a nonaggression pact, followed shortly by an assault on Poland and the Baltic republics. On the afternoon of September 3, speaking from the British Broadcasting Corporation's (BBC's) Broadcasting House, Murrow announced, "Forty-five minutes ago, the prime minister stated that a state of war existed between Britain and Germany." CBS and Murrow contended with censorship provisions established by the British military that were vetted through the BBC, but as he acknowledged, "I should be unwilling to broadcast from a nation at war without any censorship at all. The responsibility for human lives would be too great." It helped that CBS made no effort "to weigh or color the news."

The stress of war coverage wore heavily on Murrow, who smoked even more than before, acquired a gaunt appearance, and began sporting a formless raincoat that covered his otherwise immaculate suits as he rapidly traversed the London streets. Despite nervous mannerisms, Murrow nevertheless smoothly delivered his reports, which often possessed a lyrical quality. Burdett later spoke of Murrow's typical performance on the radio: "Accurate diction, economy, filed sentences, firm phrasing—these gave to his scripts a kind of magnificent clarity that bordered on the epigrammatic." The times were clearly momentous and Murrow reported on the events with characteristic clarity and eloquence. After the removal of 300,000 British troops from Dunkirk in early June 1940, Murrow declared that Prime Minister Winston Churchill prophetically "believed that these islands could be successfully defended, could ride out the storm of war and outlive the menace of tyranny. If necessary, for years. If necessary, alone."

Beginning in late August 1940, Murrow delivered his radio broadcasts on the program *London After Dark* as the German Luftwaffe conducted an intensive air campaign against London and other parts of Great Britain. As the Blitz continued Murrow declared on September 8 that "the world was upside down." He began his reports with "This is London," ended one delivery with "So long and good luck," a phrase employed by the English, but subsequently used "Good night, and good luck" as his signature sign-off. He reported from the rooftop of the BBC night after night with bombs falling all around, speaking of bombing raids and air raid shelters while indicating "not once have I heard man, woman or child suggest that Britain should throw in her hand." Murrow's steadfast delivery of news under fire, even when bombs fell on CBS headquarters, only added to his growing stature. Frequent visitors to the Murrow apartment included dignitaries such as Eleanor Roosevelt; Clementine Churchill, the wife of the British prime minister; Hollywood film star Clark Gable; and Labor Party leaders Ernest Bevin and Harold Laski. The *Christian Science Monitor* extolled *London After Dark* for its ability to offer "a message which newspapers, even with the most brilliant reporting, photography and editing, cannot deliver." Murrow met with top presidential assistant Harry Hopkins for several hours in London in early January 1941 and he also spent considerable time with John Gilbert Winant, an old friend and the new U.S. ambassador to Great Britain. Believing that if England fell to the Nazi onslaught, "we at home will tear ourselves apart within five years, probably less," Murrow initiated *Meet Uncle Sam*, a new BBC program.

After Murrow returned to the States in late 1941, CBS honored him with a dinner on December 2 at the Waldorf-Astoria in New York City. Archibald MacLeish, the poet and Librarian of Congress who was now heading the Office of Facts and Figures, a propaganda agency of the U.S. government, declared, "You burned the city of London in our houses and we felt the flames that burned it. You laid the dead of London at our doors and we knew that the dead were our dead . . . were mankind's dead . . . without rhetoric, without dramatics, without more emotion than needed be." Murrow helped to vanquish "the superstition that what is done beyond 3,000 miles of water is not really done at all." *Time* magazine sang his praises too, stating "he did more than his job" with "no bunk, no journalese, no sentimentality" while acknowledging that the British "want us in this war." After midnight on December 8, 1941, the day following the Japanese attack on Pearl Harbor and the subsequent U.S. declaration of war, Murrow and Colonel William Donovan, who soon served as director of the Office of Strategic Services, saw President Roosevelt in the Oval Office. Later Murrow wrote, "Never have I seen one so calm and so steady." In January the White House beseeched Murrow to serve with Robert E. Sherwood at the Office of War Information.

Returning instead to London that April, Murrow presented fifteen-minute radio commentaries on Sunday afternoons. He soon met General Dwight Eisenhower, U.S. commander for the European theater of operations, and directly reported on the North African campaign. In 1943 Murrow flew aboard American B-17s conducting bombing raids on Western Europe, disregarding orders to the contrary issued by CBS's Paley. One top network executive acknowledged, "There was no way to make him stop short of firing him." In mid-1943 another job offer came his way, a request by Churchill for Murrow: to head BBC programming. Paley would later ask Murrow to lead the CBS news department; the "largest paper in Washington, DC" hoped to hire him as editor. Murrow also received word that his alma mater, Washington State, wanted him to replace the outgoing president. He declined all such offers.

In late 1943 he referred to unprecedented horrors unfolding on the European continent. "One is almost stunned into silence by some of the information reaching London," he said, declaring that "what is happening is this: millions of human beings, most of them Jews, are being gathered up with ruthless efficiency and murdered." He continued, "When you piece it all together—from Holland and Norway, from Poland—you have a picture of mass murder and moral depravity unequaled in the history of the world. It is a horror beyond what imagination can grasp." Murrow spoke of thousands of Jews shipped off daily from the Warsaw ghetto while "the infirm, the old and the crippled were killed in their homes." Some were murdered in the Jewish cemetery while others were placed "in freight cars; the floors were covered with quick-lime and chlorine." The survivors ended up in death camps such as Treblinka, where "a huge bulldozer is used to bury the bodies." Murrow warned, "The Jews are being systematically exterminated throughout all Poland."

The following June he supervised the CBS account of D-Day, the mass Allied invasion of Nazi-occupied France. As for his country's servicemen, Murrow suggested they subscribed to "the old-fashioned American attitude that big bullies should pick on somebody their own size." With V-2 rocket bombs raining on London, Murrow warned that such an assault "makes complete nonsense out of strategic frontier, mountain and river barriers" and "seems to make more appalling the prospect or the possibility of another war." In late 1944, worn out by wartime pressures and conflicted about a love affair threatening his marriage, Murrow returned to the United States. After an extended vacation, he was back in London in March 1945, now knowing that Janet was pregnant, which excited him greatly. The time he spent at Buchenwald markedly affected Murrow, who finished his radio report "shaking with rage." He witnessed children with tattoos on their arms, imprinted by their Nazi captors, and saw "two rows of bodies stacked up like cordwood." Without hesitation Murrow editorialized: "I pray you to believe what I have said about Buchenwald. I reported what I saw and heard, but only part of it. For most of it I have no words." He closed by affirming, "If I've offended you by this rather mild account of Buchenwald, I'm not in the least sorry." At one point that spring, he indicated to other CBS reporters, "We've seen what radio can do for the nation in war. Now let's go back to show what we can do in peace!" When V-E Day arrived in Europe on May 8, Murrow informed his radio audience that London was "a city of celebration and song and thanksgiving." After all, "the organized killing has ended in Europe." He suggested that even as the celebration continued, "perhaps we should remember . . . that the suffering will continue for many years" and "that unspeakable crimes are still unpunished." Murrow warned "that power carries with it great responsibility. We have the power." At the same time he worried "that the hatred of Czech for Czech, Pole for Pole" surpassed that of "their hatred for their German captors and butchers . . . that is Communist versus non-Communist."

CBS boss Paley encouraged Murrow to take over the company's news division with a salary and bonuses amounting to $50,000 annually while other offers came in as well, including one to head the Carnegie Corporation and another to serve as assistant secretary of state. Murrow became CBS vice president for public affairs and purchased a townhouse on Manhattan's Upper East Side. He began putting together another group of Murrow Boys, which included Alexander Kendrick, George Polk, David Schoenbrun, Marvin Kalb, Daniel Schorr, Bob Pierpont, and Ed Bliss. Speaking to Schoenbrun, Murrow stated, "One day I could give you the biggest classroom in the world. . . . we are going to make CBS the greatest network in the world. We are going to inform and educate the people of America." Long isolationist, the United States now stood as "the world's greatest power." As Murrow explained, "That's why I see CBS as an international classroom." Paley for his part sought to make CBS "an elite network" that provided "an important forum for great public figures and great public issues, for education, for thoughtful and challenging presentation of the news." At the same time Paley wanted to supplant NBC as the top commercial radio network. Murrow expressed his belief that "radio in a democracy must be more than an industry, more than a medium of entertainment." It "must hold a mirror behind the nation and the world," unveiling "racial intolerance, economic inequality, bigotry, unemployment."

CBS hardly appeared immune to the changed political climate in the United States. A domestic version of the Cold War paralleled the rising tensions between East and West with the Chamber of Commerce urging a curbing of supposed communist influence at home, including in the media, entertainment, and public service. The Republican Party hurled charges that Democratic opponents in the 1946 congressional elections were communist sympathizers, a tactic that resulted in the GOP's capture of both houses of Congress. President Harry S. Truman seemingly responded to the changing political climate by demanding that federal employees take a loyalty oath. Left-of-center organizations, such as the Political Action Committee of the Congress of Industrial Organizations and Progressive Citizens of America, charged that a witchhunt was brewing. The dismissal of Murrow's old friend Bill Shirer led to accusations that CBS had succumbed to political pressures.

That episode possibly cemented a decision by both Paley and Murrow that Ed return to broadcasting with a weekly salary of $2,500 plus annual travel expenses of $20,000. He did so on September 29, 1947, having been away from the mike for eighteen months. *Variety* applauded the development as affording "impetus to the cause of the liberal commentator." Murrow began delivering *Edward R. Murrow with the News*, opening with "This is the news" and concluding each report with a six-minute commentary, followed by his sign-off, "Good night and good luck." In the radio booth Murrow reported on leading international and domestic events including the hearings about supposed communist influence in Hollywood being held by the House Un-American Activities Committee. In a widely critiqued statement on October 27, 1947, he insisted that the "right of dissent . . . the right to be wrong, is surely fundamental to the existence of a democratic society. That's the right that went first in every nation that stumbled down the trail toward totalitarianism." Meanwhile, the FBI tracked Murrow while the newly formed Defense Department attempted to hire him. Following an announcement that the Soviets had tested an atomic bomb, Murrow declared, "The Russians not only exploded an atomic weapon, they exploded an American myth . . . that we had, and could maintain, the secret of the bomb's construction." After the overthrow of Chiang Kai-shek's dictatorial regime in China by the communists, Murrow explained, "It is an old lesson of war that an army cannot operate successfully against guerrilla tactics unless it has the support of the local population."

In 1950 the domestic Cold War heightened following accusations by Wisconsin senator Joseph McCarthy of communists nestled in the State Department and the start of the Korean War. Murrow expressed concerns about "a witch-hunt" while insisting that the Bill of Rights shielded even the most unpopular sorts of individuals. After a government worker lost her job due to anonymous accusations that she was a communist, Murrow retorted, "She was fired for thinking supposed disloyal thoughts. A Constitution that forbids speech control does not permit thought control." An orchestrated letter campaign included charges that Murrow revealed "his own Communistic leanings" and that his sponsor displayed a readiness to financially back "Un-Americanism." After the North Korean attack across the thirty-eighth parallel in June, Murrow flew to Korea, where he spent six weeks. Murrow discovered that Campbell's Soup wanted to end its sponsorship of his prime-time program, but Paley quickly lined up new sponsors for *Edward R. Murrow with the News*. More happily the Murrows, having bought a comfortable lodge resting on fourteen acres in Quaker Hills, sixty-four miles outside of New York City, to serve as a weekend getaway, also purchased a large apartment at 580 Park Avenue in Manhattan.

Murrow had resisted the new television industry, recently questioning what form "TV news . . . is . . . likely to take after the shakedown cruise. . . . Is it to be a medium of entertainment or education?" He did not foresee television news becoming "more than a supplement to the daily newspaper." However, watching Senator Estes Kefauver's televised Senate investigation of organized crime convinced Murrow otherwise and he agreed with producer Fred Friendly to initiate a thirty-minute, weekly television program, *See It Now.* On November 18, 1951, the new program began a historic seven-year run when the forty-three-year-old Murrow, holding a lit cigarette, stated, "Good evening. This is an old team trying to learn a new trade." The first program, focusing on a platoon in the U.S. Army's nineteenth infantry, stationed in Korea, led one critic to contend that the segment offered "the first Korea picture report that actually brought the war home to us." In 1952, Murrow, having returned to the battlefield, presented a popular "Christmas in Korea" segment. Critic Gilbert Seldes referred to *See it Now* as "the most important show on the air—not only for the solutions it found to some problems, but also for the problems it tackled without finding the right answers." Nevertheless, a number of *See it Now* offerings, such as a talk with J. Robert Oppenheimer, former head of the Manhattan Project during World War II that led to the development of the atomic bomb, proved controversial. Meanwhile, CBS was on the receiving end of red-baiting when the right-wing journal *Counterattack* presented a full issue asserting Murrow was "confused on communist issues and defends those involved in communist causes." Despite such accusations, Murrow in 1953 began hosting *Person to Person*, which presented two guests weekly, speaking from their homes. The figures ranged from Brooklyn Dodgers catcher Roy Campanella and West Point football coach Earl "Red" Blaik to Massachusetts senator John F. Kennedy and his new bride, Jacqueline Bouvier Kennedy.

Drawing on the stature he had acquired over the past two decades, Murrow soon determined to confront the demagogic Joseph McCarthy, who had vilified people the broadcaster greatly admired, such as General George Marshall, Franklin D. Roosevelt's top military adviser during World War II, a former Secretary of Defense and Secretary of State, and architect of the Marshall Plan to rebuild war torn Europe. On January 22, 1953, *Edward R. Murrow with the News* criticized the demand by the new secretary of state, John Foster Dulles, for "positive loyalty to the nation's policies," pointing out the difference between "loyalty to one's country" and "blind loyalty to the policy that a particular administration happens to be carrying out." During his radio broadcast on April 29, 1953, Murrow, after referring to book burnings by American government officials overseas, charged, "The sense of superiority which we had when the Nazis were burning books can scarcely sustain us now." "The Case against Milo Radulovich, A0589839," involving an army lieutenant whom the Air Force sought to discharge because of his relatives' political beliefs, appeared on the October 20, 1953, broadcast of *See It Now*, with Murrow concluding "that the son shall not bear the iniquity of the father, even though that iniquity be proved, and in this case it was not." Murrow was hardly the first newsman to challenge McCarthyism—Walter Lippmann, Drew Pearson, Joseph Alsop, Stewart Alsop, Eric Sevareid, and I.F. Stone already had—but he was perhaps the most prominent one to do so.

On March 9, 1954, *See It Now* presented a thirty-minute special, "A Report on Senator Joseph McCarthy," later referred to by *Time* magazine as "TV's most explosive telecast." Others call it "television's finest hour." Indicating that the story would be presented "mainly" in McCarthy's "own words and pictures," Murrow presented contrasting images of the often scowling, sometimes giggling legislator. Murrow indicated that McCarthy had "terrorized" American citizens, "substantially demoralized the present State Department," and attacked military officers. While acknowledging the usefulness of congressional investigations, Murrow charged, "The line between investigation and persecuting is a very fine one and the junior senator from Wisconsin has stepped over it repeatedly." Demanding due process of law, Murrow declared, "We must not confuse dissent with disloyalty. . . . We must not walk in fear, one of another." Americans would not be "driven by fear into an age of unreason" if they recalled their heritage and remembered "we are not descended from fearful men, not from men who feared to write, to speak, to associate and to defend causes which were for the moment unpopular." Indeed, "we cannot defend freedom abroad by deserting it at home." Murrow concluded, "The actions of the junior senator from Wisconsin have caused alarm and dismay amongst our allies abroad and given considerable comfort to our enemies, and whose fault it that? Not really his, he didn't create this situation of fear, he merely exploited it and rather successfully." CBS received more than 75,000 pieces of correspondence and phone calls about the program, over 90 percent of them favorable. Critic Jack Gould of the *New York Times* declared, "Last week may be remembered as the week that broadcasting recaptured its soul." Given equal time to respond, McCarthy declared that Murrow was "a symbol, the leader and the cleverest of the jackal pack which is always found at the throat of anyone who dares to expose individual Communists and traitors." That response, coupled with the senator's abysmal performance during the televised Army-McCarthy hearings, helped to break his fever-like hold on the nation's psyche. In late 1954, the U.S. Senate voted to censure McCarthy, although not for reasons directly related to red-baiting.

Murrow remained CBS's top broadcaster for the next several years, with *See it Now* running until 1958 and *Person to Person* remaining on the air until the following year. A lengthy article, "This Is Murrow," appearing in the September 30, 1957, issue of *Time*, explained that Murrow possessed "expert technique," whose "timing can make silence more eloquent than words." His "persuasiveness" was "rooted in a prickly social conscience and a sense of mission about keeping people informed." In addition, he remained "a fine reporter with sight and sound," possessing "a gift for capturing actuality in its moods and nuances as well as its meaning." In a speech in mid-1958, Murrow spoke about the state of television: "This instrument can teach, it can illuminate; yes, and it can even inspire, but it can do so only to the extent that humans are determined to use it to those ends. Otherwise it is merely wires and lights in a box." Murrow worked with Friendly to produce *CBS Reports*, which opened in 1960, eventually including the celebrated *Harvest of Shame* about migrant workers. In 1961 he accepted President John F. Kennedy's offer to become director of the U.S. Information Agency, seeking "not to capture, but to free men's minds," remaining in the post until after Kennedy's assassination. Over the years Murrow's health deteriorated, the result of years of heavy smoking, regular drinking, relentless work, and the depression that frequently beset him. On April 27, 1965, the fifty-seven-year-old Murrow died of brain cancer. "He was a shooting star and we will live in his afterglow a very long time," Eric Sevareid proclaimed. A quarter-century later, longtime CBS anchor Walter Cronkite said of Murrow, "He's the head of the parade, he's the pinnacle of the pyramid. He led the way."

Bibliography

Bliss, Edward, and Edward R. Murrow. *In Search of Light: The Broadcasts of Edward R. Murrow, 1938–1962.* Cambridge, MA: Da Capo Press, 1997.

Clooney, George, dir. *Good Night and Good Luck.* Warner Independent Pictures, 2005.

Cloud, Stanley, and Lynne Olson. *The Murrow Boys: Pioneers on the Front Lines of Broadcast Journalism.* New York: Houghton Mifflin, 1996.

Dinnerstein, Leonard. *Antisemitism in America.* New York: Oxford University Press, 1995.

Douglas, Susan J. *Listening In: Radio and the American Imagination.* Minneapolis: University of Minnesota Press, 1999.

Edward R. Murrow Papers, 1927–1965: A Guide to the Microfilm Edition. Sanford, North Carolina: Microfilming Corporation of America, 1982.

Edwards, Bob. *Edward R. Murrow and the Birth of Broadcast Journalism.* Hoboken, NJ: John Wiley, 2004.

Fang, Irving E. *Those Radio Commentators!* Ames: Iowa State University Press, 1977.

Greenberg, Hank, with Ira Berkow. *Hank Greenberg: The Story of My Life.* Chicago: Triumph Books, 2001.

Kempner, Aviva, dir. *The Life and Times of Hank Greenberg.* Ciesla Foundation, 1998.

Kendrick, Alexander. *Prime Time: The Life of Edward R. Murrow.* Hinkley, IL: Little, Brown, 1969.

Levine, Peter. *Ellis Island to Ebbets Field: Sport and the American Jewish Experience.* New York: Oxford University Press, 1993.

Persico, Joseph E. *Edward R. Murrow: An American Original.* New York: McGraw Hill, 1988.

Ritter, Lawrence S. *The Glory of Their Times: The Story of the Early Days of Baseball Told by the Men Who Played It.* New York: Harper Collins, 1992.

Seib, Phillip. *Broadcasts From the Blitz: How Edward R. Murrow Helped Lead America Into War.* Dulles, VA: Potomac Books, 2006.

Sperber, A.M. *Murrow: His Life and Times.* New York: Smithmark, 1986.

Time. "This Is Murrow." September 30, 1957.

EIGHT

American Rebels

MARILYN MONROE AND ELVIS PRESLEY

Postwar America witnessed the flourishing of the antihero. Although this figure was no newcomer to American popular culture, images of the antihero proliferated after the war. This was hardly surprising, given the enormity of the war, which came on the heels of the worst depression in the nation's history. The revelations of man's inhumanity to his fellow man, coupled with jolting economic, political, and social events, fostered unease, anxiety, and alienation. Coming out of the war, Americans recalled images of death camps and mushroom clouds. New tensions emerged among the members of the Grand Alliance, which had defeated the fascist states and imperialist Japan. French writers Jean-Paul Sartre, Albert Camus, and Simone de Beauvoir became associated with the philosophical movement called existentialism, which called into question traditional morality and societal norms, offering instead the sensibility that individuals had to strive for personal authenticity in an age of unreason and absurdity.

Even before existentialist philosophy began to influence American intellectuals, cinema and literature in the United States provided examples of existential heroes or antiheroes. Members of the Lost Generation had presented iconic figures that moved beyond the pale, literally or otherwise. Ernest Hemingway's Jake Barnes in *The Sun Also Rises*, Frederick Henry in *A Farewell to Arms*, and Robert Jordan in *For Whom the Bell Tolls* exemplified antiheroes in their own fashion. A veteran of the American fight in Europe during World War I, Barnes returns physically and psychically scarred. Lieutenant Henry opts for his own separate peace during that conflagration, refusing to believe in the supposedly larger issues that the war purportedly represents, focusing instead on the landscape and human relationships. Jordan leaves behind college teaching to join the early fight against fascism during the Spanish Civil War, linking up with various left-wing groups that would have made him suspect had he returned from the front. F. Scott Fitzgerald's Jay Gatsby in the classic novel *The Great Gatsby* represents a seemingly amoral individual determined to win the love of a woman he idealizes, having acquired a personal fortune in undefined, illicit ways that include his association with mobsters. John Steinbeck's Tom Joad in *The Grapes of Wrath*, jailed after a manslaughter conviction, opts to fight on behalf of the people even though that again places him outside the law. Richard Wright's Bigger Thomas in *Native Son*, a young African-American man in Chicago, commits two murders, albeit one inadvertently, while serving for his communist lawyer as a symbol of class oppression.

Antiheroes thrived in American cinema virtually from the very beginning of the industry. Charlie Chaplin's good-natured Little Tramp bumbles through one epic film after another, including *The Kid*, *The Gold Rush*, *City Lights*, and *Modern Times*. A series of cinematic antiheroes appeared on the silver screen at the very height of the Great Depression. Edward G. Robinson's Enrico Bandello, James Cagney's Tom Powers, and Paul Muni's Tony Camonte are the gangster leads in *The Public Enemy*, *Scarface*, and *Little Caesar*, respectively. Boris Karloff's Frankenstein, Bela Lugosi's Count Dracula, and Claude Rains's Jack Griffin appear as different kinds of monsters in *Frankenstein*, *Dracula*, and *The Invisible Man*. By the middle of the decade, comedic protagonists could be seen in screwball films such as *My Man Godfrey*, starring William Powell as a supposedly forgotten man who turns out to be a well-educated dropout suffering from romantic angst, and *The Awful Truth*, with Cary Grant starring as the wealthy Jerry Warriner, whose open marriage threatens to implode. A different spate of cinematic antiheroes showed up in American film at the end of the 1930s, including Errol Flynn's swashbuckling bandit in *The Adventures of Robin Hood*, John Wayne's gunslinging Ringo Kid in *Stagecoach*, and Clark Gable's cynical Rhett Butler in *Gone with the Wind*. The most striking cinematic antihero, of course, was seemingly whichever character Humphrey Bogart played: escaped convict Duke Mantee in the 1935 film *The Petrified Forest*, the detective Sam Spade in *The Maltese Falcon*, antifascist fighter turned nightclub operator Rick Blaine in *Casablanca*, skipper-for-hire Harry Morgan in *To Have and Have Not*, the latter three of which appeared during World War II, and private investigator Philip Marlowe in *The Big Sleep*, released in 1946.

Along with Bogart's Marlowe, other antiheroes proved noteworthy during the early postwar era. Young writers Norman Mailer, J.D. Salinger, and Arthur Miller presented tormented protagonists such as the platoon of riflemen in *The Naked and the Dead*, teenager Holden Caulfield in *A Catcher in the Rye*, and the middle-aged traveling salesman Willy Loman in *Death of a Salesman*. Howard Hawks's 1948 film *Red River* starred Montgomery Clift as Matt Dunson, the stepson of cattleman Tom Dunson, appropriately enough played by John Wayne, by now the iconic American hero, at least in cinematic guise. Buffed, shirtless, and sporting tight-fitting jeans, Marlon Brando took on the role of the sociopathic Stanley Kowalski in the 1951 cinematic version of Tennessee Williams's play *A Streetcar Named Desire*. Having appeared as the Mexican revolutionary in *Viva Zapata!*, which came out in 1952, Brando showed up the following year in *The Wild One*, becoming identified with the character of Johnny Strabler, a motorcycle gang leader who takes to the road with no aim in mind other than to experience as many kicks as possible. When asked at one point, "What are you rebelling against?" a laid-back Johnny responds, "Whaddaya got!," the classic example of a rebel hardly searching for a cause. Johnny-like juvenile delinquents, whether Hell's Angels or not, garnered attention from both sociologists and psychologists, in addition to concerned parents. James Dean offered film versions of troubled youth in both *Rebel Without a Cause* and *East of Eden*, in which his characters battle with parents and other authority figures while attempting to remain true to themselves. Marilyn Monroe's real-life struggles, along with her appearances in films like *Niagara* and *Bus Stop*, demonstrated how American women wrestled with gender-rooted constraints in an age that glorified monogamy, domesticity, and the nuclear family.

Identifying with outcasts and bohemians, small circles of friends on the East and West Coasts, in places like New York City's Greenwich Village, San Francisco's North Beach, and Venice, California, held aloft the notion of "a New Vision" or "the New Consciousness," which involved "trying to look at the world in a new light, trying to look at the world in a way that gave it some meaning." Eventually called the beats, individuals like Jack Kerouac, Allen Ginsberg, and Neal Cassidy sought in classically existentialist fashion to live according to their own codes of behavior while they deliberately challenged conventional ways, sexually and otherwise.

In many ways the beginning of the 1950s hardly appeared to be a propitious time for dissenting voices in the United States. The domestic Cold War intensified, the Korean War unfolded, and pressure to conform heightened. Nevertheless, that proved to be the very period when antiheroes thrived, ranging from film stars like Brando, Dean, and Monroe, to rock and roll artists Elvis Presley, Chuck Berry, Jerry Lee Lewis, and Little Richard. To a certain extent, Monroe and Presley both represented figures outside the pale. The strikingly beautiful Monroe, with her blonde hair and exquisite body, represented the latest version of the American sex goddess, albeit in a period when puritanical values supposedly prevailed. The handsome Presley, the seeming personification of the poor-boy-makes-good myth, transformed American music and culture with his swagger, sensuality, and ability to meld white and black music. Together Monroe and Presley stood as American antiheroes in a period when classic heroes still dominated, like President Dwight D. Eisenhower; the most celebrated astronauts of the Mercury Project, Alan Shepard and John Glenn; and sports stars Stan Musial, George Mikan, and Johnny Unitas.

MARILYN MONROE

The fabled Hollywood actress Marilyn Monroe was born Norma Jeane Mortenson on June 1, 1926, in Los Angeles, California, to Gladys Baker and an unknown father. Gladys's depression and financial difficulties led to Norman Jeane's being placed in foster homes, an orphanage, and, for a spell, the home of Grace McKee, a good friend of her mother who urged the young girl to dream of becoming a movie star. When Grace moved to West Virginia, fifteen-year-old Norma Jeane had the choice of returning to the orphanage or marrying twenty-one-year-old Jimmy Dougherty. After Dougherty went overseas with the Merchant Marines in 1944, Norma Jeane resided with his parents and worked in a defense plant. An American photographer shot her picture, and she soon signed with a model agency. By the spring of 1945, her photographs, including some with her newly lightened blonde hair, could be seen in *Yank* and *Stars and Stripes*, the army newspapers, and on the covers of several national magazines. She divorced Dougherty in 1946, and signed with Twentieth Century Fox for $125 a week, soon operating under the name of Marilyn Monroe. Only a couple of bit parts came her way and Fox failed to renew her contract. Throughout this period Monroe relied on her physical charms to increase her chances of making it in Hollywood. She became involved in a "party circuit" that resulted in her involvement with numerous men, some of whom proved violent. When later questioned if tales regarding the casting couch were valid, Monroe answered, "They can be." Still, she insisted, "You can't sleep your way into being a star, though. It takes much, much more. But it helps. A lot of actresses get their first chance that way." Monroe operated in this fashion in the very period when Americans remained conflicted about sexuality and women's roles in general.

Fears that an economic downturn might result in a return of the Great Depression undoubtedly helped to shape Americans' attitudes regarding sexual practices and relationships between men and women. Another cult of domesticity emerged throughout the early postwar period, as Americans married early and experienced a baby-making binge. While few critics went as far as Philip Wylie had during the war, when he castigated women in *Generation of Vipers*, many Americans believed that the proper sphere for women was the home and that having and nurturing children was women's greatest responsibility. In fact, as had occurred after World War I, a number of women remained in the workplace in the late 1940s and early 1950s because of desire or necessity. Many found themselves stuck in low-end jobs, receiving lower salaries than men did for the same or similar work. Most women attending institutions of higher learning were believed to be doing so in order to acquire spouses. For those gainfully employed outside the home, the glass ceiling remained in place in business, the academy, and government service. Nevertheless, seeds of a sexual revolution were being planted. *Sexual Behavior in the Human Male*, also known as the *Kinsey Report*, was published in 1948. Spearheaded by sexologist Alfred Kinsey, the report offered mathematical data purportedly indicating that the American male was sexually complex, with the vast majority of men engaging in premarital intercourse, most paying prostitutes for sex, a large portion having extramarital affairs, and over one-third engaging in homosexual activity. *Time* magazine reported that the "itch" for the book was "most notable among urban intellectuals and college students."

Hardly comfortable with the resurgent cult of domesticity, Monroe still was a very young woman who relied on men, often lovers, to help her break into Hollywood. Columbia Pictures gave her a small role in *Ladies of the Chorus*, released in 1948, which led the *Hollywood Reporter* to acclaim her as "cute and properly naïve" and the *Motion Picture Herald* to proclaim, "One of the bright spots is Miss Monroe's singing. She is pretty and, with her pleasing voice and style, she shows promise." More important, film agent Johnny Hyde convinced Fox to re-sign her in 1949. He also induced Monroe, who had previously had her uneven teeth straightened, to undergo plastic surgery on her chin. In June 1950 she appeared in John Huston's film noir classic *Asphalt Jungle*, which led to a favorable mention in *Photoplay*: "There's a beautiful blonde too, name of Marilyn Monroe, who . . . makes the most of her footage." Monroe also had a small part in the Oscar-winning *All About Eve*, which came out in October 1950, produced a comment from *Daily Variety* that she was one of the film's "standouts," and led to a seven-year contract with Twentieth Century Fox and her appearance on stage during the Academy Awards ceremony. The U.S. military newspaper, *Stars and Stripes*, named Monroe Miss Cheesecake of 1950. By early 1951 Monroe was having an affair with director Eliza Kazan and becoming involved with the playwright Arthur Miller. She also was relying on drugs, including both barbiturates and amphetamines. Monroe enrolled for classes at UCLA while awaiting greater film opportunities. The September 8, 1951, issue of *Collier's* contained a full-length article on Monroe, titled "1951's Model Blonde." For writer Robert Cahn, she spun a story of her difficult times as an orphan and a foster child who had struggled mightily to overcome distress.

By early January 1952, Harry Brand, Fox's publicity director, told columnist

Hy Gardner, "I want you to talk with this girl. We're grooming her—or maybe I should say she's grooming herself—to be the sexiest thing in pictures since Jean Harlow." Brand admitted that Fox was worried about one thing, the fact that Monroe had posed nude for a photographer. When rumors began to spread that she was the naked woman in a calendar, Monroe refused the advice of most studio executives and admitted, "Oh, the calendar's hanging in garages all over town. Why deny it? You can get one anyplace." She almost defiantly continued, "Besides, I'm not ashamed of it. I've done nothing wrong. I was told I should deny I'd posed . . . but I'd rather be honest about it." Largely favorable responses awaited the article that appeared with Marilyn's reaction. She appeared to have acquired a sense of what the public would accept, no matter the prevailing mores that supposedly dominated American society at the time. On March 17, 1952, Fox reported that Monroe was seeing Joe DiMaggio, the recently retired New York Yankees center fielder. On April 7, 1952, the sultry actress appeared on the cover of *Life* magazine with the title, "Marilyn Monroe: The Talk of Hollywood." The article predicted that "the genuine article is here at last—a sensational glamour girl, guaranteed to entice people from all lands to the box office." Monroe now showed up in a number of films, including *Clash by Night* and *Don't Bother to Knock*, in which she had her first substantial role. Her part in *Clash by Night* led the *New York World-Telegram and Sun* to call Monroe "a forceful actress, a gifted new star, worthy of all that fantastic press agentry. Her role here is not very big, but she makes it dominant." Cast as a sociopathic individual in *Don't Bother to Knock*, she received mixed reviews at best, with the *New York Post* writing, "They've thrown Marilyn Monroe into the deep dramatic waters, sink or swim, and while she doesn't really do either, you might say that she floats. With that figure, what else can she do."

She performed her smaller part in Howard Hawks's comedy *Monkey Business* as her relationship with DiMaggio ebbed and flowed. The affair between the stunning, twenty-five-year-old actress and the peerless ballplayer, twelve years her senior, captured the nation's imagination. DiMaggio had led the Yankees to ten pennants and nine World Series titles in a thirteen-year career, abbreviated by wartime service and injuries, and he held the major-league record with a consecutive fifty-six-game hit streak. Monroe was at the time still a starlet, albeit an extremely ambitious one. While in New York she spent time with DiMaggio and friends at his favorite hangout, Toots Shor's restaurant on West Fifty-first Street. One friend, sportswriter Jimmy Cannon, referred to the couple as the "whole country's pets."

In the last few months of 1952 Monroe shot scenes for *Niagara* and *Gentlemen Prefer Blondes*, directed respectively by Henry Hathaway and Howard Hawks. Starring opposite Joseph Cotton, Monroe offered a sultry performance as his wife in Hathaway's film noir. The studio's publicity for *Niagara* suggested that Monroe's character evoked "a raging torrent of emotion that even nature can't control," while asserting that the film and the femme fatale were "the two most electrifying sights in the world." *Niagara* opened in January 1953, quickly proving to be a box-office smash, while *Gentlemen Prefer Blondes* was still being shot. The *New York Times* referred to "the grandeur that is Marilyn Monroe," who like Niagara Falls left "little to be desired by any reasonably attentive audience" although she was admittedly "not the perfect actress at this point." *Niagara*'s success, along with that of *Gentlemen Prefer Blondes* and *How to Marry a Millionaire*, one of the first films to employ the new widescreen CinemaScope, allowed Monroe to share top billing with Jane Russell, Lauren Bacall, and Betty Grable and made her Hollywood's hottest star by the end of the year. The latter two films cast Monroe in the role of the ditzy blonde: Lorelei Lee in the adaptation of Anita Loos's 1925 classic about a gold digger and the nearsighted but vain Pola Debevoise, who states, "Men aren't attentive to girls who wear glasses." In a gorgeously choreographed scene, Monroe sings and dances to the tune of "Diamonds Are a Girl's Best Friend" in *Gentlemen Prefer Blondes*. Wearing a form-fitting red dress, Monroe exudes beauty and sexuality, but the songs' lyrics challenge sexist stereotypes: "Men grow cold/As girls grow old/And we all lose our charms in the end/But square-cut or pear-shape/These rocks don't lose their shape/Diamonds are a girl's best friend." Monroe and Russell appeared on the cover of *Life* magazine wearing tight red dresses that showed off their shapely legs. *Box Office Magazine*, which called Monroe and Russell "the nation's favorite glamour girls," referred to Marilyn as "the box office bombshell" who "acts the dim-witted blonde to perfection—in a manner to make the male patrons drool." In his review of *How to Marry a Millionaire*, the *New York Times*' Bosley Crowther referred to "the famously shaped Miss Monroe" and praised her comedic flair. *Photoplay* magazine named Monroe—who had long indicated, "I want to be a big star more than anything"—the Best New Actress of 1953.

The complicated relationship of Americans with sexuality influenced the film public's response to Monroe. The same year that she became a major motion picture star witnessed release of the second Kinsey report, *Sexual Behavior in the Human Female*, which landed the sexologist on the cover of *Time* magazine in mid-September 1953 alongside a picture of "the birds and the bees." The study focused on women's sexual activity, pointing to premarital sex, masturbation, and orgasms. Dr. John Bancroft, a later director of the Kinsey Institute, contended that the new report "was undoubtedly a milestone in the fascinating, but often troubling, history of the sexuality of women." It "forever changed the way the world viewed women's sexuality" while revealing changes in behaviors and attitudes already taking place. *Sexual Behavior in the Human Female* contested the ongoing practice of double standards regarding the sexuality of men and women. That development, *Newsweek* reported, resulted from a number of factors including "the 'emancipation' of the female," greater knowledge about contraception, the impersonal nature of modern urban life, a reduction of venereal diseases, the viewing of other societies by American soldiers, and campaigns against prostitution. *Time* and the London *Mirror* both referred to the release of the latest study as "K-Day." A congressman from New York complained about Kinsey's "hurling the insult of the century against our mothers, wives, daughters and sisters."

With furor still swirling about *Sexual Behavior in the Human Female* and as Monroe's films proved top box-office draws, enabling her to become the hottest item in Hollywood, another firestorm threatened to erupt. In December 1953, Hugh Hefner, a cartoonist from Chicago, published the first issue of a new men's magazine, *Playboy*, which sold for fifty cents. With a revealing dress split in the front, Monroe graced the cover of *Playboy* and also appeared inside in an airbrushed nude shot as the magazine's first centerfold. Hefner delivered his worldview in articulating the *Playboy* philosophy: "We like our apartment. We enjoy mixing up cocktails and an *hors d'oeuvre* or two, putting a little mood music on the phonograph and inviting in a female acquaintance for a quiet discussion on Picasso, Nietzsche, jazz, sex. . . . If we are able to give the American male a few extra laughs and a little diversion from the anxieties of the Atomic Age, we'll feel we've justified our existence." While Monroe's appearance in *Playboy* proved controversial, it merely solidified her standing as the nation's number one sex symbol. In a different fashion than other recent female embodiments of sensuality, such as Lillian Russell and Jean Harlow, and somewhat more like Clara Bow, Monroe also came across as strikingly vulnerable.

With her Sweetheart of the Month pictorial and three hit movies, Monroe's celebrity only increased in the months ahead. On January 14, 1954, she married Joe DiMaggio in a small civil ceremony conducted at San Francisco City Hall. When DiMaggio informed reporters he would like to have at least one child, Monroe piped up with the comment, "I'd like to have six." At the end of the month the couple flew off to Honolulu and then Tokyo, encountering raucous crowds eager to see the movie star and her husband, in Japan to promote the new baseball season. While DiMaggio attended to business, Monroe flew to Korea to visit American troops stationed there. During four days and ten performances she entertained more than 100,000 soldiers who were thrilled by the sight of the gorgeous film star. Wearing a low-cut dress, Monroe sang "Diamonds Are a Girl's Best Fried," "Bye Bye Baby," and "Do It Again." Delighted by the response, she told a friend, "I never felt like a star before, in my heart. It was so wonderful to look down and see a fellow smiling at me." DiMaggio was less pleased with his wife's South Korean adventure: when she recounted her triumph and asked, "Joe, do you have any idea what that's like? Did you ever have ten thousand people stand up and applaud you?" DiMaggio reportedly responded unemotionally, "Seventy-five thousand," referring to the number of fans at well-attended games at Yankee Stadium who had invariably cheered the Yankee Clipper when he roamed in center field, effortlessly darted around the bases, and stroked one of the hits that enabled him to carve out a lifetime .325 batting average.

The marriage lasted only nine months. It proved tempestuous and possibly resulted in physical as well as verbal abuse. Monroe and DiMaggio resided in his San Francisco home and a rented house in Beverly Hills. DiMaggio proved excessively jealous while Monroe felt isolated from the movie industry. Ironically, given Monroe's obvious standing as a leading sex symbol, DiMaggio resented the attention she received, much of it clearly based on her physical beauty. He also apparently wanted her to give up her career, which she refused to do. As her marriage disintegrated, Monroe additionally suffered something of a sophomore slump as evidenced by the pair of films she appeared in that year, *River of No Return* and *There's No Business Like Show Business*. Reviewing the latter film, *New York Times* film critic Crowther indicated that Monroe's "wriggling and squirming to 'Heat Wave' and 'Lazy' are embarrassing to behold." More happily she was cast in Billy Wilder's *The Seven-Year Itch*, which began production in August. The camera rolled on September 14, and DiMaggio, along with 2,000 spectators, watched as Monroe stood at Fifty-second Street and Lexington Avenue in New York City, with bursts of wind from a subway grating forcing up her dress. The following month Monroe received the divorce she sought, on grounds of "mental cruelty." She admitted, "When I married him, I wasn't sure of why I married him, I have too many fantasies to be a housewife."

Determined to acquire a new image and become a serious actress, Monroe jumped her contract with Fox and began studying with Lee Strasberg at his Actors' Studio in New York City. She stayed at the Waldorf Towers and spent time with writers Carson McCullers, Tennessee Williams, and Truman Capote. Monroe also began seeing Arthur Miller again, although she attended the New York premiere of *The Seven Year Itch* on June 1, 1955, her twenty-ninth birthday, with DiMaggio. Crowther, in his *New York Times* review, wrote that from her opening appearance in the film, "the famous screen star," wearing "a garment that drapes her shapely form as though she had been skillfully poured into it . . . emanates one suggestion," as indicated by the title. Movie mogul Darryl Zanuck finally caved in at the very end of the year, acceding to Monroe's demand for a new, far more generous contract, which allowed her to approve of the directors who shot her films and enabled her to appear in other studios' productions.

Returning to Hollywood, Monroe began shooting *Bus Stop*, adapted from the play by William Inge, and made her first appearance on the cover of *Time* on May 14, 1956. On June 21 Miller testified before the House Un-American Activities Committee, refusing to give the names of other Hollywood radicals. Nine days later Monroe and Miller married at the Westchester County Courthouse in White Plains, New York. The following month Congress cited him for contempt. After trips to England to begin filming *The Prince and the Showgirl* with Laurence Olivier, and to Jamaica for a honeymoon, the couple eventually resided at an apartment at 444 East Fifty-seventh Street in Manhattan. In early September Monroe received word of a rave review of *Bus Stop* by the *Times* film critic, Bosley Crowther, who began by stating, "Hold onto your chairs, everybody, and get set for a rattling surprise. Marilyn Monroe has finally proved herself an actress in 'Bus Stop.' She and the picture are swell!!" Director Joshua Logan, Crowther suggested, had gotten Monroe "to be the tinseled floozie, the semimoronic doll," who nevertheless retained a "small flame of dignity." Monroe was nominated for a Golden Globe as the Best Actress in a Musical or Comedy.

Viewed as a serious actress for the first time, Monroe attempted to carve out a loving relationship with Miller and his children. "Marriage," Monroe informed one interviewer, "makes me feel more womanly, more proud of myself. It also makes me feel less frantic. For the first time I have a feeling of being sheltered." More threatening was the federal grand jury indictment Miller suffered in February 1957, which led to a $500 fine and a one-month jail sentence that the federal judge suspended. Reviews of *The Prince and the Showgirl* came out, with the *New York Times* contending, "Miss Monroe mainly has to giggle, wiggle, breathe deeply and flirt. She does not make the showgirl a person, simply another of her pretty oddities." Soon her marriage was falling apart, little helped by a series of miscarriages, affairs, and mounting disdain on both sides.

As the 1950s neared a close, Monroe's stardom had hardly diminished. In December 1958 she posed for famed photographer Richard Avedon, who shot a series of pictures that appeared in *Life* magazine. Marilyn posed as other screen temptresses including Lillian Russell, Theda Bara, Clara Bow, Marlene Dietrich, and Jean Harlow. For Miller the photographs produced "a kind of history of our mass fantasy, so far as seductresses are concerned." A month earlier Monroe had finished the filming of *Some Like It Hot*. The shooting of the film proved trying for actors Tony Curtis and Jack Lemmon and director Billy Wilder, who had to contend with Monroe's muffed lines and frequent delays. Yet prior to the release of *Some Like It Hot*, Wilder admitted that

Monroe "has a certain indefinable magic that comes across which no actress in the business has." The film appeared to critical acclaim and garnered a Golden Globe for its lead actress. The *New York Times* indicated that Monroe "contributes more assets than the obvious ones to this madcap romp," proving "to be the epitome of a dumb blonde and a talented comedienne."

In late 1959 and early 1960—the year that the contraceptive pill helped to recast Americans' sexual practices—Monroe filmed *Let's Make Love* with Yves Montand. The turmoil in Monroe's life heightened, exacerbated by drug use, depression, and the further deterioration of her marriage. For the first time she no longer appeared luminous on the screen, to the astonishment of those who viewed the rushes. Film critics proved little more receptive, with the *New York Daily Mirror* declaring, "Miss Monroe, basically a first-rate comedienne, doesn't have a single bright line." The shooting of John Huston's film, *The Misfits*, hardly went more smoothly, with Monroe continually making co-star Clark Gable wait on set. The now fading actress ended up hospitalized, purportedly because of exhaustion. This had become a frequent occurrence for Monroe, brought on by her often-fraught emotional state. In November 1960 Miller moved out of their apartment only days following Gable's death and shortly before the premiere of *The Misfits*. The film appeared in late January to mixed reviews. The *New York Times* called Monroe "completely blank and unfathomable as a new divorcee who shed her husband because 'you could touch him but he wasn't there.'" Although her star now appeared to be dimming, Monroe was the subject of a glowing write-up by Alice McIntyre in *Esquire*. McIntyre considered Monroe

> like nothing you have ever seen or dreamed. She is astonishingly white. . . . Indeed, there seems the awful possibility . . . that MM is a manifestation of the White Goddess herself . . . she becomes at once the symbol of impartial and eternal availability, who yet remains forever pure—and a potentially terrible goddess whose instinct could also deal death and whose smile, when she directs it clearly at you, is exquisitely, heartbreakingly sweet.

As her divorce approached, Joe DiMaggio reappeared in her life. She also became involved with Frank Sinatra and, through Sinatra's friendship with Peter Lawford, brother-in-law of President John F. Kennedy, with the nation's chief executive himself. On May 19, 1962, before a crowd of over 15,000 people at Madison Square Garden, Monroe, attired in a skintight dress, sang a sultry version of "Happy Birthday" to Kennedy. Columnist Dorothy Kilgallen spoke of Marilyn's "making love to the president in the direct view of forty million Americans." Four days after the Madison Square Garden incident, Monroe was back in the news, having been photographed in the nude as she departed from a swimming pool in Los Angeles. The following month, Fox, concerned about cost overruns caused by her missing work and difficulties with another film, *Cleopatra*, starring Elizabeth Taylor, fired Monroe from *Something's Got to Give*. When co-star Dean Martin refused to continue shooting without Monroe, the studio rehired her, planning to begin filming in October. However, on August 5, 1962, Monroe, recently turned thirty-six, died of an apparent overdose of barbiturates while sleeping in her home in Brentwood, California. Director Lee Strasberg eulogized her: "Marilyn Monroe was a legend. In her own lifetime she created a myth of what a poor girl from a deprived background could attain. For the entire world she became a symbol of the eternal feminine."

ELVIS PRESLEY

Elvis Aaron Presley was born in a two-room house on January 8, 1935, in East Tupelo, Mississippi, to spunky, twenty-three-year-old Gladys Love Smith, a sewing machine operator, and silent, sullen, unambitious, eighteen-year-old Vernon Presley, a truck driver. Elvis's twin brother, Jesse Garon, was stillborn, and he grew up an only child, but was surrounded by numerous relatives with German, Scottish, Native American, and Irish roots. Convicted of forgery, Vernon went to jail for eight months beginning when the well-loved Elvis was three years old, compelling Gladys and her son to reside with Vernon's parents. The Presleys, particularly Gladys, were religious, regularly attending the Pentecostal First Assembly of God Church, where Elvis sang in the choir. At the age of eleven, the dreamy, playful Presley began playing the guitar. In 1948 the family relocated to Memphis, Tennessee, where Vernon worked at the United Paint Company. The Presleys dwelled in either public housing units or low-rent homes in poor neighborhoods, including when Elvis, largely a loner, went to high school. Gospel, black, and country music appealed to Presley, such as the work of Muddy Waters, B.B. King, Roy Acuff, and Ernest Tubb. He spent time on famed Beale Street, considered the birthplace of the blues. He adopted the look of black singers, including long hair that he slicked back, long sideburns, a bolero jacket, striped pants, a pink suit, and white shoes. After graduating from high school in 1953, Presley worked at a series of jobs that included driving a delivery truck. Attending night school, the pompadour-sporting Presley thought of becoming an electrician but continued to be drawn to music. That same year he paid four dollars to record two songs by the Ink Spots, "That's When Heartache Begins" and "My Happiness," at the Memphis Recording Service, home station of Sun Records, as a birthday present for Gladys.

On January 4, 1954, Presley recorded "Careless Love" and "I'll Never Stand in Your Way," although the experience proved less successful than the previous one. That spring he met the producer Sam Phillips, founder of Sun Records. Phillips, known for having worked with Howlin' Wolf, B.B. King, and Junior Parker, among others, and hoping to find "a white man with the Negro sound and the Negro feel," listened as Presley recorded "Without You." Soon Presley proved to have the very combination of talents that Phillips sought, along with an ability to draw from country, country blues, gospel, bluegrass, and popular music. He possessed the ability to meld black and white music, or "race" and "hillbilly," in the very period when Americans were notably grappling with their troubled racial history. In May 1954 the U.S. Supreme Court issued its ruling in *Brown v. the Board of Education*, which prohibited segregation in public schools. That decision, delivered by Chief Justice Earl Warren, emboldened blacks in many sectors of the old South while infuriating recalcitrant whites, who were determined to hold onto a particular way of life that harked back to the "peculiar institution," as historian Kenneth M. Stampp referred to slavery. This social and cultural zeitgeist could hardly help but influence a new, incompletely formed music that drew from both white and African-American sources, attracted white and black listeners, and featured white and black performers, although generally not on stage together.

Returning to Sun Studio in July 1954, Presley sang a speeded-up version of "That's Alright Mama," written by Arthur "Big Boy" Crudup eight years earlier. Now Presley had guitarist Scotty Moore and bass player Bill Black as his sidekicks. The three recorded the Crudup tune along with a faster rendition of "Blue Moon of Kentucky," written in 1946 by Bill Monroe, which together became the first of five 78-rpm singles Presley delivered for Sun Records. Thus Presley's first recording contained a song by Crudup, a top black rhythm and blues performer, and one by Monroe, the country giant. Dewey Phillips, a top local disc jockey, played the song repeatedly and thousands of requests poured forth while the song flew to the top of the Memphis charts, selling 20,000 copies. Presley enjoyed such success even though some white disc jockeys refused to play his recording of "That's Alright Mama," believing it was sung by a black singer. Regardless, Marion Keisker of Sun Records stated that "the odd thing about" the release "is that both sides seem to be equally popular on popular, folk, and race record programs." Referring to Presley, Keisker continued, "This boy has something that seems to appeal to everybody." Presley continued working at Crown Electric Company while his band, the Blue Moon Boys, performed in small clubs across the South, driving on dusty roads from concert to concert. In late August "Blue Moon of Kentucky" became the third hottest song on the country and western Territorial Best Sellers list.

Hank Snow helped Presley land a spot at the Grand Ole Opry, the jewel of country music. While some critics have referred to that performance as a bust, Sam Phillips was elated that Presley had appeared at the mecca of country and western, winning congratulations by Bill Monroe himself. On October 16, 1954, the band, with its lead singer, sometimes called "The Hillbilly Kid" or "The King of Western Pop," appeared on the *Louisiana Hayride*, a radio program that delivered country music on Saturdays to nearly 200 stations in thirteen states. Nevertheless, Phillips purportedly continued to have difficulty convincing certain disc jockeys in the South to play Presley's records, in contrast to black areas in the upper Midwest and in California, where his songs were well received. Presley began making regular appearances on the *Louisiana Hayride* and signed a one-year contract in November to show up weekly. Through the program Presley met a former carnival promoter and country music manager, the self-proclaimed Colonel Tom Parker, who had worked with Hank Snow and Eddy Arnold and would help to shape Elvis's career. In January 1955 Presley and his band began touring with Hank Snow, the Carter Sisters, Mother Maybelle, and the comedian Whitey Ford.

Presley's on-stage performances demonstrated that change was in the air, that the conservatism, conformity, and complacency that had enveloped America in the early Cold War years seemed to be abating. Moreover, an ill-defined youth culture seemed to be emerging. It drew strength from the sheer number of young people, including the older siblings of boomers, eager for something new. It became possible because of the nation's general affluence that had continued for a full decade after the end of World War II, belying concerns that the country would slide back into an economic depression. It received sustenance from the cult of the antihero that strengthened during the very period when Americans sported "I like Ike" buttons during presidential campaigns, remained confused about sexual practices, listened to religious leaders evangelize about proper values, and adhered to rigid anticommunist beliefs. Notwithstanding such a conservative backdrop, duck-tailed motorcyclists tore down America's highways, teenage girls sported tight sweaters intended to highlight their physical attributes, and black Americans demanded fair treatment as full, equal citizens. Presley for his part represented many of the cultural changes the nation was enduring. On meeting Presley, Hank's son Jimmy Rodgers Snow was taken aback. Elvis wore "a chartreuse jacket and black pants with a white stripe down the side." Moreover, "the kids were just going wild." As Snow remembered, "I'd never seen anyone quite like him." Watching Presley from the audience, Roy Orbison viewed him as "this punk kid. Just a real raw cat singing like a bird," who spat, told bad jokes, and spoke like a truck driver. Presley also clearly recognized the appeal he had for girls and young women, which bordered on the electric. In March

1955 Presley made his first appearance on television, performing on a local broadcast of *Hayride*. In April the singer traveled to New York City, where he unsuccessfully auditioned for the popular television program *Arthur Godfrey's Talent Scouts*. Within a month a Presley show in Jacksonville, Florida, led to a riot, when fans tried to grab his clothing and his song "Baby, Let's Play House" began its march onto the country and western top ten list, ending up as the number five song on the *Billboard* charts. The magazine reported that "Presley continues to gather speed over the South" and was "the teenager's favorite wherever he appears." He also began acquiring countless girlfriends and lovers.

During the last several months of 1955, Presley turned into a genuine pop cultural star, although nothing like the sensation he would soon become. In September his offering of "I Forgot to Remember to Forget" was his first record to top the country best-seller list. Presley toured with Bill Haley, viewed as "the Nation's No. 1 Rhythm & Blues Artist" ever since the film *The Blackboard Jungle* had featured his song "Rock Around the Clock." Elvis headlined his own Elvis Presley Jamboree, which included Johnny Cash and Porter Wagoner, while Buddy Holly opened one show. Two months later Colonel Parker purchased Presley's contract from Sun Records. Strapped for cash, Sam Phillips decided to let Presley go, choosing instead to concentrate on other stars in his stable, including Johnny Cash, Roy Orbison, Carl Perkins, and Jerry Lee Lewis. Like Presley, they all were considered rockabilly performers who drew from the blues, boogie-woogie, jazz, folk, gospel, and country and western music. Lewis, Perkins, Cash, and Presley would be called Sun's "Million Dollar Quartet," but the company hardly reaped the bounty of Presley's stardom. Phillips received but $35,000 and Presley pocketed only $5,000, possibly for unpaid royalties; still the total was the largest yet offered for a recording artist. The December 3 issue of *Billboard*, which named him "most promising C & W artist," referred to Presley as "one of the most sought-after warblers this year."

In early January he began recording in Nashville at the RCA studio, soon producing versions of "Heartbreak Hotel" and Ray Charles's "I Got a Woman," which his band had been playing for some time. Presley made his national television debut on *Stage Show* on January 28, 1956, a variety program hosted by brothers Tommy and Jimmy Dorsey, big-band conductors from the 1930s. A New York radio disc jockey introduced Presley, said to have come "out of nowhere to be an overnight star." Presley sang Big Joe Turner's "Shake, Rattle and Roll" and "Flip, Flop and Fly." Back in the studio, Presley recorded Arthur "Big Boy" Crudup's "My Baby Left Me" and "So Glad You're Mine." He appeared regularly on *Stage Show* over the next several weeks, belting out "Tutti Frutti" and "Baby, Let's Play House" during his second appearance, and both "Heartbreak Hotel" and "Blue Suede Shoes," already a big hit by Carl Perkins. By the time he made his final appearance on *Stage Show*, Presley proved far more comfortable on television, offering a scintillating version of "Heartbreak Hotel," which was shooting up the charts, along with his own rendition of "Blue Suede Shoes." The "Heartbreak Hotel" single approached the top of the pop, country, and rhythm and blues charts, a feat previously achieved only by Perkins's recording of "Blue Suede Shoes." In late March, Presley completed a screen test with Hollywood producer Hal Wallis. With Colonel Parker now officially his manager, the singer appeared on the *Milton Berle Show* on April 3 and then on the *Steve Allen Show*, where he sang "Hound Dog." That same month Presley arrived in Las Vegas, where he performed at the New Frontier Hotel. After a slow start audiences generally warmed up to the young singer, although some continued to resist Presley's sound, denouncing it as "nigger music." While *Variety* indicated that his Las Vegas stay had been less than successful, *Life* featured an article on Presley, titled "A Howling Hillbilly Success," in its April 30 issue. Hysterical girls, thunderous applause, and an occasional riot began to greet Presley and his band. Women flocked to him, his parents now resided in a new home he had purchased for them, he possessed a Harley Davidson motorcycle and three Cadillacs, and royalties poured in from record and album sales. His debut album, containing "Blue Suede Shoes," "Tutti Frutti," and "Blue Moon," topped *Billboard*'s Best Selling Popular Albums chart on May 5. An article in the May 14, 1956, issue of *Time* referred to Presley's "sensuously" swinging hips, quivering body, and "petulant, full-lipped face." Titled "Teenage Hero," it also referred to his style—"partly hillbilly, partly socking rock 'n' roll"—and indicated that the "tight-trousered young man" could "drive teenage girls wild." Presley's "I Want You, I Need You, I Love You" headed the pop chart by June, while "Heartbreak Hotel" and "I Forgot to Remember to Forget" stood astride the rhythm and blues and country charts, respectively, and his album stayed atop the *Billboard* list for ten weeks.

Increasingly Presley came to be identified less with country and western or rhythm and blues music and more with rock and roll. That musical genre borrowed from rockabilly and from pop as it melded black and white music in a previously unprecedented manner. The name of the genre suggested various meanings, including those pertaining to spirituals, dancing, and, in double entendre fashion, sex. Few African-American rhythm and blues performers possessed crossover appeal, although many early white rockers covered song after song written and initially performed by black counterparts. Nevertheless, the soulful rhythm and blues presented by Muddy Waters and Chester "Howlin' Wolf" Burnett, along with The Wolf's electrifying stage performances, antedated the musical explosion that lay just ahead. In the early 1950s, Cleveland disc jockey Alan Freed began referring to rock and roll music. Freed put on a series of concerts, frequented by both blacks and whites, before moving on to New York City, where he hosted the "Rock and Roll Party" on radio beginning in 1954. By that point teenagers and their somewhat younger siblings could listen to their favorite songs on portable, transistorized radios and in their family cars. Bill Haley and the Comets' "Rock Around the Clock" was the initial rock and roll song to head the *Billboard* chart, but Haley lacked the sex appeal and charisma that a pop cultural star required. Nevertheless, he became the first white musician during the decade to intertwine white and black music while influencing popular music. As rock historian Paul Friedlander indicates, Haley "introduced teenage America to classic rock and roll." Black rhythm and blues performer Bo Diddley came out with "Bo Diddley" and "I'm a Man" in 1955, while doo-wop groups like the Dominoes, the Drifters, and the Teenagers, made up of ghetto youngsters who presented their brand of urban-based angst, continued marching up the charts. That same year Chess began recording Chuck Berry, including his boogie-woogie classic "Maybelline," soon followed by "Roll Over Beethoven," with its implicit proclamation of youthful rebellion. In early 1956, another handsome black performer ramped up the intensity level of the new musical genre, as Little Richard presented "Tutti-Frutti."

That summer rock and roll grabbed the nation's attention as never before thanks to performances by that young man from East Tupelo, Mississippi. On July 2, 1956, Presley recorded a song written by Jerry Leiber and Mike Stoller that Big Mama Thornton had turned into a rhythm and blues hit, "Hound Dog." Speeding up Thornton's rendition, Presley delivered a pulsating tune that hardly fit into the classic country and western or rhythm and blues modes, sounding more like the version he had heard performed in Las Vegas by Freddie Bell and the Bellboys. Three days after his recording session Presley appeared on the *Steve Allen Show*, where he sang the song to a hound dog, gyrating his hips in the process. *America*, the Catholic magazine, responded with an article titled "Beware Elvis Presley." The publication admitted that "if his 'entertainment' could be confined to records, it might not be too bad an influence on the young." However, Presley made live appearances too, and a recent performance in La Crosse, Wisconsin, led the local newspaper to warn that young concertgoers "literally 'went wild'" at his "strip-tease with clothes on," some "actually rolling in the aisles." Conservative social critics charged that Presley and his kind were helping to spawn juvenile delinquency, a problem that Americans were increasingly concerned about during the 1950s. In the meantime Presley conducted his own examination, which only cemented his identification with rebel culture. He informed writer

Lloyd Shearer, "I've made a study of Marlon Brando. I've made a study of poor Jimmy Dean. I've made a study of myself, and I know why girls, at least the young 'uns, go for us. We're sullen, we're broodin,' we're something of a menace." Presley, like rock and roll, was controversial too because of the way his songs took from both white and black music. Referring to his own brand of music, Presley acknowledged, "The colored folks been singing it and playing it just like I'm doin' now, man, for more years than I know. They played it like that in their shanties and in their juke joints and nobody paid it no mind 'til I goosed it up. I got it from them."

Television host Ed Sullivan, who initially claimed that Presley was "unfit for a family audience," now signed the star to a $50,000 contract to make three appearances on his nationally syndicated program. On September 9, 1956, Presley, introduced by guest host and Oscar-winning actor Charles Laughton because Sullivan was recuperating from an automobile accident, appeared on *The Ed Sullivan Show* for the first time as a record audience of 60 million people tuned in, nearly 83 percent of potential viewers. Presley first sang "Don't Be Cruel," resulting in cries and screams from the television audience at the CBS studio in Los Angeles, where he was filming *Love Me Tender*. Then he sang the title song from the movie to complete his first set. Presley returned later in the show to sing "Ready Teddy," a Little Richard number, with the camera withdrawing as Elvis began dancing. Presley's performance concluded with a couple of verses from "Hound Dog" as the studio audience erupted. Laughton asked television onlookers, "Music hath charms to soothe the savage breast?" In his account of the show, *New York Times* music critic Jack Gould wrote, "Mr. Presley has no discernible singing ability. . . . His one specialty is an accentuated movement of the body that heretofore has been previously identified with the repertoire of the blonde bombshells of the burlesque variety." The Reverend Billy Graham, a leading televangelist, declared, "From what I've heard, I'm not so sure I'd want my children to see him." Various communities across the country restricted the public playing of rock and roll music, while some parents torched effigies of Presley.

The hysteria surrounding the singer, also known as "Elvis the Pelvis," continued as he began touring again and when he returned to *The Ed Sullivan Show* on October 28, 1956, appearing far more relaxed and polished as he performed and exchanged light banter with Sullivan. Colonel Parker maintained his efforts to turn the singer into a one-man industry, signing a new contract with RCA that ensured Presley would receive substantial royalties for many years to come. *Variety* deemed the singer a millionaire, while Parker arranged for a California merchandiser, Hank Saperstein, to promote a vast array of items and products using Presley's name. *Look* magazine referred to "the Great

Elvis Presley industry" and noted "how the money rolls in!" Presley's movie *Love Me Tender* opened on November 21, doing better at the box office than Marilyn Monroe's most recent films, and leading *The Hollywood Reporter* to lump the rock star with Brando and Dean. The magazine bemoaned the emergence of a hero who boasted "mannerisms by Brando out of the Actor's Studio . . . slouches, ambles . . . minces," along with "tentative, incomplete" hand gestures. The *Reporter* continued, "The new hero is an adolescent. Whether he is twenty or thirty or forty, he is fifteen and excessively sorry for himself. He is essentially a lone wolf who wants to belong." On December 8 *Elvis* began a five-week run as *Billboard*'s top-selling pop album, including songs such as "Rip It Up" and "Long Tall Sally," both performed earlier by Little Richard, and "So Glad You're Mine," another tune written by Arthur Crudup. The December 31, 1956, edition of the *Wall Street Journal*, reporting that merchandise associated with the singer had pulled in $22 million in sales in the past years, affirmed that "Elvis Presley today is a business." Seven days later Presley made his final appearance on *The Ed Sullivan Show*, singing "Don't Be Cruel" and several other numbers. Having been won over, Sullivan, in introducing Presley for a second set, declared, "I want to say to Elvis Presley and the country that this is a real decent, fine boy, and wherever you go, Elvis, . . . we want to say that we've never had a pleasanter experience on our show with a big name than we've had with you."

In March 1957 Presley purchased a beautiful mansion, Graceland, in Memphis for $100,000, where his parents would live and Elvis resided when he was in town. At the end of the month, he appeared in a gold-leaf suit that cost $2,500 for a concert in Chicago, the start of a tour that resulted in hysterical fans and hyperbolic commentary from reporters. Presley's second movie, *Loving You*, premiered in July, featuring Elvis's rendition of "Teddy Bear" and landing in the box-office top ten. That same month RCA released *Loving You*, which soon began another ten-week run at the top of the pop chart. The album included "Teddy Bear" and "Blueberry Hill," which was a big hit for Fats Domino. *Jailhouse Rock*, with Presley playing the lead as a teenage rock star, opened in mid-October, proving to be another smash hit. *Jet* magazine praised Presley in its August 1 issue, stating that "to Elvis, people are people regardless of race, color or creed." In December *Elvis' Christmas Album* landed atop the *Billboard* chart. In late January, Presley began filming *King Creole*, in which he delivered his finest acting performance as a musician struggling to make it in New Orleans.

On March 24, 1958, the U.S. Army welcomed rock's biggest star into its ranks. "The King" informed a reporter from *Life*, "Heaven knows, I want to live up to what people expect of me." The next day he received a GI haircut, soon followed by the start of basic training in Fort Hood, Texas, where he achieved sharpshooter and marksman badges. *New York Herald Tribune* columnist Hy Gardner applauded Presley's willingness to serve his country: "Where else could a nobody become a somebody so quickly, and in what other nation... would such a rich and famous man serve alongside you other draftees without trying to use influence to buy his way out?" Granted emergency leave in August, Presley returned to Memphis to be with his dying mother, who was only forty-six years old. In September he sailed to Germany, where he was stationed in Friedberg for eighteen months, eventually being discharged as a staff sergeant. During that period the state legislatures of Mississippi and Tennessee honored him.

Presley's entrance into the military coincided with an end to the first golden era of rock and roll. As if replicating the biblical Samson, Presley appeared to lose a good deal of his rebellious quality on having his hair shorn, but more important, he and Colonel Parker made a conscious decision to tone down his image after his military service, opting for more romantic ballads. Meanwhile, rock suffered other blows, including the imprisonment of Chuck Berry for having violated the Mann Act, which prohibited transporting underage females across state borders for illicit purposes; Little Richard's decision to relinquish performing in favor of the pulpit; Jerry Lee Lewis's marriage to his thirteen-year-old cousin; the deaths of rockers Buddy Holly and Eddie Cochran; payola scandals involving Alan Freed and Dick Clark, the host of television's *American Bandstand*; and the greater emphasis on Top 40 music, which tended to favor homogenized songs and unthreatening performers. The Special House Subcommittee on Legislative Oversight explored payola, which involved disc jockeys' receiving gifts as an inducement for promoting records, leading Clark to denounce the effort as a "witchhunt." Fortunately, by the time Presley departed from the army and issued *G.I. Blues*, which landed on the top of the charts in early December 1960, various stellar singers and groups were making their mark in the world of American rock, while others soon would. Having become familiar names before Presley entered the military, Ricky Nelson, Fats Domino, and the Everly Brothers continued to produce quality work, as did Sam Cooke and a host of "girl groups," such as the Ronnettes and the Marvelettes. Markedly influencing the worlds of rock and pop music were gifted black performers, particularly those associated with Berry Gordy's Motown Records, which featured the Temptations, Smokey Robinson and the Miracles, Martha and the Vandellas, and many others. Meanwhile Presley remained the biggest pop star, although *Something for Everybody*, released in July 1961, and *Blue Hawaii*, which came out five months later, were his only albums to reach number one for the next four years. Rock had changed altogether by that point, thanks to the Beatles, Bob Dylan, and the Byrds, among other seminal musicians of that period.

Concentrating on his movie career, which proved largely forgettable, Presley stopped delivering stage performances in 1961, but continued producing singles and albums that never again stood at the cutting edge of popular music. He undertook various comebacks along the way, returning to the top of the *Billboard* charts in both 1965 and 1973, again staging live performances in Las Vegas and elsewhere that drew sellout crowds, and receiving Grammy Awards for gospel records. His three network television specials, particularly the one in 1968, received critical acclaim. Reportedly as many as 1.5 billion people worldwide watched his 1973 special: *Elvis: Aloha from Hawaii*. Married to Priscilla Beaulieu in 1966, the two had one child, Lisa Marie, but divorced seven years later. In the last years of his life, Presley mushroomed to 250 pounds, canceled live performances, became addicted to prescription drugs, and suffered from social isolation. He died on August 16, 1977, at his Graceland mansion, the victim of heart failure apparently induced by ingesting a large quantity of drugs. Former Beatle John Lennon asserted, "The King is dead. But rock 'n' roll will never die. Long live the King." In 1986 Presley became one of the original inductees into the Rock and Roll Hall of Fame and subsequently entered both the Country Music Hall of Fame and the Gospel Music Hall of Fame. He sold more multiplatinum, platinum, and gold albums, along with more gold singles, than any other artist. Thousands of Presley fans visit Graceland each year to commemorate the birthday of "The King."

Bibliography

Clayton, Marie. *Elvis Presley: Unseen Archives*. London: Paragon, 2003.
———. *Marilyn Monroe: Unseen Archives*. London: Paragon, 2003.
de Vito, John. *The Immortal Marilyn: The Depiction of an Icon*. Lanham, MD: Scarecrow Press, 2006.
Friedlander, Paul. *Rock and Roll: A Social History*. Boulder, CO: Westview Press, 2006.
Guiles, Fred Lawrence. *Legend: The Life and Death of Marilyn Monroe*. Chelsea, MI: Scarborough House, 1992.
Guralnick, Peter. *Careless Love: The Unmaking of Elvis Presley*. London: Abacus, 2000.
———. *Last Train to Memphis: The Rise of Elvis Presley*. Hinkley, IL: Little, Brown, 1995.
Hopkins, Jerry. *Elvis: A Biography*. Medford, NJ: Plexus, 1971.
Keogh, Pamela Clarke. *Elvis Presley: The Man, the Life, the Legend*. New York: Atria Books, 2004.
Leaming, Barbara. *Marilyn Monroe*. New York: Crown, 1998.
McCann, Graham. *Marilyn Monroe*. New York: Oxford University Press, 1987.
Morrison, Craig. *Go Cat Go! Rockabilly Music and Its Makers*. Champaign: University of Illinois Press, 1996.

Nash, Alanna. *The Colonel: The Extraordinary Story of Colonel Tom Parker and Elvis Presley*. New York: Simon & Schuster, 2003.

Spoto, Donald. *Marilyn Monroe: The Biography*. Lanham, MD: Cooper Square Press, 2001.

Steinem, Gloria. *Marilyn: Norma Jeane*. New York: MJF Books, 1988.

Summers, Anthony. *Goddess: The Secret Lives of Marilyn Monroe*. New York: New American Library, 1986.

Tracy, Kathleen. *Elvis Presley: A Biography*. London: Robson Books, 2006.

Weatherby, W.J. *Conversations with Marilyn*. New York: Mason/Charter, 1976.

American Icons
in a Time of Unrest

JOHN F. KENNEDY AND MUHAMMAD ALI

During the 1960s new kinds of American icons emerged, ones who displayed the characteristics of classic heroes but appeared in different guises, exuding youthful verve, a seeming willingness to challenge traditional ways, and controversy. World War II archetypes faded as Americans no longer sported "I like Ike" buttons, the still popular former commander of American forces in Europe left the Oval Office, two-time Democratic Party presidential nominee Adlai Stevenson failed to capture his party's nomination yet again, and John Wayne's stature as a cinematic embodiment of American values diminished, at least in the eyes of many filmgoers and critics. Other motion picture stars also faded, including Clark Gable, Jimmy Stewart, Cary Grant, and Bette Davis, along with the five-star generals from the fight against fascism and Japanese imperialism, such as Dwight Eisenhower, George Marshall, Douglas MacArthur, and Omar Bradley. As occurs in each generation, the luster of many sports giants also diminished, including that of the Cleveland Browns quarterback Otto Graham and coach Paul Brown, New York Yankees manager Casey Stengel and National League skipper Leo Durocher, batting champions Ted Williams and Stan Musial, golfers Ben Hogan and Sam Snead, and boxers Rocky Marciano and Sugar Ray Robinson.

In their place emerged other individuals who often embodied the antiheroic traits associated with rebel culture even as they became iconic figures for a new generation. In realms ranging from high political office to the sports arena, time-honored values and virtues were called into question. Although the Cold War remained the political and cultural backdrop, the unease and uncertainty engendered by the East-West divide led a few Americans at first and then many more to examine the policies and practices that threatened global annihilation while stoking greater alienation. While most Americans supported their government during the Cuban missile crisis early in the decade, more came to question U.S. foreign policy particularly as involvement in Southeast Asia turned into an extended, unhappy quagmire. As an antiwar movement burgeoned, military service—long viewed as an inevitable rite of passage for American males—no longer carried the same stature it had so recently, nor did military leaders on the order of Generals William Westmoreland and Creighton Abrams, who led American forces in Vietnam. American popular culture foreshadowed the changed perceptions with films like the postnuclear, apocalyptic *On the Beach*; the chilling *Manchurian Candidate*, grappling with the themes of brainwashing and political assassination; *Fail-Safe* and *Dr. Strangelove, or I Stopped Worrying and Learned to Love the Bomb*, dealing with nuclear armaments; and *Seven Days in May*, involving an attempted military coup in the United States.

American society and culture underwent other sweeping changes during the period, as the challenge to Jim Crow practices broadened, activists battled against gender-based discrimination, and some insisted on the need for wholesale alterations of institutions and humankind itself. Drawing on the epochal changes ushered in by Jackie Robinson in the national pastime—major-league baseball—and fueled by the Warren Court's rulings in *Brown v. the Board of Education* and a series of other cases, the civil rights movement demanded that black Americans be treated as full, equal members of the body politic. Harking back to Jesus Christ, Henry David Thoreau, and Mahatma Gandhi, Baptist minister Martin Luther King Jr. wielded the weapon of nonviolent resistance to contest segregation practices. Young activists in organizations like the Student Nonviolent Coordinating Committee (SNCC) and the Congress of Racial Equality (CORE) initially adopted similar tactics in invoking the ideal of the beloved community, but the Black Muslims led by Elijah Muhammad and Malcolm X and later the Black Panthers refused to follow a pacifist stance, seemingly believing as militant H. Rap Brown did that "violence was as American as cherry pie." At first white activists, particularly those in Students for a Democratic Society (SDS), again followed the lead of their black counterparts in calling for greater student engagement through participatory democracy. American popular culture paralleled such developments, with black and white artists contesting hidebound ways. James Brown, Marvin Gaye, and Aretha Franklin soulfully captured life in the inner city and the psyche of African-Americans, while Bob Dylan, the Byrds, and Jefferson Airplane represented the counterculture that the beats and the Beatles helped to spawn. This generational culture that the United States experienced during the 1960s and thereafter built on the rebel culture of the immediate postwar period.

As much as any other figures, the nation's top officeholder and a boxing champion represented the shifting currents of American culture, beginning with the early 1960s. During his run for the Democratic Party nomination in 1960, throughout the thousand days of his administration, and following his tragic death, John Fitzgerald Kennedy, the youngest man ever elected to the presidency, captivated the imagination of the country. So too did Cassius Clay, the brash, outspoken young man from Louisville, Kentucky, who rode an Olympic championship into a heavyweight run that led to an unexpected world title, which in turn was followed by his renouncement of his "slave" name and adoption of one more befitting his Black Muslim faith, Muhammad Ali. It is hardly exaggerating to suggest that these two handsome, charismatic individuals triggered a revolution in national consciousness that proved enduring in many ways. Kennedy fostered youthful determination to participate in the affairs of one's community, whether local, national, or international, while Ali compelled Americans to rethink racial beliefs no matter what difficulties that process entailed. Both exhibited genuinely heroic characteristics and antiheroic ones too, including those involving relationships with women and people from other nations. Although other presidents accomplished more in office, Kennedy's legacy or at least his image proved enduring even as it underwent alterations with the passage of time. Other boxers, including heavyweight champions, compiled better records than Ali although his fame eventually surpassed that of any other athlete and perhaps any other individual. In the end, both men remained heroic figures, however flawed, while demonstrating something of the antiheroic persona that appealed to so many people in the United States and outside the country's boundaries as well.

John F. Kennedy

John Fitzgerald Kennedy was born in Brookline, Massachusetts, on May 29, 1917, the second of nine children of Rose Fitzgerald and Joseph Patrick Kennedy, both the grandchildren of impoverished Irish Catholics who, propelled by the potato famine, came to America in the middle of the nineteenth century. Rose was the vivacious, deeply religious daughter of ex-congressman and Boston mayor John F. "Honey Fitz" Fitzgerald. Good-looking Joe, the son of Patrick Kennedy, a former state legislator and top Boston banker, was a graduate of Harvard College and a business leader already well on his way to acquiring his first million. Joe made a fortune in commodities and the stock market during the 1920s, cashing in his stocks a year before the crash began in late 1929. He also made money during Prohibition through Somerset Importers, the lone American agent for leading Scotch and gin distillers, and as a Hollywood film producer. As the end of Prohibition approached, Joe parlayed his liquor investment into real estate holdings, which eventually enabled him to become one of the wealthiest men in the country. He also became a top figure in the Democratic Party. His early backing of Franklin Delano Roosevelt for the presidency led to Joe's appointment as chair of the Securities and Exchange Commission in 1934. Joe later served as ambassador to Great Britain from 1937 to 1940.

His second son, who almost succumbed to scarlet fever when he was only two, graduated from the Choate School, an elite boarding school in Wallingford, Connecticut, where his academic performance proved mediocre yet he was selected "most likely to succeed." In 1935 he enrolled first at the London School of Economics and then at Princeton University, but bouts of jaundice, induced by the unacknowledged presence of Addison's disease, resulting in weight loss and stomach ailments, compelled him to withdraw in both instances. Waiting until the fall of 1936 to enter Harvard University, Kennedy began to apply himself as he majored in political science, competed on various athletic teams, served on the *Harvard Crimson*, joined the prestigious Hasty Pudding Club, dated countless women, and graduated cum laude in 1940. His father ensured Jack's first real celebrity by helping to bring about publication of his son's senior thesis, which appeared in August 1940, shortly after the fall of France, as *Why England Slept*. The book contained an introduction by the publisher Henry Luce, whose *Time* magazine termed the book "startlingly timely" and "strenuously objective" in refuting Joe's isolationist views and convincing Americans of the need for preparedness. While acknowledging that *Why England Slept*, which became a best seller, contained nothing that was factually new, *Time* insisted that the book provided "a terrifying record of wishful thinking about peace when peace was impossible, or shilly-shallying about rearmament when war was inevitable." Moreover, it served as "a warning and a challenge" to those who reasoned that democracy's moral superiority would enable it to prevail over fascism. In September 1940, Kennedy entered Stanford Business School, considered transferring to Yale Law School, and finally decided instead to undertake a trip to South America, along with his sister Kathleen and mother Rose.

Learning that his older brother, Joe Jr., having just completed his second year at Harvard Law School, had enlisted in the Naval Reserve, Jack attempted during the spring of 1941 to get into either the army's Officer Candidate School or the navy but failed both physicals. Joe Kennedy called on Rear Admiral Alan G. Kirk, a well-placed family friend, who was head of naval intelligence, and Jack took another physical, enabling him to enter the Naval Reserve as an ensign in October 1941. He soon was working at a low level for the Office of Naval Intelligence in Washington, DC. A beautiful blonde reporter for the *Washington Times-Herald*, Inga Arvad, interviewed Kennedy for a column she wrote on the U.S. mobilization effort. In her article on Kennedy, the Danish native wrote, "If former Ambassador Joe Kennedy has a brilliant mind . . . charm galore and a way of walking into the hearts of people . . . then son No. 2 has inherited more than his due. . . . here is really a boy with a future." The two became lovers but an FBI report warned that she clearly sympathized with the Nazis. Kennedy soon found himself transferred out of the capital. Despite a ruptured disc, he determined to head out to sea. During a midshipman's course orchestrated by the Great Lakes Naval Training Station in the summer of 1942, Kennedy learned of the possibility of skippering his own PT boat. Although initially tagged to remain as an instructor at the training center, Kennedy received his desired appointment shortly after meeting later that year with his state's senior senator, David I. Walsh, a member of the Naval Affairs Committee.

On August 2, 1943, a Japanese destroyer near the Solomon Islands sliced Lieutenant Kennedy's boat, PT-109, in half. Two crewmembers drowned, but Jack saved another by towing him by a life jacket strap in his teeth for several hours. Days later, having swum to various islands, the crew was rescued. Kennedy received a Purple Heart along with the Navy and Marine Corps Medal, but not the Silver Star recommended by his squadron commanding officer. Signed by Admiral W.F. Bull Halsey, the citation, which noted Kennedy's personal "heroism," concluded, "His courage, endurance and excellent leadership contributed to the saving of several lives and was in keeping with the highest traditions of the United States Naval Service." By early September he returned to action, skippering a PT-59 boat. Suffering from a stomach ailment and bothered by his aching back, Kennedy returned to the States on January 7, 1944. He soon met John Hersey, whose lengthy, straightforward article, "Survival," in the June 7 issue of the *New Yorker*, describing Kennedy's heroics when PT-109 went down, brought additional attention to the young lieutenant. Kennedy soon heard of his brother Joe's death, which occurred on a bomber, laden with explosives, bound for Europe. Receiving his honorable discharge in early 1945, Jack agreed to pursue the path his father now planned for him: high elective office. Kennedy first had to contend with his aching back and a bout of malaria that led to a stay at a health resort near Phoenix and a visit to the Mayo Clinic in Rochester, Minnesota. With Joe Kennedy again pulling strings, Kennedy received a request from the *Chicago Herald-American*, a Hearst publication, to report on the United Nations Conference in San Francisco, offering the perspective "of the ordinary GI." The Hearst syndicate next sent Kennedy to Britain to cover the national elections, which led to Winston Churchill's defeat in early July, less than two months after the end of the war in Europe. Kennedy then went to Ireland, where he spoke with Eamon De Valera, president of the Irish Free State, and to Paris, Berlin, and Frankfurt, where he met Dwight

D. Eisenhower. Back in London he again experienced stomach problems, accompanied by a fever.

Returning to Massachusetts, Kennedy ran for a congressional seat, the first step in his father's determined bid to see his son become the nation's first Irish Catholic president. As the campaign progressed, Kennedy's early, halting steps receded and he acquired greater confidence in speaking with potential voters. Joe Kennedy's financial resources and political ties proved enormously helpful; the soon-to-be-famous Kennedy political machine was put together, and the ex-ambassador declared, "We're going to sell Jack like soap flakes." Joe's son, running as a veteran and delivering 450 speeches, bested ten other candidates in the Democratic Party primary for the Eleventh Congressional District, which contained Cambridge, the intellectual center housing Harvard University, just outside Boston, but also blue-collar sectors with Irish and Italian immigrants. *Time* reported that "grave, earnest, teetotaling Jack Kennedy" won the primary, a virtual guarantee of a congressional seat given the district's overwhelmingly Democratic makeup. The general election saw the "boyish looking" twenty-nine-year-old Kennedy garner 73 percent of the vote, enabling him to become one of many freshmen—who included Orange County's Richard Nixon in their midst—in the Eightieth Congress that convened in Washington, DC, in January 1947.

Over the next six years Kennedy compiled a largely liberal record on social and economic affairs. He supported national health care, slum clearance, public housing projects, subsidized housing for veterans, organized labor, restrictions on wiretapping, and aid to the disabled, the elderly, and dependent children. As the Cold War resulted in the collapse of the wartime alliance between Great Britain, the USSR, and the United States, Kennedy backed the Truman Doctrine, which effectively expressed his country's willingness to oppose aggression by the Red Army or by left-wing guerrillas. However, he worried about the effectiveness of the Marshall Plan in revitalizing war-torn Western Europe and blasted what he considered the loss of China to the communists. Kennedy questioned U.S. backing for the French war effort in Indochina and insisted that France should depart from Algeria. On overseas trips he met Yugoslav leader Joseph Tito, Israel's founder David Ben-Gurion, Indian premier Jawaharlal Nehru, and former Vietnamese emperor Bao Dai, among others. On a lighter note, he continued dating and bedding numerous women, including a string of movie stars.

In 1952, Kennedy, whom *Time* referred to as "a redoubtable opponent," ran for the U.S. Senate against the handsome, aristocratic incumbent, Henry Cabot Lodge. The hard-fought race featured a mid-September debate in Waltham, hosted by the League of Women Voters. Women made up almost the entire audience and appeared to be enamored of the dapper young congressman, who held his own against the more experienced Lodge. The two candidates met once more on October 5 in a televised debate, enabling Kennedy to be seen by many voters who were unfamiliar with him. Weeks before the election *The Nation* magazine indicated that "the youthful Kennedy" was "more than a match for the Senator" when it came to "charm, wealth, and social prestige." In November Kennedy won by 70,000 votes, notwithstanding Eisenhower's easy triumph over Democratic Party nominee Adlai Stevenson in the state's presidential vote.

On June 13, 1953, the *Saturday Evening Post* featured a story, "Jack Kennedy: The Senate's Gay Young Bachelor." As suggested by the title, the article hardly amounted to a serious examination of the new senator, but did present quotes in which he denied being a liberal and indicated he was uncomfortable with the kinds of people drawn to liberal organizations such as Americans for Democratic Action and the American Veterans Committee. Twelve days later the *New York Times* announced the engagement of the thirty-six-year-old Kennedy to twenty-three-year-old Jacqueline Bouvier. Later that year the newlyweds appeared on *Person to Person*, the CBS interview program hosted by Edward R. Murrow, one of the earliest examples of how television and politics were becoming increasingly interdependent. During a speech on the Senate floor in April 1954, Kennedy, in referring to French Indochina, warned, "No amount of American military assistance can conquer an enemy which is everywhere and at the same time nowhere." Beset by excruciating back pains, Kennedy opted the following October to undergo a spinal fusion operation, which his doctors opposed because of his Addison's disease. At one point, a priest delivered last rites. His hospital stay enabled Kennedy to avoid voting on a motion to censure the virulently red-baiting Senator Joseph McCarthy, a friend of the family but now out of political favor; the Senate voted to censure McCarthy, deeming his behavior "contrary to senatorial traditions." Surgeons performed yet another back operation on Kennedy in mid-February 1955. During his hospital stays and afterward, he worked on a book originally titled *These Great Men* but soon renamed *Profiles in Courage*, dealing with political statesmen who had performed heroically in difficult circumstances.

Then, in 1956, he made a bid for the vice presidential nomination of the Democratic Party. An article in the July 9 issue of *Newsweek* indicated that Kennedy's "political attractiveness" was "not merely a regional phenomenon." The story suggested that his "casual dress" and "boyishly earnest face" might help to dispel images of boss-driven politics. The article called his family background "impeccable," referred to the Kennedys' wealth and experience in public affairs, and mentioned his "strikingly beautiful" wife. It also noted that "the senator's cerebral assets" were "impressive" as indicated by the long run of *Profiles in Courage* on the best-seller list. The *Newsweek* offering presented an image of Kennedy that would recur later, including his "disarming" informality, propensity to go about without money in his pockets, readiness to play touch football, and ability to display "his old vim" through other athletic endeavors, notwithstanding his recent spinal operation, said to have been necessitated by the PT-109 incident. The article concluded that Kennedy would "expect to win. The Kennedys always have." During the Democratic nominating convention in mid-August, television audiences watched Senator Kennedy narrate *The Pursuit of Happiness*, a history of the party. Kennedy lost the vice presidential nomination to Tennessee senator Estes Kefauver, but Adlai Stevenson, the party's standard bearer yet again, later acknowledged that Jack would be "the one person people will remember from the convention." In fact, in a subsequent spate of publicity, Kennedy often was featured on the covers of mass circulation magazines.

Kennedy soon obtained a much-desired seat on the Senate Foreign Relations Committee, where he criticized Eisenhower's foreign policy, insisting on the need to pay greater attention to so-called Third World or underdeveloped countries. That same year, *Profiles in Courage*, which Theodore Sorensen helped Kennedy to write, took the 1957 Pulitzer Prize for biography after Joe again brought his influence to bear. That award engendered controversy: columnist Drew Pearson charged on *The Mike Wallace Interview*, run on ABC, that Kennedy was "the only man in history . . . who won the Pulitzer Prize on a book which was ghostwritten for him, which indicates the kind of public relations buildup he's had." Pearson reported too that some of Kennedy's colleagues purportedly informed him, "Jack, we wish you had a little less profile and more courage." Infuriated, Kennedy hired Clark Clifford, a former top assistant to President Truman, to threaten legal action against ABC. The television network issued a retraction, but scholars and nonscholars continue to debate whether Kennedy truly authored the prize-winning book. At the time the award added luster to his name and convinced many Americans that he possessed the gravitas to make a bid for higher political office. At least equally fortunate, Jacqueline, who had recently suffered a miscarriage, gave birth to a daughter, Caroline, and soon became pregnant again.

Time presented a lengthy essay on Kennedy that ran in its December 2, 1957, issue, under the title "Democrats: Man Out Front." An artist's rendering of Kennedy graced the front cover while the article began by quoting the mayor of Daytona Beach, Florida, who referred to Jack as "the future President of the U.S." A coed at the University of Minnesota reported that all of her sorority sisters sent Kennedy their "love" and promised to vote for him. Students at the University of Kansas mobbed him. In Oklahoma City a woman exclaimed, "I've come to-see him because I think he's wonderful." In Jackson, Mississippi, even though Kennedy expressed support for the *Brown v. Board of Education* ruling by the U.S. Supreme Court, the state's governor termed him the Democrats' "best presidential prospect for 1960" and offered, "I am all for him." The same was true in Kansas, where the governor supported Kennedy even though he had failed to support agricultural subsidies popular in the region. *Time* referred to Kennedy as a member of "a legendary family that surpasses its legend," "an authentic war hero and a Pulitzer-prizewinning author," an athlete, and a man with considerable intellectual qualifications. During his undeclared but obvious bid for his party's next presidential nomination, Kennedy had "left panting politicians and swooning women" throughout the country. The magazine declared that Kennedy was "certainly the only member of the U.S. Congress who could—as he did—make a speech with his shirttail hanging out and get gallery ahs instead of aws."

Running for reelection to the U.S. Senate in 1958, Kennedy took 74 percent of the vote, thereby achieving the largest plurality in state political history and immediately catapulting him near the top of the list of those viewed as potential Democratic Party presidential candidates. His victory led to his reappearance on the cover of *Time*, alongside others, including Texas senator Lyndon B. Johnson, presented as "Democratic Hopefuls." Increasingly viewed as his party's front-runner, Kennedy delivered speeches across the country, generally to large crowds, many containing obviously enamored young people. The April 27, 1959, issue of *Life* reported that "students at Beloit College hung on his every word. They followed him outdoors as if he were the Pied Piper, then stood in an ogling semi-circle until he drove away." Less happily the grande dame of the Democratic Party, Eleanor Roosevelt, criticized Kennedy for having failed to challenge Joseph McCarthy. Kennedy in her estimation was "someone who understands what courage is and admires it, but has not quite the independence to have it."

Speaking in the U.S. Senate Caucus Room on January 2, 1960, forty-two-year-old John Fitzgerald Kennedy declared his candidacy for the presidency, which he called "the most powerful office in the Free World." The nation's top political figure, he declared, would affect the arms race, the status of newly independent states, and the American economy. Twelve days later, at the National Press Club, Kennedy contended that the American people demanded "a vigorous proponent of the national interest" as "the challenging revolutionary sixties" began. The White House, he insisted, had to "be the center of moral leadership," offering the kind of "bully pulpit" that Teddy Roosevelt had favored. As the new decade developed, the American president, Kennedy suggested, should be capable of leading "his national constituency to its finest hour," requiring necessary sacrifices. With a well-oiled political machine—

one possessing "the smooth rhythm of a delicate watch," columnist Rowland Evans Jr. remarked—Kennedy captured all seven of the presidential primaries he ran in before the Democratic nominating convention in Los Angeles. He deftly handled the one issue that might derail his nomination: his Catholicism, which led some to fear that he would accede to mandates from the Vatican. Fielding a query from a reporter at a press conference in Los Angeles regarding whether a Catholic could be elected president, Kennedy responded, "If he is prepared to answer questions about the separation of church and state, I see no reason to discriminate against him." The more than 400 reporters in attendance rose and delivered a standing ovation.

After winning his party's nomination, Kennedy spoke to the gathered throng at the Los Angeles Coliseum, applauding the Democratic platform that propounded "'The Rights of Man'—the civil and economic rights essential to the human dignity of all men." He insisted that following "eight years of drugged and fitful sleep," the United States required a "strong, creative Democratic" chief of state, one capable of dealing with a changing world. Kennedy referred to revolutionary pressures in former colonial lands and at home, where a nonviolent campaign for human rights was spreading. The time was ripe, he declared, "for a new generation of leadership" that could tackle the New Frontier and new challenges confronting the planet. He urged all "to be pioneers of that New Frontier" while reaching out "to the young in heart, regardless of age," who were ready to choose "between the public interest and private comfort—between national greatness and national decline."

Controversies regarding Kennedy's faith soon resurfaced. Protestant minister Norman Vincent Peale, warning that "our American culture is at stake," formed a group of Protestant clergy that denied that Catholics possessed the requisite independence to lead the nation. Speaking to the Greater Houston Ministerial Association on September 12, Kennedy affirmed, "I am not the Catholic candidate for President. I am the Democratic Party's candidate for President, who happens also to be a Catholic. I do not speak for my Church on public matters—and the Church does not speak for me." Television rebroadcasts of the ten-minute address helped to diminish the impact of the religious issue on the election, although it never subsided entirely.

Analysts agree it was the still relatively new world of television that ensured Kennedy's narrow victory over the Republican nominee, Vice President Richard M. Nixon. The two men met in a series of four televised debates, although by all accounts the initial one on September 26, involving domestic issues, proved most instrumental. Nixon arrived at the debate site in Chicago confident because he had been a champion debater in college and had used television to save his political career earlier. During the presidential campaign in 1952, Nixon had spoken on television to squelch floating rumors that he had benefited from a slush fund. In the famous Checkers address, Nixon referred to the "good Republican cloth coat" that his wife Pat wore and the dog Checkers that his daughter had received as a present, while never altogether refuting the accusations. Nevertheless, the public response compelled Dwight Eisenhower to keep Nixon on the Republican ticket. Now, eight years later, the two-term vice president confidently awaited the first debate with Senator Kennedy. However, he appeared haggard and drawn, having lost twenty pounds because of a recent illness. By contrast, the movie-star-handsome Kennedy seemed to literally shine and more than held his own with his more experienced opponent during the debate. Those who listened via radio considered the result to be a draw at best, but television viewers overwhelmingly favored Kennedy over his sweating foe, whose makeup failed to cover an unattractive five o'clock shadow.

Given the narrow margin of victory that Kennedy achieved in November, the first televised debate quickly became part of political folklore. At a minimum it suggested the potential that television possessed to alter American politics in the same manner it had clearly transformed cultural and social affairs. Not only during the campaign but also throughout his presidency, Kennedy used television skillfully, becoming the third occupant of the Oval Office in the twentieth century to deftly use media. Earlier presidents, including Founders George Washington and Thomas Jefferson and Civil War president Abraham Lincoln, had acquired legendary status because of the gravitas they possessed. In a different fashion, Andrew Jackson became a celebrity figure of a kind, thanks to his military prowess, identification with the frontier, and seeming connection to Providence, as evidenced by his ability to win duels and ward off assassination attempts. At the beginning of the twentieth century, Theodore Roosevelt, the youngest man ever to become president, proved to be a popular cultural icon thanks to his bushy mustache, glasses, and bravado, as well as his readiness to use the nation's highest political office as a bully pulpit. Mass-produced teddy bears appeared after Teddy refused to shoot a small bear cub during a hunting expedition. His distant cousin Franklin was the next chief executive to employ the media brilliantly; thousands of photographs of the handsome president, often sporting a long, lighted cigarette, and thirty fireside chats confirmed his popularity. Harry Truman and Dwight Eisenhower called on television, but it was Jack Kennedy who proved to be wholly comfortable with the new medium. It hardly hurt that Kennedy possessed youth, looks, and glamour or that he had a stunningly beautiful young wife and two children, Caroline and John Jr., who was born in 1960.

Kennedy's presidency, which began in January 1961, lasted only about a thousand days. Historians still debate about the effectiveness of his tenure, although his reputation is ascending once more. Some claim that the period was marked by Cold War tensions, a failure to address the blight of racism, and the startling denouement that overshadowed Kennedy's performance as president. Others claim that Kennedy faltered initially, as evidenced by the Bay of Pigs fiasco, involving the aborted attempt to overthrow Cuba's Fidel Castro, and a difficult session with Russian premier Nikita Khrushchev in Vienna, but impressively grew in stature. His increasing experience enabled him to skillfully manage the Cuban missile crisis when nuclear war threatened, to undertake the space program that landed an American astronaut on the moon by the end of the decade, to bring the federal government's power to bear on behalf of civil rights, and to instill hope and ambition in his countrymen, particularly the nation's youth, as part of his administration's attempt to carve out a New Frontier for America. Kennedy initiated the Peace Corps, tapping into the idealism of the young; began the Alliance for Progress, which offered much needed (however incomplete) economic support to Latin American states; and introduced sweeping civil rights legislation in Congress.

Along the way he repeatedly called on the media to connect with his fellow Americans, to impart a sense of duty and urgency, and to steer public policy in the direction he felt it should head. Kennedy's inaugural address on January 20, 1961, is considered among the most memorable in American presidential history. It contained the moving lines, "Let the word go forth from this time and place, to friend and foe alike, that the torch has passed to a new generation of Americans," as well as the famous exhortation, "And so, my fellow Americans, ask not what your country can do for you—ask what you can do for your country." Very early in his administration, Kennedy skillfully employed press conferences, displaying intelligence, wit, and humor, albeit admittedly during a period when certain matters remained unexplored because of courtesies then accepted. Kennedy's extramarital affairs, including one with Marilyn Monroe, never became the subject of those sessions, which were used rather to highlight domestic and foreign policy concerns and to display the handsome Kennedy family to good effect. The Kennedys engendered energy and vigor in welcoming to the White House dignitaries from the worlds of art, science, literature, and sports. Photographs captured the Kennedy children playing in the presidential office; the president sailing; and the first lady in glamorous attire. Jackie Kennedy hosted an enormously popular one-hour special on the White House, presented by CBS. *The First Family*, a comedy album by Vaughan Meader that parodied the Kennedys, became the top-selling record in the country.

In a more serious vein, Kennedy spoke forcefully to the nation and the world, first about threats of a global cast, and later regarding the need to move beyond Cold War paranoia in order to prevent a worldwide conflagration. After

East Germany erected the Berlin Wall to divide the city into East and West zones, Kennedy told a huge crowd of West Germans, "All free men, wherever they may live, are citizens of Berlin, and, therefore, as a free man, I take pride in the words *'Ich bin ein Berliner.'*" During the Cuban missile crisis as the U.S. government learned about the Soviet Union's secret plan to place missiles in Cuba, Kennedy warned that the United States would "regard any nuclear missile launched from Cuba against any nation in the Western Hemisphere as an attack by the Soviet Union on the United States." Speaking at American University in Washington, DC, on June 10, 1963, the president called for a test ban treaty and urged a reexamination of Americans' attitudes toward the communist state. He praised "the Russian people for their many accomplishments" and recalled the fact that "no nation in the history of battle lost more than the Soviet Union" had during World War II with at least 20 million of its people killed. While acknowledging the large differences between the United States and the Soviet Union, particularly the communist philosophy Americans considered "profoundly repugnant," Kennedy urged movement toward helping to "make the world safe for diversity. For, in the final analysis, our most basic common link is that we all inhabit this planet. We all breathe the same air. We all cherish our children's future. And we are all mortal." Having signed the nuclear test ban treaty, Kennedy declared in October 1963, "Today the fear is a little less and the hope is a little greater."

Kennedy also addressed the issue of domestic racism, highlighted by the attempts of black students to integrate lunch counters and state universities across the South. On June 11, 1963, speaking to a nationwide television audience about the indignities suffered by black Americans, Kennedy asked, "If an American, because his skin is dark, cannot eat lunch in a restaurant open to the public, if he cannot send his children to the best public school available, if he cannot vote for the public officials who represent him, if in short, he cannot enjoy the full and free life for which all of us want, then who among us would be content to have the color of his skin changed and stand in his place?" Kennedy proceeded to support passage of strong civil rights and anti-poverty legislation.

Looking ahead to the upcoming presidential campaign and hoping to heal rifts in the Texas Democratic Party, Kennedy toured the Lone Star state in late November 1963. Large friendly crowds greeted the president and first lady. As the presidential motorcade passed through downtown Dallas, shots rang out, including one that tore apart Kennedy's head. Within an hour newscasters reported that President Kennedy, the youngest man ever elected to the nation's highest office, was dead. On hearing of the slaying, civil rights leader Martin Luther King Jr. exclaimed to his wife Coretta, "This is what is going to happen to me. This is such a sick society." The next day the British journalist Alistair

Cooke noted, "This is the first assassination of a world figure that took place in the age of television, and every network and station in the country took up the plotting of the appalling story." *New York Times* columnist James Reston wrote, "What was killed was not only the president but the promise. . . . The death of youth and the hope of youth, of the beauty and grace and the touch of magic. . . . He never reached his meridian: we saw him only as a rising sun." A stunned nation, glued to television sets, watched the shooting of Kennedy's purported killer, Lee Harvey Oswald, two days after the assassination. Television also captured the anguish experienced by many Americans, including the Kennedy family, during the funeral procession. Thus the medium that had helped to shape Kennedy as a political figure, that catapulted him into the presidency, that defined his 1,037 days in office, also elicited grief and shock following the assassination. The killing itself initiated a wave of such murders, which eventually cost the nation the services of Malcolm X, Martin Luther King Jr., and the president's brother Robert F. Kennedy.

Almost immediately Jacqueline Kennedy began working to shape the remembrances of her husband and his administration, and authors like Theodore H. White began referring to the Kennedy presidency as America's Camelot, akin to the golden period in English history involving King Arthur and his Round Table. Kennedy's successor, Lyndon B. Johnson, established the Warren Commission, headed by Chief Justice Earl Warren, which concluded that Oswald was the lone gunman. Nevertheless, controversies and rumors continued to swirl about multiple shooters and conspiracies supposedly involving intelligence agencies, right-wing fanatics, oilmen, the Mafia, Fidel Castro, or anti-Castro Cubans. In March 1967, Kennedy's grave was placed at a special site at Arlington National Cemetery, ringed by plaques bearing the words of the slain president. His name was used for the Kennedy International Airport in New York, the Kennedy School of Government at Harvard, and the presidential library in Boston. Best-selling works, including large tomes by Arthur Schlesinger Jr. and Theodore Sorensen, sang his praises, while Seymour Hersh's later *The Dark Side of Camelot* called into question Kennedy's heroic stature. Hollywood offered big-budget films about Kennedy and the assassination, including Oliver Stone's *JFK*. Numerous tales emerged regarding Kennedy's sexual antics, health difficulties, and use of procaine, amphetamines, and other psychotropic drugs, but he continued to be lauded by Democratic and Republican politicians alike. For many people around the globe, John F. Kennedy remained an iconic figure, representing youthful possibilities and idealism. For many, too, his death ushered in a wave of disillusionment, soon heightened by racial disturbances, the Vietnam War, and a wholesale distrust of the Establishment that Kennedy had so eloquently represented and urged to change.

MUHAMMAD ALI

Muhammad Ali, another icon of the 1960s whose stature lasted long after that decade, was born Cassius Marcellus Clay Jr. in Louisville, Kentucky, on January 17, 1942. He was the first of two sons born to a sign painter and artist, Cassius Clay Sr., and Odessa Clay, who sometimes served as a domestic for wealthy white families. The Clays, whose family members had lived in Louisville for six generations, were considered middle-class, having earlier purchased their five-room, red brick house, situated in a black neighborhood in the city's West End. Their children, who helped out with odd jobs or assisted Cassius Sr. with his sign painting, never lacked for shelter, clothing, or food. The family surname came from a nineteenth-century abolitionist farmer who freed his own slaves and provided housing for Cassius's great-grandfather. Odessa's racial ancestry was mixed, resulting in her own light skin. The large extended family doted on the voluble young Cassius. Cassius Sr. was, as Ali biographer David Remnick relates, "a braggart, a charmer, a performer," a womanizer prone to violence after he drank, and a frustrated artist who expressed resentment about whites and spoke fondly of Marcus Garvey, the Jamaican immigrant who headed the Back to Africa campaign in the 1920s that proved highly popular among urban blacks in the United States. Young Cassius early learned something about Louisville's racial sensibilities, recognizing that certain downtown stores, hotels, movie theaters, schools, parks, and neighborhoods altogether were off-limits to blacks. In the summer of 1955 Clay heard from his father about one of the most horrific incidents that characterized the region's racial inequities, the brutal slaying in Money, Mississippi, of Emmett Till, a fourteen-year-old black boy who had paid the price for flirting with a white woman.

By that point Clay had already determined to become a boxer, believing that the sport "was the fastest way for a black person to make it in this country." A mediocre student at best, Clay wanted to avoid hanging out in the streets with other young men who seemingly had no place to go. He apparently first thought about becoming a fighter after his new, $60 Schwinn bicycle was stolen when he was twelve years old. Seeking a police officer, he went to a boxing gym run by Joe Martin, a white patrolman, who also offered *Tomorrow Champions*, a Saturday afternoon television program featuring amateur boxing. Encouraged by Martin, Clay began training and had his first fight only six weeks later. After winning a three-round fight through a split decision against a white boy, Clay roared that he would "be the greatest of all time." Clay also began to toss out the kind of rhyming comments he would later be noted for, declaring at one point, "This guy must be done/I'll stop him in one." Immediately drawn to the sport of boxing, Clay spent as much

189

time as possible at Martin's Columbia Gym, displaying quickness, remarkable reflexes, and a strong work ethic. Declining to smoke or drink, he began each day with a lengthy run and adhered to a rigid diet. By the time he graduated near the bottom of his high school class, Clay was already renowned as an amateur fighter, having won 100 of 108 bouts, six Kentucky Golden Glove titles, a pair of national Golden Glove middleweight titles, and two national Amateur Athletic Union light heavyweight championships.

In May 1960, he knocked out Alan Hudson in the Olympic trials in San Francisco to win the light heavyweight division. That summer, Clay, although terrified of flying, traveled to Rome to compete in the Olympics, where he met the famed singer-movie star Bing Crosby and heavyweight boxing champion Floyd Patterson, interacted easily with foreign athletes, and flirted shamelessly. *Time* magazine later reported that "if anyone had held an election for mayor of the Olympic Village, Cassius Clay would have been a prime candidate." In the ring the 178-pound light heavyweight won four bouts, including the championship match, winning a unanimous decision over twenty-five-year-old Zbigniew Pietrzykowski to take the gold medal. *Time* magazine termed Clay "the most promising amateur in the United States," who operated "with lightning speed, firing rights and lefts in stunning combinations." Following the awards ceremonies, Clay fielded a question from a Soviet reporter about race relations back home. He responded, "Tell your readers we've got qualified people working on that problem, and I'm not worried about the outcome. To me, the U.S. is still the best country in the world, counting yours." Back home in Louisville, Clay purchased a pink Cadillac, which he drove around town while exclaiming, "I am Cassius Clay! I am the greatest!" He became drawn to the separatist Black Muslims, who made him recall all the times he had witnessed whites abusing blacks, which had caused him to hate being black.

Although not everyone was impressed by Clay's boxing style, light heavyweight champion Archie Moore expressed interest in managing Clay, as did former Olympic champion Pete Rademacher and Patterson's manager, Cus D'Amato. Declining those offers and unsuccessfully seeking out the legendary boxer Sugar Ray Robinson as a trainer, Clay also avoided falling into the trap that had snared many boxers who became connected to mobsters. Instead he turned to a group of eleven well-heeled white businessmen, all but one from Louisville, who offered him $10,000 up front, an annual salary of $4,800, payment of all expenses, and an even split of boxing purses; fortunately, 15 percent of Clay's earnings would be placed in a pension fund that could be drawn on only when he turned thirty-five. The syndicate eventually selected the well-regarded trainer Angelo Dundee to hone Clay's boxing skills. His professional boxing career as a heavyweight opened on October 29, 1960, with a disappointing six-round decision over Tunney Hunsaker, a policeman from

West Virginia. Fighting in Miami Beach on December 27, Clay knocked out Herb Siler in four rounds. Three weeks later he did the same to Tony Esperti in three rounds, followed by a one-round knockout of Jim Robinson on February 7, 1961, both bouts also held in Miami Beach. He fought there again on February 21, knocking out Donnie Fleeman in the seventh round. Dundee later admitted that at this stage the top boxing writers remained unconvinced about his fighter, believing "he bounced around too much and did everything wrong. They figured he was all mouth and no talent."

By contrast, Ferdie Pacheco, Clay's physician after he moved to Miami, reported that the boxer "was the most perfect physical specimen I had ever seen, from an artistic and an anatomical standpoint, even healthwise." Clay's boxing stature appeared to improve, at least among the local boxing audience, after he sparred with Ingemar Johansson, the former heavyweight champion who was meeting Patterson for the third time. As Clay jabbed and danced away, he taunted Johansson, "I'm the one who should be fighting Patterson, not you! Come on, sucker, what's the matter! Can't you catch me!" *Sports Illustrated* staffer Gil Rogin watched in amazement, thinking, "Jesus Christ! What have we here?" Shortly after Clay knocked out Lamar Clark in the second round in Louisville on April 19, the *New York Times* reporter Arthur Daley recalled that Clay, back in the Olympic Village, had predicted to heavyweight champion Patterson that the two would meet "in about two more years." Daley now called Clay "enormously appealing" and reported that he had grown into "a solid 195-pounder." The reporter termed Clay "a compulsive talker with the engaging personality of a youthful Archie Moore": Daley declared, "This good-looking boy is a charmer and is so natural that even his more extravagant statements sound like exuberance instead of braggadocio. On him they look good." While Clay obviously exulted in publicity, Daley noted, "he also attracts it with the inexorability of a magnet drawing steel filings." Clay decisioned Duke Sabedong in ten rounds in Las Vegas on June 26 while also encountering the professional wrestler Gorgeous George, who urged him to act as outrageously as possible to maintain attention. Back in Louisville, Clay fought three more times that year, competing against ranked heavyweights, winning the first match with another ten-round decision and the other pair by mid-fight knockouts.

Boxing analysts remained mixed in their evaluations of Clay. *Sports Illustrated* writer Huston Horn, who had panned a recent Clay fight, examined the boxer in an article that appeared on September 25, 1961. Referring to him as "still just an unsophisticated Olympic gold medalist," Horn indicated that it remained uncertain how skillful a fighter Clay would prove to be. The October 16, 1961, issue of *Sports Illustrated* quoted Clay who expressed his desire to become "the youngest heavyweight champion in history" while offering that his latest fight "showed he can fight almost as much as he can talk." The *New Yorker*'s A.J. Liebling crafted a lengthy piece in March 1962 on the six-foot-two, 195-pound Clay. Liebling, who had long delivered essays on boxing for the prestigious publication, recalled considering Clay's performance during the Rome Games "attractive but not probative," remembering that he had been more impressed by Floyd Patterson's showing two Olympics earlier. Liebling called Clay a poet and a butterfly. After watching him dispose of Sonny Banks in four rounds, Liebling indicated that he "was the kind of Hero likely to be around for a long while."

Clay fought six more times in 1962, knocking out each of his opponents including the aging Archie Moore, who recently had been stripped of his light-heavyweight crown. A prohibitive favorite against Moore, Clay predicted he would win easily: "When you come to the fight, don't block the aisle, and don't block the door. You will all go home after round four." Clay came through just as he had prophesied and Moore acknowledged, "He's definitely ready for Liston," referring to Sonny Liston, the heavyweight champion who had taken the crown by flattening Patterson in the first round. Clay won two more fights in early 1963, one by a third-round knockout and the other, which took place at Madison Square Garden on March 13, by decision. While in New York City, Clay appeared at the Bitter End nightclub in Greenwich Village, where he proclaimed, "Cassius Marcellus Clay/Will be the noblest Roman of them all."

Although his New York fight had been something of a disappointment, it ran his record to 18–0 and was soon followed by a *Time* magazine cover that featured the young fighter and a pair of boxing gloves. The corresponding article quickly noted that Clay considered himself "the Greatest" and declared, "This is a story about a man/With iron fists and a beautiful tan/He talks a lot and boasts indeed/Of a powerful punch and blinding speed." In the piece, Clay admitted that Dundee had taught him the jab but then insisted, "The rest is me. What changed the most was my own natural ability." *Time* suggested that boxing had been in the doldrums since the retirement in the mid-1950s of undefeated heavyweight champ Rocky Marciano, while mobsters and the fighters they controlled had alienated fans. Then the man arrived whom sportswriters dubbed "The Louisville Lip, "Mighty Mouth," and "Cassius the Brashest," able to attract spectators back to the sport, regardless of whether they loved or hated him. Only three weeks earlier Clay and heavyweight champion Liston had been both training at Miami Beach's Fifth Street Gym. In characteristic fashion, Clay began harassing Liston, declaring, "You ain't so hot." Liston replied, "Yeah? I could leave both legs at home and beat you." Asserting "I can lick you," Clay began to enter the ring, only to fall back when Liston charged. A delighted Clay heard Liston cry out, "I'm not training for Patterson—I'm training for Clay."

Clay's next fight took him to London, where he battled against Henry Cooper on June 18 before 55,000 fans gathered at Wembley Stadium. Although landing on the canvas for the second time in his professional career, Clay rebounded to knock out Cooper in the fifth round. The next month found Clay in Las Vegas, the site of the Liston-Patterson rematch. Clay waltzed into the gym where Liston was watching a sparring session and began taunting the champ. Later that evening at a casino, Liston finally turned on his tormentor, first verbally threatening him, then slapping a stunned Clay in the face. Determined to force Liston to give him a title fight, Clay showed up at Sonny's Denver home at three in the morning in a passenger bus with the horn blaring and the slogans "World's Most Colorful Fighter" and "Liston Must Go in Eight," painted on the side. The atmosphere remained highly charged until the police arrived, shooing away Clay and his compatriots. Finally, in early November, representatives for the two fighters agreed to a title match to be held in Miami in late February. In an article that appeared shortly afterward under his name in *Sports Illustrated*, Clay admitted that people had heard of him because he could "throw the jive better than anybody you will probably ever meet anywhere." Jive was the reason he was slated to fight Liston and "why they took my picture looking at $1 million in cold cash," indicating how much "a southern colored boy has made . . . just as he turns 22." Predicting he would win the heavyweight crown in the eighth round, Clay insisted that "Liston will be worn out by then." Clay's bus now sported signs reading "Big Ugly Bear," "Bear-Hunting Season," "Too Pretty To Be A Fighter," and "Bear Must Fall."

Only days before the fight Clay met the four young Englishmen who had taken America by storm. "Hello, there, Beatles," greeted Clay, adding, "We oughta do some road shows together." Photographers positioned the Beatles and Clay in the ring where the boxer pretended to launch a punch that floored them all. When Liston's plane arrived in Miami, Clay, seeking to garner publicity and to mess with his foe, greeted the champion, "Chump! Big ugly bear! I'm gonna whup you right now!" Clay also followed Liston's car until Sonny got out and confronted him. Now Clay refused to back down, yelling, "Come on, chump, right here!" At the weigh-in, Clay, pretending to have a nervous breakdown, began screaming, "You ain't no giant! I'm gonna eat you alive!" and acting like he was going to attack Liston. On February 25, 1964, Clay, a 7–1 underdog who had promised to "float like a butterfly and sting like a bee," met Liston at the Fontainebleau Hotel in Miami Beach, amazingly enough with only 8,300 spectators on hand and as many empty seats. Quickly the older, lumbering champion appeared outmatched by his younger, faster, more limber, and bigger opponent. The 210-pound, six-foot-three Clay, "backpedaling, bobbing, weaving, ducking," took the opening round and Liston the second. Clay's incessant punching produced a welt under Liston's left eye, which opened up in the next round. Liston connected more readily in the fourth round, but Clay's constant jabs left additional bruises on his face. Nevertheless, at the close of that round Clay indicated that he was blinded and called for the fight to stop. Ignoring the request, Dundee worked on his fighter, then pushed him back into the ring, shouting, "This is the big one, Daddy. We aren't going to quit now!" Hardly able to see, Clay somehow avoided Liston, who looked foolish trying to land punches. In round six Clay took the upper hand once more, delivering eight consecutive punches at one point and rocking Liston with a pair of left hooks. As the two men returned to their corners, Clay seemed fresh and charged while Liston appeared haggard. Soon it became evident that the thoroughly battered Liston was quitting and Clay began dancing around, hollering, "I'm the greatest. I shook up the world! I am the greatest thing that ever lived! . . . . I'm the king of the world!"

At the next day's news conference and in the days that followed, Clay revealed that he was associated, in some fashion at least, with the Black Muslims, the highly controversial separatist group led by Elijah Muhammad, which had been damned in a CBS documentary, *The Hate That Hate Produced.* A *Newsweek* article presciently suggested that based on his religious beliefs, Clay, who had failed a series of Army preinduction qualifying tests, "might well claim to be a conscientious objector," while concluding that "there is no limit to his horizon." He soon appeared in New York City with Malcolm X, the eloquent Black Muslim who had become estranged from Elijah Muhammad. Malcolm praised the new world heavyweight champion highly: "Clay is the finest Negro athlete I have ever known, the man who will mean more to his people than any athlete before him. He is more than Jackie Robinson was, because Robinson is the white man's hero." Robinson himself was one of the few who refused to condemn the fighter's decision, declaring that "Clay has just as much right to ally himself with the Muslim religion as anyone else has to be a Protestant or a Catholic." Elijah Muhammad soon announced on radio that he had given Clay a new, nonslave name: Muhammad Ali. Many sportswriters and fans alike refused to accord Ali his new name, still referring to him as Cassius Clay, although influential sports broadcaster Howard Cosell steadfastly respected Ali's wishes. The furor failed to dissipate with Ali damned for his association with a group that subscribed to the idea of black supremacy. Hardly troubled by the controversy, Ali undertook an overseas venture in which he toured Africa and the Middle East, meeting Ghana's Prime Minister Kwame Nkrumah and Egypt's President Gamal Abdel Nasser.

The October 1964 issue of *Playboy* contained an extended interview with Ali conducted by the African-American writer Alex Haley, but it too referred to the boxer as Cassius Clay. Ali, acknowledging that he had been involved with the Black Muslims since the 1960 Olympics, believed that his association had, as he put it, "pulled me up and cleaned me up as a human being." When Haley asked if whites should worry about the heavyweight champ belonging to the Black Muslims, Ali retorted, "Look, the black man that's trying to integrate, he's getting beat up and bombed and shot. But the black man that says he don't want to integrate, he gets called a 'hate teacher.'" Contending that civil rights legislation would result in bloodshed, Ali argued instead "that the black man needs to get together with his own kind," which was why he had chosen to reside in Harlem, where he was "around unity, rhythm and soul." Admitting he was a Muslim, Ali declared, "moved me from the sports page to the front pages. I'm a whole lot bigger man than I would be if I was just a champion prizefighter." He had been "elevated from the normal stature of fighters to being a world figure, a leader, a statesman," sought out by African diplomats. Returning home, he married Sonji Roi, a beautiful black woman, but the marriage, the first of four for Ali, quickly became rocky.

A rematch with Liston approached in November 1964 with oddsmakers again favoring the more experienced boxer. Just three days before the fight, a severe hernia compelled Ali to cancel. On February 21, 1965, three gunmen murdered the thirty-nine-year-old activist Malcolm X. Declaring that the assassinated leader had been his friend, Ali refused to talk about him anymore. Three months later Ali was back in the ring with Liston, fighting in Lewiston, Maine. One minute into the fight, Ali tossed an overhand right that snapped back Liston's head, and the contender fell to the canvas. Towering over Liston, Ali shouted, "Get up and fight, you bum! You're supposed to be so bad! Nobody will believe this!" With the crowd yelling, "Fix! Fix!" the confused referee, Jersey Joe Walcott, himself a former heavyweight champion, failed to deliver the count. Over twenty seconds passed before Liston finally got up. Seeking a knockout, Ali pursued Liston with a series of blows until Walcott walked over to the ring apron where Nat Fleischer, editor of the top boxing magazine *Ring*, cried that the fight had ended, as the referee soon informed the fighters. Although the punch that floored Liston would be called a "phantom" shot and rumors about a dive continued, slow-motion replays demonstrate that Ali delivered a devastating blow that left Liston still wobbly long after he got off the mat. While some sportswriters continued to insist that the fight was a fraud, most viewed it as legitimate.

After a series of exhibition matches, including several with sparring partner Jimmy Ellis, Ali fought Patterson in Las Vegas on November 22, 1965. Enraged by Patterson's embittered charge that "the image of a Black Muslim as the world heavyweight champion disgraces the sport and the nation," Ali deliberately toyed with the former two-time champion, delivering a merciless beating. Considering Patterson "a deaf dumb so-called Negro who needs a spanking," Ali withheld the knockout punch, preferring instead to taunt his opponent as an Uncle Tom. Ali finally knocked out Patterson in the twelfth round. The next year saw Ali fight five times, outpointing George Chuvalo in Toronto and winning four times—twice in London and once each in Frankfurt and Houston—by knockout.

While his professional boxing record remained unblemished, Ali remained a source of controversy both in the ring and outside of it. Some boxing analysts continued to question his reputed lack of punching power or at least the absence of the kind of knockout punch that had characterized great heavyweights such as Joe Louis and Rocky Marciano, but also damned him for cruelly toying with ring opponents. Many remained angry about Ali's ties to the Black Muslims, while the federal government began wrestling with the boxing champ over the question of military service. Now reclassified as I-A by the Selective Service, Ali exclaimed, "Man, I ain't got no quarrel with them Vietcong." Ali termed the Vietnam War a white man's fight that involved the killing of darker-skinned people. Sportswriter Jimmy Cannon condemned Ali wholeheartedly in a soon-to-be-famous passage that ironically nicely summarized a good bit of generational culture by the midpoint of the 1960s:

> He fits in with the famous singers no one can hear and the punks riding motorcycles and Batman and the boys with their long dirty hair and the girls with the unwashed look and the college kids dancing naked at secret proms and the revolt of students who get a check from Dad, and the painters who copy the labels off soup cans and surf bums who refuse to work and the whole pampered cult of the bored young.

Other critics blasted Ali as "a self-centered spoiled brat of a child" and "a sad apology for a man." In *Sports Illustrated*, Jack Olson presented "A Case of Conscience," a five-part series on Ali, whom he still referred to as Cassius Clay. Olsen declared that Ali, "the best-known sports figure in the world," had "become the most hated figure in sport." Reacting to early indignities and purportedly schooled in hatred of whites by his father and Elijah Muhammad, Ali had developed a perspective on race, Olsen insisted, that amounted to "a tortured confusion of truth, half-truth and untruth."

Ali decisioned Ernie Terrell in a fifteen-round bout in Houston on February 6, 1967, a performance that led Tex Maule to declare, "It was a wonderful demonstration of boxing skill and a barbarous display of cruelty." Muhammad knocked out Zora Folley in the third round in New York City on March 22. He continued battling with the Selective Service and was investigated by the Federal Bureau of Investigation. Affirming his own opposition to the Vietnam War, Martin Luther King Jr. declared, "Like Muhammad Ali puts it, we are all—Black and Brown and poor—victims of the same system of oppression." Hardly further endearing himself to either his critics or the U.S. government, Ali posed the question in a statement that had been carefully crafted in advance:

> Why should they ask me to put on a uniform and go ten thousand miles from home and drop bombs and bullets on brown people in Vietnam while so-called Negro people in Louisville are treated like dogs? No, I'm not going 10,000 miles from home to help murder and burn another poor nation simply to continue the domination of white slave masters of the darker people the world over.

Compelled to appear at the induction center in Houston, Ali refused to respond when his name was called. Informed that he could face a fine and a five-year prison sentence, Ali offered a statement that said, "I refuse to be inducted into the armed forces of the United States because I claim to be exempt as a minister of the religion of Islam." Civil rights and peace activist Julian Bond, a member of the Georgia state legislature, affirmed the importance of Ali's action: "When Ali refused to take that symbolic step forward everyone knew about it moments later. . . . People who had never thought about the war—Black and white—began to think it through because of Ali." In June 1967, an all-white jury in Houston handed out the maximum sentence to Ali: five years in prison and the loss of his passport. The boxing commission stripped him of his title as the appeal process occurred. Out on bail, Ali spoke frequently at college and university campuses, opposing the war and affirming his commitment to the stand he had taken. Writing in *Esquire* magazine, Ali contended that black athletes should use their "fame for freedom." He also called on the government to issue $25 billion in reparations to construct homes for blacks in Georgia, Mississippi, and Alabama. By 1970 the increasingly radicalized Ali acknowledged, "I was determined to be one nigger that the white man didn't get." He exhorted others, "Go on and join something. If it isn't the Muslims, at least join the Black Panthers. Join something bad."

Allowed to return to the ring in 1970, Ali won two late-year fights by knockout. On March 8, 1971, he battled Joe Frazier in Madison Square Garden for the heavyweight championship. Billed as "The Fight of the Century," the fight went fifteen rounds, watched by celebrities in attendance including Frank Sinatra, Barbra Streisand, Norman Mailer, Diana Ross, and Hugh Hefner. Both fighters were former Olympic gold medalists, undefeated in their professional careers, and guaranteed $2.5 million. The fight became a battle of attrition with Frazier, earlier blasted by Ali as an "Uncle Tom," prevailing in a unanimous decision. Writing about the contest, Norman Mailer termed Ali

"America's Greatest Ego" as well as "the very spirit of the twentieth century
. . . the prince of mass man and the media." In late June, the U.S. Supreme
Court unanimously ruled in favor of Ali's request for conscientious objector
status. The following July, Ali knocked out former sparring partner, Jimmy
Ellis, in the twelfth round to win the North American Boxing Federation
heavyweight title. Ali won twice more that year and then swept through six
matches in 1972, including, amazingly enough, a rematch with Floyd Patterson. In 1973 Ali won an early fight, then suffered a broken jaw in losing
to Ken Norton on March 31. When the two fought again in early September,
Ali prevailed this time in twelve rounds. He took another fight the following
month, preparing for a rematch with Frazier in late January 1974, which Ali
won. On October 30 Ali fought against the seemingly invincible heavyweight
champion George Foreman in "The Rumble in the Jungle," a match held in
Kinshasa, Zaire. Billboards, hiding squatter camps, read, "Zaire: Where Black
Power is a Reality." Wearing Foreman down with a "rope-a-dope" strategy, Ali
knocked him out in the eighth round to regain the heavyweight title. *Sports
Illustrated* named Ali its 1974 Sportsman of the Year. After three title defenses
in the first half of 1975, Ali fought Frazier again in "The Thrilla in Manila,"
with Frazier's trainer's throwing in the towel after the fourteenth round. Later,
Ali claimed, "This must be what death feels like." His autobiography, titled
The Greatest: My Own Story, came out that year.

Time out of the ring, age, and the vicious fights with Norton (including
another one in 1976) and Frazier, in particular, took something out of Ali
although he managed six more successful title defenses. In mid-February
1978, Ali lost to Leon Spinks, whom he defeated eight months later to win
the heavyweight championship for a record third time. Ali announced his
retirement from the ring in June 1979. On October 2, 1980, Larry Hol-
mes, a former sparring partner, became the first fighter to knock out Ali.
Ali fought once more, late in 1981, but was decisioned by a journeyman
fighter. The pounding he took in the ring, particularly after his skills diminished, undoubtedly contributed greatly to the onset of Parkinson's disease.
Slurred speech and slowed motor skills now characterized Ali. As his once
magnificent body began to fail him, he acquired the kind of near universal
acclaim that had previously eluded him. In 1996, *We Were Kings*, a film
about Ali's fight with Foreman in Zaire, won the Academy Award for best
documentary. Some 3.5 billion people across the globe watched Ali with his
trembling hands light the Olympic torch to initiate the 1996 Summer Games
in Atlanta. The British Broadcasting Corporation (BBC) in 1999 named Ali
Sportsman of the Century. The BBC observed that "at the height of his powers, Muhammad Ali was probably the most famous person on the planet"
as "his fame simply transcended sport." Three years later the BBC termed

Ali "a phenomenon" and declared he "has transcended the bounds of sport, race and nationality." In 2002 *Ring Magazine* placed Ali third, just behind Sugar Ray Robinson and Henry Armstrong, but above other heavyweights, including the great Joe Louis, in a list of the 80 Best Fighters of the Last 80 Years. In November 2005, Ali received the Presidential Medal of Freedom; the citation included the observation that "his deep commitment to equal justice and peace has touched people around the world." That same month the Muhammad Ali Center opened in Louisville to foster "peace, social responsibility, respect and personal growth."

Bibliography

Chomsky, Noam. *Rethinking Camelot: JFK, the Vietnam War, and U.S. Political Culture*. Cambridge, MA: South End Press, 1993.

Dallek, Robert. *An Unfinished Life: John F. Kennedy 1917–1963*. London: Little, Brown, 2003.

Early, Gerald Lyn, ed. *The Muhammad Ali Reader*. New York: Ecco Press, 1998.

Ezra, Michael. *Muhammad Ali: The Making of an Icon*. Philadelphia: Temple University Press, 2009.

Giglio, James. *The Presidency of John F. Kennedy*. Ann Arbor: University of Michigan Press, 1991.

Gorn, Elliot, ed. *Muhammad Ali: The People's Champ*. Champaign: University of Illinois Press, 1995.

Hauser, Thomas. *Muhammad Ali: His Life and Times*. New York: Simon & Schuster, 1991.

Hellmann, John. *The Kennedy Obsession: The American Myth of JFK*. New York: Columbia University Press, 1997.

Hersh, Seymour. *The Dark Side of Camelot*. London: Little, Brown, 1998.

Kram, Mark. *Ghosts of Manila: The Fateful Blood Feud Between Muhammad Ali and Joe Frasier*. New York: Harper Collins, 2001.

Mailer, Norman. *The Fight*. London: Little, Brown, 1975.

Martin, Ralph G. *A Hero for Our Time: An Intimate Story of the Kennedy Years*. New York: Random House, 1983.

Muhammad Ali. *The Soul of a Butterfly: Reflections on Life's Journey*. New York: Simon & Schuster, 2004.

Parmet, Herbert. *JFK: The Presidency of John F. Kennedy*. Ann Arbor: University of Michigan Press, 1983.

Perrett, Geoffrey. *Jack: A Life Like No Other*. New York: Random House, 2002.

Reeves, Thomas. *A Question of Character: A Life of John F. Kennedy*. New York: Random House, 1997.

Remnick, David. *King of the World: Muhammad Ali and the Rise of an American Hero*. New York: Vintage Books, 1999.

Renehan, Edward J., Jr. *The Kennedys at War, 1937–1945*. Ann Arbor: University of Michigan Press, 2002.

Schlesinger, Arthur M., Jr. *A Thousand Days*. New York: Houghton Mifflin, 1965.

Sidey, Hugh. *John F. Kennedy, President.* Berkeley: University of California Press, 1964.

Sorensen, Theodore C. *Kennedy.* New York: HarperCollins, 1965.

Strober, Gerald S., and Deborah H. Strober. *"Let Us Begin Anew": An Oral History of the Kennedy Presidency.* Ann Arbor: University of Michigan Press, 1994.

Torres, Jose. *Sting Like a Bee: The Muhammad Ali Story.* Ann Arbor: University of Michigan Press, 1971.

Wills, Gary. *The Kennedy Imprisonment.* New York: Houghton Mifflin, 1982.

Zirin, Dave. *What's My Name, Fool? Sports and Resistance in the United States.* Chicago: Haymarket Books, 2005.

TEN

American Dreamers

MICHAEL JORDAN AND JENNIFER LOPEZ

To the dismay of its critics over the years, American popular culture has proved tremendously influential on a global basis while serving as a unifying force in the United States. Over the span of several generations and in the face of ethnic, racial, and class divides at home and ideological divisions overseas, it has helped to shape attitudes and beliefs, to foster desires and hopes, and to instill dreams and expectations. It has sustained the idea of the American Dream, of economic advancement for American families within an atmosphere of general political freedom, all while millions suffered deprivation, exploitation, and other hardships. Even in the worst of times in the United States, such as the economic collapse of the 1890s and the Great Depression, success stories dotted the landscape and American popular culture reflected that fact. Indeed, in songs, stage performances, and visual imaginings, artists frequently served as exemplars of those who had succeeded, having overcome obstacles of different sorts. Consequently, perhaps as much as any other factor, popular culture served to lessen tensions and disharmony even as facets of the genre agitated, probed, and provoked society as a whole and powerbrokers in particular, whenever possible. Ultimately popular culture helped to spread the gospel of America, of the American Dream, both at home and outside the boundaries of the United States. When Iron Curtain–styled walls collapsed, along with the Cold War, they were fueled by the desire of millions not only for freedom, but also for the chance to partake more fully of popular culture in all its guises.

By the last decade of the twentieth century, the possibility of achieving the American Dream appeared greater than ever based on the makeup of those who had obviously attained it. For most of American history, the likeliest individuals and families to acquire such success tended to be Caucasians of European ancestry, although others occasionally managed to approach the loftiest rungs of material achievements. Over several generations, Catholics whose families earlier hailed from Ireland, France, or Italy joined Anglo-Saxon Protestants in positions of preeminence, albeit at lesser rates. Then immigrant Americans of Eastern European extraction began to garner fame, particularly in the field of entertainment. African-Americans began a slow but steady upward march although not at the same pace as immigrants from the Far East. Finally, during the century's last segments, those who traced their family roots back to Hispanoamerica likewise began to make their mark, although again in a fashion demonstrating less obvious success than many others had.

Still, by the opening stages of the twenty-first century, Americans of color, including those who were black and brown, boasted luminous figures who dotted the cultural landscape and altered perceptions of what might be possible for other African-Americans and Hispanics. In the realm of popular culture, two such shining lights were the peerless black basketball player and commercial pitchman Michael Jordan and the multitalented actress-singer-dancer-entrepreneur Jennifer Lopez. Notwithstanding a twenty-month hiatus from the game, Jordan garnered five most valuable player (MVP) awards and ten scoring titles during his career as he led his Chicago Bulls to six National Basketball Association (NBA) championships. Equally important, he transformed the sport, relying on unparalleled athleticism and grace as he drove relentlessly to the hoop or flew above the rim before honing a deadly jump shot as he became an older, more mature player. Along the way, Jordan followed in Muhammad Ali's footsteps in becoming the world's most recognized figure, while achieving financial success that dwarfed that of the great boxing champion. In the process he shattered racial barriers and stereotypes regarding the commercial viability of black celebrities as his smiling visage became identified with Nike, Wheaties, Gatorade, and McDonald's, among other corporate giants. *Forbes* magazine indicated that the beautiful Lopez, a pop, Latin pop, and rhythm and blues performer, was the richest Latin American artist in Hollywood. Her records reached the top of the charts. She offered a thriving clothing line, JLO. She owned a swanky Cuban restaurant, Madre's, in Pasadena, California. Her fragrance lines surpassed sales of $500 million worldwide. She was one of the top-paid actresses in the film industry. Like Jordan, who shattered many remaining racial barriers in popular culture, Lopez helped overcome stereotypes that had long precluded Hispanic Americans from achieving starring roles in Hollywood and other entertainment venues.

MICHAEL JORDAN

On February 17, 1963, Michael Jeffrey Jordan was born in Brooklyn, New York, the fourth of five children of James R. Jordan Sr. and Deloris Jordan. At the age of five, Michael nearly cut off his bare big toe as he tried to chop wood. Luckily a neighbor thought to douse the toe with kerosene, which somehow enabled it to heal. The Jordan family relocated to Wilmington, North Carolina, when he was seven years old. Seeking to provide their children with a decent standard of living, James Sr. worked for an electric plant and Deloris had a job at a local bank. Michael played various sports, including baseball, football, and basketball, but was unable to make the varsity basketball team at Laney High School as a sophomore when he stood five-foot-eleven. Playing for the junior varsity squad, Jordan averaged twenty-five points a game. Over the summer he shot up four inches and practiced constantly.

He made the varsity team his junior year and averaged about twenty-one points a game, earning an invitation to Dean Smith's basketball camp the following summer. Three gym sessions left Roy Williams, then a graduate assistant to the fabled University of North Carolina coach who later took Smith's old job, impressed with Jordan's work ethic, intensity, and obvious athleticism. He informed another North Carolina staffer, "I think I've just looked at the best six-foot-four high school player that I've ever seen." Doug Moe, an assistant with the Denver Nuggets, informed the NBA team's general manager that Jordan was "great. I'm talking Jerry West and Oscar Robertson," referring to the players then considered the finest guards in NBA history. Thanks to Williams, Jordan enrolled at Howard Garfinkel's Five-Star Camp, which boasted seventeen high school All-Americans, in Pittsburgh. After watching Jordan for a few minutes on court, Garfinkel realized that "Michael Jordan was the most explosive young player he had ever seen." Jordan went on to average 29.2 points, 11.6 rebounds, and 10.1 assists, his senior year at Laney High, when he landed on the McDonald's All-American Team. Playing in the McDonald's All-American Game in Wichita, Jordan scored thirty points, sinking thirteen out of nineteen shots.

Jordan enrolled at the University of North Carolina in the fall of 1981. In contrast to several other leading schools, North Carolina under Smith refused to offer players or their families anything under the table, highlighting instead the quality of the university and its tradition of basketball excellence. Smith emphasized team ball even when he had extraordinary athletes like James Worthy and Jordan. North Carolina, starring Worthy, Sam Perkins, and freshman Jordan, made it to the National Collegiate Athletic Association (NCAA) title game, encountering Georgetown, coached by John Thompson and led by seven-foot center Patrick Ewing. Invariably sticking out his tongue when driving to the basket, Jordan grabbed nine rebounds, more than any other player, and "the ice-bucket cool" freshman made three of the last five North Carolina buckets, including a seventeen-foot jumper—the "shot," it would be called in North Carolina—in the final seconds to win the championship, Smith's first. In each of the next two years, Jordan, who had shot up to six-foot-six and was now running the forty-yard dash in under 4.4 seconds, a blistering time, was named the top player in college basketball although North Carolina failed to repeat as NCAA titlist. During his junior year, *Sports Illustrated* featured Jordan, whom it referred to as "merely the finest all-around amateur player in the world," along with Perkins, on its cover, the first of the record forty-nine times he would appear there.

Jordan opted to become eligible for the NBA draft following his junior season although he would honor Dean Smith's determination that his players take their education seriously by returning to Chapel Hill to complete his degree. The NBA was in the midst of a revival led by the Los Angeles Lakers' dynamic six-foot-nine guard Magic Johnson and the Boston Celtics' great shooting forward Larry Bird, who entered the league in 1979. They joined the most important franchises in the NBA, which had become known for plummeting attendance figures, drug scandals, and surly athletes. By the time the 1984 NBA draft was held, Johnson and Bird were the game's brightest stars, having already led the Lakers and Celtics to two league titles apiece. Standing at the podium at the Felt Forum on June 19, 1984, NBA commissioner J. David Stern announced that Michael Jordan was the third selection behind centers Hakeem Olajuwon and Sam Bowie. An ensuing "love of the game" clause allowed Jordan to play basketball whenever he chose to, including on blacktops in his home state.

Before his rookie year with the Chicago Bulls, Jordan starred for the U.S. Olympic team coached by Indiana University's fiery Bobby Knight. Following the competition in Barcelona, which resulted in an easy gold medal performance by the United States, Jordan completed a stellar campaign for the Bulls in which he averaged 28.2 points a game, the third highest total in the league, along with 6.5 rebounds and 5.9 assists, and was named Rookie of the Year. Jerry West, now general manager with the Los Angeles Lakers, stated, "He's the only player I've seen who reminds me of me." *Sports Illustrated* placed Jordan, wearing his jersey number 23, on its cover early in his first season, declaring, "A Star Is Born." Jordan appeared to be literally taking the game to new heights, often undergoing seemingly instantaneously alterations of his body as he flew past opponents or left them in his path on his way to the basket. Others, particularly Julius Erving, when he played in the American Basketball Association, had demonstrated an acrobatic quality, but Jordan appeared still more fluid and graceful than even the celebrated Doctor J. Attendance at Bulls' games more than doubled and television networks now altered their schedules to feature the Bulls. Jordan's celebrity soared outside the basketball court with help from his agent, David Falk, and a new pair of Nike sneakers, called Air Jordans, which turned that company into a corporate powerhouse.

In the third game of his sophomore season with the Bulls, Jordan suffered a broken bone in his left foot, sidelining him for sixty-four games. Returning late in the year, Jordan, who had honed his outside shot during the off-season, spearheaded the Bulls' drive to the playoffs where they met the Boston Celtics, who were experiencing a magical season led by Bird, Kevin McHale, and Robert Parish. The Celtics swept the Bulls in three straight games, although Jordan averaged 47.7 points. More striking, he set a playoff record with sixty-three points in an overtime contest that awed even seasoned observers of the sport. Bird informed a sportswriter, "That was God disguised as Michael Jordan." Following the season, the young black filmmaker Spike Lee, who had created the Air Jordan–loving character of Mars Blackmon for his low-budget film *She's Gotta Have It*, directed and co-starred in television commercials with Jordan for Nike that became classics. In the estimation of journalist-historian David Halberstam, they also made Jordan virtually "unique as a cultural icon," affording him the power exhibited by Hollywood stars.

During his third year in the NBA, Jordan scored forty points in nine consecutive games at one point on his way to his first scoring title as he averaged 37.1 points, the fifth-highest total in the league's history (Wilt Chamberlain achieved the top four). That season he captured his first of two consecutive Slam Dunk crowns in All-Star competition. Jordan twice scored sixty-one points in a game, once against the Detroit Pistons and again against the Atlantic Hawks, when he tallied an NBA-record twenty-three points in a row. Rick Telander, in *Sports Illustrated*, explained why fans and sportswriters alike loved Michael Jordan: "For the same reasons we love Peter Pan. Because he can fly." The 1987–1988 campaign ended with Jordan having averaged thirty-five points a game while the Bulls, strengthened by the addition of forwards Scottie Pippen and Howard Grant, compiled a 50–32 regular season mark, ten games better than the previous season. The man called "Superman in Shorts" shone during the Slam Dunk competition at Chicago Stadium, defeating Dominque Wilkins, who had nipped him in the 1985 finals, in the last round. Jordan was named MVP of the All-Star game after scoring forty points in the contest, then was chosen NBA Defensive Player of the Year and MVP, the first player to win both awards in the same year. He blistered Detroit for fifty-nine points in a late-season contest, leading Piston coach Chuck Daly to devise "the Jordan Rules" in which the Pistons, particularly topflight defenders Joe Dumars and Dennis Rodman, double- and triple-teamed Jordan in brutally physical fashion. Jordan scorched the Cleveland Cavaliers with back-to-back fifty-point games in a first-round playoff series during which he averaged 45.2 points a game. The Bulls, who had finished only four games behind the Pistons in the Eastern Conference's Central Division, lost to Detroit in the best-of-seven conference semifinal, four games to one. Critics wondered aloud if Jordan could ever elevate the play of his overshadowed teammates in the fashion of Bird and the Lakers to take them to a league championship.

Early in the 1988–1989 campaign, *Time* magazine offered a lengthy write-up on Jordan by Sally B. Donnelly, titled "Great Leapin' Lizards! Michael Jordan Can't Actually Fly, But." Donnelly asserted that Jordan was "the hottest player in America's hottest sport." Since he had turned pro the NBA's revenues had nearly doubled while attendance was up 40 percent. Undoubtedly helpful was the fact that Jordan obviously relished playing basketball, affirming that he had "the best job in the world." His fierce determination to succeed shone as well. If necessary, Jordan found motivation in perceived insults, declaring to himself, "Someone is trying to take something from me, to make a name for himself by outplaying Michael Jordan." On the court Jordan began wearing longer shorts, a fashion statement soon adopted throughout the NBA. Away from the court Jordan thrived too, particularly as a commercial pitchman for Nike, McDonald's, Johnson Products, Coca-Cola, Wheaties, and Chevrolet, among other corporate giants. His non-NBA earnings dwarfed his $4 million annual salary with the Bulls. That season, the Bulls, whose regular season record faltered a bit, finished sixteen games behind the Pistons in the Eastern Conference Central Division, even though Jordan again led the league in scoring with a 32.5 point-per-game mark. In the final game of the first-round playoff series against Cleveland, in which he averaged 39.8 points a game, Jordan scored forty-four points and, after double-pumping, sank a fifteen-foot jumper—soon referred to as the "shot" in Chicago—past Craig Ehlo to win the contest 101–100. The Bulls eventually advanced to the Eastern Conference finals, where they met their nemesis, the Detroit Pistons, who won in six games. The next year, the Bulls, now coached by Phil Jackson, again came in second to the Pistons in the Eastern Conference Central Division, four games back, despite having won fifty-five regular season contests. They fell to Detroit one more time in the conference finals, losing the decisive seventh game. Jordan's league-leading scoring average for the season shot back up to 33.6 points a game, including sixty-nine in one outing against the Cavaliers, who refused to double-team him, and he also topped the NBA with 2.8 steals a game. Following the season Jordan married Juanita Vancy, with whom he would have three children.

The Chicago Bulls, relying on a triangle offense that sought to involve all five players, finally broke through the following year to win their first NBA championship. The Bulls completed the regular season with a franchise-record sixty-one games, eleven games better than the Pistons, in spite of a slow start when Jackson attempted to reduce Jordan's offensive output. After Jordan began pouring the ball into the hoop again, reporters asked whom he had consulted about playing more aggressively. Jordan responded quickly, "I talked it over with myself." Now sporting a completely shaved head, Jordan once more was the scoring titlist with 31.5 points a game, ably assisted by the greatly improved Pippen, who was rapidly becoming the second brilliant act in the Bulls' lineup. In the opening playoff round, Chicago swept the New York Knicks, then beat Charles Barkley and the Philadelphia 76ers, four games to one, with Jordan averaging almost forty-three points a game, before sweeping Detroit in the conference finals. After dropping the initial game in the NBA finals against Magic Johnson and the Los Angeles Lakers, the Bulls won four in a row led by regular season and finals MVP Jordan. Jack McCallum of *Sports Illustrated* noted that Jordan's performance in the finals was "probably the finest all-around" in NBA history as he averaged 31.2 points, 11.4 assists, 6.6 rebounds, 2.8 steals, and 1.4 blocked shots a game.

During the fall of 1991 journalist Sam Smith published a book, *The Jordan Rules*, threatening to alter the hitherto unsullied image of Jordan by relating embittered battles with team management, especially general manager Jerry Krause, and on-the-floor squabbles with teammates. Smith indicated that Jordan, defying the strategy of Coach Jackson, who he was certain wanted to ensure that he would not repeat as scoring champion, picked up his scoring pace in the opening quarters of several games. Jackson, who appreciated Jordan's brilliant competitiveness, offered that "it was a curse in some ways . . . to be so good, to be a comet racing across the game with everyone light-years in your wake." Nevertheless, as the 1991–1992 season unfolded, the Bulls began to achieve on-court harmony that Jackson believed resembled that of the Bill Russell-led Boston Celtics dynasty of the 1960s. Still, Jordan and Pippen often resorted to freelancing, discarding the triangle offense. Beginning in the second-round playoff series against the 76ers, Jordan seemed to adapt better to a team-oriented game, shooting less and calling for set plays for his teammates, whom he referred to as his "supporting cast," conserving energy for the last few minutes of contests.

Sports Illustrated proclaimed Jordan its Sportsman of the Year for 1991. Writer Jack McCallum declared that Jordan was perched on the "mountaintop, unquestionably the most famous athlete on the planet and one of the most famous citizens of any kind." By now endorsements and other commercial dealings paid Jordan over $21 million annually. Jordan had achieved unparalleled popularity on a global scale while surpassing previous standards involving the celebrity of sports figures. Moreover, he had generally done so "with a preternatural grace and ease that have cut across lines of race, age and gender." Many were already proclaiming him the finest basketball player ever.

The Chicago Bulls roared through the 1991–1992 regular season, capturing sixty-seven games, with Pippen becoming an All-Star starter and MVP Jordan again leading the league in scoring with 30.1 points a game. The Bulls swept the Miami Heat in a first-round playoff series, held on to beat the rugged Knicks in a best-of-seven conference semifinal matchup, then defeated the Cavaliers in the conference finals, winning in six games, before accomplishing that same feat in the NBA finals against the Portland Trailblazers. MVP runner-up Clyde Drexler led the Trailblazers but Jordan shut down the Portland star after stories floated that Drexler might well be the game's best. Jordan set the tone in the opening half of game one when he scored an NBA playoff record of thirty-five points, including six three-point shots in a row. One signature moment occurred during that stretch when Jordan canned a three pointer, then spotted Magic Johnson at the broadcast station alongside court. Jordan smiled at his recently retired former rival, raised his eyes, and held up his hands as if to indicate he failed to understand how he could be that good. As the Bulls captured their second straight NBA title, Jordan became only the fourth player—Kareem Abdul-Jabbar, Johnson, and Bird were the others—to win multiple finals MVP awards and the first to do so in consecutive years.

Immediately following the finals, Jordan joined Johnson (who briefly came out of retirement), Bird, eight other NBA stars, and a top college player on the United States Olympic team, the so-called "Dream Team," in heading for the Olympic Games in Barcelona. Head coach Chuck Daly admitted, "It was like Elvis and the Beatles put together. Traveling with the Dream Team was like traveling with 12 rock stars. That's all I can compare it to." Other athletes deferred to the NBA stars, then at the height of their fame as the sport had become quite possibly the world's most popular. On the court Jordan once again stood out; his opponents watched in wonderment, even applauding his dunks. Sweeping through eight games, the American squad won by an average of nearly forty-four points a contest, although starters like Jordan played relatively few minutes. The United States easily defeated Croatia in the championship game, 117–85, with Jordan scoring a game-high twenty-two points.

The 1992–1993 regular season was somewhat tougher for the Chicago Bulls, who compiled a 57–25 mark, ten games worse than the previous year and only three in front of the Cleveland Cavaliers in the Eastern Conference Central Division. Jordan averaged a league-leading 32.6 points and 2.8 steals a game. His scoring title was his seventh in a row, duplicating the feat earlier achieved by Wilt Chamberlain. The supposedly more vulnerable Bulls again raced through the preliminary playoff series, whitewashing the Atlantic Hawks, and then blanked the Cavaliers in the conference semifinals. Both the conference finals and the NBA championship series proved tougher, but the Bulls came out on top for the third straight year, beating first the New York Knicks and then the Phoenix Suns. Jordan scored a playoff high of fifty-five points in game four and passed to John Paxon, who hit the game-winning jumper, to give the Bulls the deciding sixth game. Once again Jordan was named the finals MVP, thereby duplicating Johnson's feat of winning the award three times.

A series of unfortunate developments doomed chances of a four-peat. Concerns about his gambling flooded the airwaves during the 1993 NBA playoffs, angering Jordan, who recognized the double-edged nature of his enormous celebrity. More tragically, Jordan's father, James Jordan, was killed in August 1993 by a pair of hoodlums as he was returning home from a funeral. Rumors floated that James's death was related in some manner to Michael's gambling problems. With the 1993–1994 training camp about to open, Jordan announced his retirement. Most athletes, even the very finest ones like quarterback Johnny Unitas and heavyweight champion Muhammad Ali, hold on too long, after their once peerless skills have evaporated. Jordan's retirement hardly appeared to diminish his commercial appeal; according to one advertising expert, "Michael is truly in the league of legends. Whether he is playing or retired, he is still going to be a tremendous draw." The league, *Time's* Richard Stengel suggested, would miss Jordan most because he was viewed by many as the NBA's savior, helping move it "into the promised land of perpetually full arenas and high Nielsen ratings." Seemingly everyone wanted to "be like Mike," as the Gatorade commercial said.

Still enormously competitive, Jordan astonished the sports world by joining a baseball team, the Birmingham Barons of the Southern League. Having been away from the game for nearly two decades, Jordan foundered, batting only .201 with just three homers as a light-hitting outfielder. In the spring of 1995, Jordan delivered a brief statement—"I'm back"—and rejoined the Bulls for the final seventeen games of the regular season. Later he explained, "Eventually I just decided that I loved the game too much to stay away." His baseball debacle seemed only to humanize Jordan, who until then had appeared virtually invincible. Without Jordan, but led by Pippen, the Bulls had won fifty-five games during the previous season, advancing into the second round of the playoffs where they lost a deciding game seven to the Knicks. When the 1994–1995 regular season opened, the Bulls were playing at the new United Center, which featured a statute of Jordan outside the arena. Now lacking Howard Grant as well as Jordan, the Bulls compiled a mediocre record until Jordan returned to the team. In his fifth game back, played at Madison Square Garden, Jordan poured in fifty-five points and delivered an assist to center Bill Wennington to cinch a 113–111 victory. At times Jordan's play appeared every bit as spectacular as before; after a brilliant game against the Charlotte Hornets, sportswriter Phil Taylor wrote, "Michael Jordan is so breathtakingly balletic on a basketball court that it is easy to forget that he is also a predator." Although Jordan averaged 31.5 points in the playoffs, Chicago fell to the Miami Heat in the conference semifinals, where Michael clearly demonstrated that he had not regained his stamina.

Fired up by the Bulls' setback and perhaps by his baseball debacle, Jordan was about to undertake another three-year reign at the top of NBA basketball. When that period concluded, he had won three more scoring titles, a pair of MVP trophies, and three additional NBA crowns. Recognizing that he could no longer drive to the basket as frequently as he had in his younger years, Jordan honed a jumper that became possibly the most feared weapon in the sport. The 1995–1996 version of the Bulls included starring roles for Pippen, now clearly recognized as one of the NBA's greatest players, and Dennis Rodman, an extraordinary rebounder and, like Pippen and Jordan, virtually tireless as a peerless defender. The media coverage was more intense than ever as the Bulls compiled an NBA record of seventy-two victories during the regular season, including one stretch when they won thirty-one of thirty-two games. MVP Jordan led the league in scoring with 30.4 points a game, and then averaged 30.7 in the playoffs. Pippen joined Jordan on the first All-NBA team, and the two, along with Rodman, who topped the circuit in rebounding, made up three-fifths of NBA's All-Defensive starting quintet. The Bulls avenged the previous season's loss to Miami, routing the Heat in three straight games, before beating the Knicks 4–1 and the Orlando Magic 4–0 in the conference semifinals and finals, respectively. The NBA finals matched the Bulls against Gary Payton and the Seattle Seahawks, with the Bulls winning in six and Jordan again named playoff MVP. The following year was almost equally spectacular with the Bulls delivering a 69–13 regular season mark; Jordan led the league in scoring with 29.6 points a game, his lowest average for a full season since his rookie year. The Bulls completed a first-round sweep of the Washington Bullets, and then routed both Atlanta and Miami in five games, before notching a 4–2 triumph over the Utah Jazz, led by John Stockton and Karl Malone. Averaging 29.6 games against Utah, Jordan was named finals MVP for a record fifth time.

By this point in his career, Jordan had become, as author David Halberstam records, "a very good teammate." His early impatience with less gifted players, which sometimes translated into taunting and outright cruelty, had largely vanished. Jordan seemed to better appreciate the skills of his on-the-court mates, particularly Pippen, who was fighting through an ankle injury and contract difficulties. After a slow start the Bulls managed a 62–20 record to tie the Jazz for the league's best mark during the 1997–1998 regular season, with Jordan, who averaged 28.7 points a game, leading the league in scoring for the tenth time. *Seattle Post-Intelligencer* columnist Art Thiel declared that Jordan had become "the universal measuring device in appraising greatness" in American culture. He was "ubiquitous in popular culture," Thiel reported, suggesting that only pop music stars such as Frank Sinatra, Elvis Presley, and the Beatles had achieved similar iconic status.

Having blanked the New Jersey Nets in round one, the latest version of the Bulls took care of the Hornets in five games before barely edging past the Indiana Pacers, coached by Larry Bird, in seven hard-fought games in the Eastern Conference finals. For the third straight year, the Bulls captured the NBA title in six games, again defeating Utah, with Jordan, who averaged 28.7 games, selected the finals MVP. Trailing in game six against the Jazz, who were playing at home, Jordan stole the ball from Malone with 18.9 seconds remaining on the clock, dribbled down court, faked defender Bryon Russell out of position, and canned a jumper, following through with perfect form that he held in place, all to the dismay of the Utah faithful. When the game's final 6.6 seconds ran out, the Bulls, led by Jordan's forty-five points, including sixteen in an exhausting final quarter, had triumphed once more. Utah coach Jerry Sloan stated that Jordan was simply "the greatest player who ever played the game."

Jordan again had the opportunity to walk away from his sport while still its finest and certainly most clutch performer and as his commercial appeal seemed stronger than ever. The June 22 issue of *Fortune* magazine featured a smiling photograph of Jordan along with the title, "The Jordan Effect." The inside story by editor at large Roy S. Johnson reported that Jordan had helped to generate over $10 billion for the U.S. economy. *Fortune* pointed to Jordan's impact on the NBA as well as licensed products connected to the league, Nike, and various other brands associated with his name. A 1996 movie, *Space Jam*, starring Jordan and Bug Bunny, had made over $400 million worldwide. Michael Jordan Cologne pulled in over $150 million in the first few months of 1998. Nike president Phil Knight stated, "Michael Jordan is the greatest endorser of the 20th Century." Jordan's popularity spurred the NBA to record television audiences for the sport.

As the century neared an end, sportswriters offered analyses of the greatest athletes in history. Jack McCallum referred to Jordan as "the most written about, the most watched athlete of all time." His greatest feat, McCallum wrote, "was that he was always better than his hype." ESPN completed a survey of media representatives, athletes, and other figures connected to the sports world to determine the greatest sports stars of the twentieth century. Topping even Babe Ruth and Muhammad Ali was Michael Jordan. In a special to ESPN.com, Larry Schwartz stated that "Michael Jordan transcends hoops." The iconic Jordan, Schwartz wrote, "is the first man of the planet," whose "fame and skill were intertwined," in the fashion of Ruth and Ali. For *Sports Illustrated*, Jordan served as "the First Celebrity of the World," not only because of his basketball genius but due to "a unique confluence of artistry, dignity and history."

Just as Babe Ruth epitomized the Roaring Twenties and Jackie Robinson the social changes America experienced in the postwar era, Michael

Jordan appeared to be "the right, best athlete for us now," when his country reigned as the world's lone superpower, Frank Deford suggested. After all, he asked, "Is not Jordan a figure as cultural as he is athletic?" With the death of Princess Diana, Jordan possessed "the most familiar face on the planet Earth." He now seemed "positively ubiquitous, the human Hard Rock Café T-shirt." In the manner of General Colin Powell, comedian Bill Cosby, and political powerbroker Vernon Jordan, the basketball legend appeared to have surmounted race, Deford believed. In Michael Jordan's case, "his engaging persona" and his "remarkably dignified" makeup certainly helped. So too did the fact, Deford stated, that Jordan's mythology resulted from genuine accomplishments. Other analysts proved more critical of Jordan, asking why he failed to criticize Nike's exploitative labor policies overseas, which led to low wages, child labor, sweatshops, and anti-union abuses. For historian Walter LaFeber, Nike and Jordan made a "Faustian bargain" with the media to avoid these subjects. Humanities professor Michael Eric Dyson charged that Jordan had turned "cultural capital into cash" while seemingly disavowing his blackness. Other critics would accuse golfer Tiger Woods of similar disingenuousness.

Jordan returned again to the NBA in 2001, this time as a part owner and player for the Washington Wizards, who remained largely inept despite his attempted stewardship. Jordan's skills were clearly diminished although he averaged 22.9 and 20.0 points in his two seasons back while occasionally displaying his longtime court brilliance, as when he tallied forty points just days after turning forty. When he retired for the third and final time, Jordan held numerous records, including the career scoring average of 30.1 points a game during the regular season and 33.4 points in the playoffs. He had landed on ten All-NBA first teams, received nine All-Defensive First Team honors, and appeared in fourteen All-Star games. On CBS's top-rated news program, *Sixty Minutes*, Ed Bradley reported that Jordan had become "a name brand whose face has sold everything from soft drinks to sneakers, from fast food to underwear." Endorsements still paid him $35 million a year, while Jordan accessories, clothing, and sneakers made $500 million annually for Nike. Regarding criticisms that he refused to tackle social problems as Jackie Robinson, Muhammad Ali, and tennis star Arthur Ashe had, Jordan responded, "It's a heavy duty to try to do everything and please everybody. My job was to go there and play the game of basketball as best I can and provide entertainment for everyone." In 2006 Jordan became a part owner and managing member of basketball operations of the Charlotte Bobcats. In late December Juanita and Michael Jordan divorced, thereby ending their sometimes tumultuous seventeen-year marriage. They agreed to joint custody of their three children. This was reported to be one of the "10 Most Expensive Celebrity Divorces" and one that cost Jordan $168 million. In mid-December 2007 he took to the basketball court once more, during a practice drill, in an effort to encourage the slumping Bobcats. The following spring, reports circulated that he was searching for a new home in Jupiter, a wealthy beach community in Palm Beach County, Florida, whose residents included golfer Tiger Woods, actor Tom Cruise, and talk show host Oprah Winfrey. Jordan was named to the Naismith Memorial Basketball Hall of Fame in 2009.

JENNIFER LOPEZ

Jennifer Lynn Lopez was born in the Castle Hill section of the Bronx on July 24, 1969, to Guadalupe Rodriguez, a kindergarten teacher, and David Lopez, a computer technician. Jennifer was the second of the three daughters of Guadalupe and David, both of whom were born in Ponce, Puerto Rico. From the age of five Lopez took singing and dancing lessons, becoming exposed to a number of musical genres, including salsa, meringue, bachata, pop, hip-hop, and rhythm and blues, while she attended Catholic schools for twelve years. At an all-girls high school, she competed in softball, track and field, tennis, and gymnastics. Following high school Lopez attended Baruch College for one semester and worked in a legal office, while taking dance classes and auditioning for dance roles. She appeared in a number of music videos by rap artists before relocating to Los Angeles, where she soon acquired a part as a "Fly Girl" dancer on Fox's comedy, *In Living Color*, choreographed by Rosie Perez. After two years on that program Jennifer appeared on CBS's *Second Chances* as Melinda Lopez, a character later moved over to another program, *Malibu Road*. She also played Lucy, a co-op market worker, on Fox's *South Central* and performed as a backup dancer for Janet Jackson. She got a number of small acting parts, including in a 1993 television movie, *Nurses on the Line: The Crash of Flight 7*.

Lopez began garnering spots in Hollywood productions including the Francis Ford Coppola–produced *My Family*, a tale about Mexican immigrants in Los Angeles, and *Money Train*, in which she played a transit cop, in 1995. She also appeared as a Latina schoolteacher in *Jack*, which Coppola directed, and as a Cuban mistress of the male protagonist in *Blood and Wine* the following year. She starred in the 1996 production of *Selena* about the Tejana recording artist Selena Quintanilla Perez, the emerging crossover star who had been murdered by a crazed fan the previous year. The first Latina to receive $1 million for a film, Lopez played the part of the mature Selena, receiving plaudits from film critics. Director Gregory Nava said, "We were thrilled to have Jennifer star in this very special story. The combination of her enormous talent, warmth, appeal and strength made her the ideal candidate to portray Selena." The role enabled Lopez to display her abilities as stage and musical performer. She acknowledged, "One of the biggest challenges was the dance part. It's very hard to unlearn everything your body is accustomed to doing and that it does naturally. I had to learn what Selena did, which is very different from my own dance instincts." In his review of the film, Roger Ebert wrote that Lopez delivered "a star-making performance." Having recently offered "strong work as the passionate lover of Jack Nicholson in . . . 'Blood and Wine,' here she creates a completely different performance, as a loyal Quintanilla who does most of her growing up on a tour bus with her dad at the wheel." The film succeeded, Ebert declared, "through Lopez's performance, in evoking the magic of a sweet and talented young woman." In his review, James Beradinelli termed Lopez "radiant" and "masterful" in the lead role, able to demonstrate "the boundless energy and enthusiasm that exemplified Selena, while effectively copying not only her look, but her mannerisms." Lopez's acting stint in *Selena* led to a short-lived marriage to Ojani Noa, who proposed to Lopez on the dance floor during the shooting of the film. It also resulted in her nomination for the Golden Globe Award for Best Actress in a Motion Picture Musical or Comedy and a nomination for an MTV Movie Award for Best Actress. Less noteworthy were the next films she appeared in, *Anacaonda* and Oliver Stone's *U Turn*, which appeared in 1997. *People* magazine selected her one of the "50 Most Beautiful People in the World."

Her co-starring role with George Clooney in Steven Soderbergh's acclaimed *Out of Sight*, a 1998 release that resulted in a $2 million paycheck, led Ebert to emphasize her "star quality." For Ebert, her earlier work underscored that fact and her latest effort demonstrated that "she has only grown." The critic noted, "Here she plays a role that could be complex or maybe just plain dumb, and brings such a rich comic understanding to it." The *New York Times'* Janet Maslin wrote that Lopez "has her best movie role thus far, and she brings to it both seductiveness and grit." Kenneth Turan, film critic of the *Los Angeles Times*, declared that "Lopez, an actress who can be convincingly tough and devastatingly erotic," cemented "her position as a woman you can confidently build a film around." In Woody Allen's wonderful animated feature *Antz*, Lopez provided the voice of the love interest of a soldier ant; the film also featured the voices of Allen, Sharon Stone, Danny Glover, Sylvester Stallone, Gene Hackman, and Christopher Walken.

A feature article titled "Latin Music Pops" in the May 24, 1999, issue of *Time* magazine began by stating, "We've seen the future. It looks like Ricky Martin. It sings like Marc Anthony. It dances like Jennifer Lopez. Que bueno!" The article referred to the popularity of Latin pop, which followed on the heels of previous Latin incarnations including salsa, rumba, and mambo as delivered by stars ranging from Ritchie Valens to Gloria Esteban. The latest development offered a new generation of Latin performers brought up on Spanish radio, comfortable with mainstream pop, who sang in English. *Time* declared, "Of this group, Martin is the hottest; Lopez, 28, the most alluring; Anthony, 29, the most artistic." As Hispanics readied to become the nation's largest minority group, Latin pop promised to become "the sound of your future," *Time* predicted. The music was cutting-edge, exhibiting, as Lopez did on a recent CD track, "the street edge of hip-hop." Shakira, the Colombian-born pop artist, spoke of Latin pop's secret power: "That treasure is fusion. The fusion of rhythms, the fusions of ideas. We Latinos are a race of fusion, and that is the music we make." Claiming that Puerto Rico was where that fusion began, *Time* noted that Martin, Lopez, and Anthony all had roots on the Caribbean island. In the States, Spanish-language radio flourished, providing a "terrific launching pad for Latin crossover artists." Spurred by the overwhelming response to the death of Selena, record companies increasingly sought out Latin pop stars. *Time* predicted that the Latina "best positioned to grab hold of a Selena-proportioned success" was Lopez, who starred in the film account of the slain artist's life. Her involvement in the making of *Selena* induced Lopez to undertake a music career of her own. The talent of singer-actress-dancer Lopez appeared virtually unbounded.

On June 1, 1999, Lopez branched out, releasing her first album, the Latin pop *On the 6*, which landed on *Billboard*'s top-ten chart. The album featured "If You Had My Love," a song that stood at number one for nine weeks; "Waiting for Tonight," another song that ended up in the top ten; and "*No Me Ames*," sung with Marc Anthony, which proved an international smash. Two songs from the album, "Let's Get Loud" and "Waiting for Tonight," pulled in Grammy Award nominations. The album's success, along with her movie career, made Lopez one of the nation's leading Latin artists. Lopez won the 1999 VH1/Vogue Fashion Award for Most Fashionable Female Artist and received a Grammy nomination for "*No Me Ames.*" Nevertheless, controversy swirled about Lopez, thanks to her relationship with rapper Sean "Puffy" Combs, known as P. Diddy; a shooting incident outside a nightclub in New York City in December 1999 landed her in jail for fourteen hours. Other news reports indicated that she had insured her backside for $300 million and her full body for $1 billion.

The next year found Lopez back on the silver screen as a child psychologist in *The Cell*, a role for which she received $4 million and that led the *New York Times* to applaud her "provocative and nuanced performance." Lopez felt compelled at one point during the filming of *The Cell* to talk at a press conference about tabloid stories. She said, "You laugh it off, you get upset for a little while, you're human and you let it go." The FHM list of 100 Sexiest

Women had Lopez at the head of the class, a feat that would be repeated for the first time the next year. Her salary bumped up to $9 million for each of her next two films, *The Wedding Planner* and *Angel Eyes*, which came out in 2001. Although it became the top box-office release, *The Wedding Planner* garnered mixed reviews, with *USA Today*'s Mike Clark opening with the observation, "Jennifer Lopez works hard to squeeze some fun out . . . but she lacks the knack of her old pal the anaconda." Bob Graham of the *San Francisco Chronicle* indicated that Lopez "tops what must be, man for man and woman for woman, the most downright gorgeous cast out there right now," including Matthew McConaughey and Bridgette Wilson-Sampras. Graham noted that since her performance in *Out of Sight*, "there's been no doubt of Lopez's screen poise or acting chops," but he questioned if her role as a wedding planner provided her with the proper forum to delve into comedy. Examining Lopez's role as a tough police officer in *Angel Eyes*, *Entertainment Weekly* referred to her as "a quick-minded and intuitive actress" who, however, failed to approach "the fluky inner fire" she had displayed in *Out Sight*; instead, she had "honed her body and personality into that of an officially empowered pop superstar." The *Entertainment Weekly* reviewer called for Lopez "to be redeemed from trash like this." However, Mick LaSalle of the *San Francisco Chronicle* contended that audiences would experience "a new relaxation in Jennifer Lopez. She takes her time. She really listens. She reacts. She doesn't try to control scenes or control her face. She lets moments happen." For LaSalle her performance demonstrated a new maturity on her part: Lopez was "now an actress who can do things other movie stars can't. She doesn't push, just thinks, and her thoughts and emotions burn into the film." The *Washington Post* deemed *Angel Eyes* "a romantic mystery that's built entirely around Jennifer Lopez's appeal—dramatic and otherwise," and saluted her "earthy, straightforward performance."

As her film stardom continued to rise, notwithstanding the mixed reviews of the movies she appeared in, Lopez also became a bigger pop figure in 2001 with her second album, *J. Lo*, which appeared in late January and shot to the top of the *Billboard* 200 list, as *The Wedding Planner* was the top box-office release. In the process she became the first actress to have an album and a movie positioned at number one during the same week. Lopez's "Love Don't Cost a Thing" became the top-selling single in the United Kingdom, while remixed versions of "I'm Real" and "Ain't It Funny" ended up at the front of the pop charts. *Time* noted her willingness to appear on talk shows even if questions about boyfriend Combs came up, suggesting that "she simply has unsquashable *cojones*." At a minimum it demonstrated "she's got It. She is what the old movie moguls would have called a game gal." The *Ladies' Home Journal* named Lopez the thirtieth most powerful woman in the country. In

February 2002 Lopez reissued her second album, now titled *J to tha L-O!: The Remixes* and including backing from P. Diddy, Fat Joe, and Nas, which debuted at the top of the *Billboard* 200. That album also opened at number one, the first remixed album to head the charts. Later that year Lopez put out *This Is Me . . . Then*, which became the second-best-selling album in the country; it contained several singles, including "Jenny from the Block" and the number one smash, "All I Have," a duet with LL Cool J. Now paid $12 million and easily among the ten most highly paid actresses in Hollywood, she appeared in *Maid in Manhattan*, playing the part of a single mom who works as a maid in a luxury hotel in New York City, where she encounters a Senate candidate played by Ralph Fiennes. Despite panning the movie, the *Philadelphia Inquirer* deemed it "an achievement that Lopez, that ubiquitous face of today's media, believably plays invisible." *Newsday* declared that "Lopez isn't that interesting a physical presence onstage," while James Berardinelli of ReelViews wondered, "Whatever happened to Jennifer Lopez, actress?" He continued, "Seductive, charismatic, and energetic, she electrified the screen in movies like *Selena* and *Out of Sight*." Berardinelli likened "the woman masquerading as her in *Maid in Manhattan*" to "the one who stole her name for such lackluster fare as *The Wedding Planner*, *Angel Eyes*, and *Enough*." He then surmised, "Perhaps the advent of J. Lo, pop personality, has crushed all but a few remaining vestiges of the woman's acting ability." In one of the few favorable reviews, William Arnold of the *Seattle Post-Intelligencer* acknowledged that Lopez had acquired "the reputation of being such a demanding diva," but indicated that she won him over immediately: "The camera loves her, she exudes intelligence and charm . . . and there's something riveting about the presence."

A cascade of media accounts surrounded Lopez around this time. Her perfume, Glow, became the top-selling one in several countries, and she set up a clothing line, JLO by Jennifer Lopez. She declared, "Just because you dress sexy doesn't mean you're a bad girl. It just means you know how to dress." Lopez believed, "It's time for the world to wear my look." As she rationalized, "It is difficult for women who are curvaceous to find clothes in stores that fit. The voluptuous woman is almost ignored." In April 2001, she linked up with Andy Hilfiger to establish Sweetface Fashion Company, which soon branched out to sell the soon-to-be record-setting and top-selling fragrance at Macy's, Glow by JLO, Still Jennifer Lopez, Body Glow by JLO, and Miami Glow, among other product lines. Soon Sweetface possessed international outlets while Lopez delivered a new clothing line named Sweetface, designed for full-figured women. By the following year JLO was taking in $130 million in retail sales, with higher earnings projected. Her relationship with Sean Combs having ended, she became involved with and then married her onetime backup dancer, Cris Judd, in late September 2001. The marriage ended the following June shortly after she opened a posh Cuban restaurant, Madre's, in Pasadena, California. By that point she was linked with the actor Ben Affleck, and popular magazines and entertainment media delighted in referring to the pair as "Bennifer." The two became engaged in October 2002 when Affleck gave her a ring purportedly worth $3.5 million. The animated television comedy *South Park* contained a segment titled "Fat Butt and Pancake Head," obvious references to Lopez and Affleck, that aired in mid-April 2003. Lopez and Affleck appeared together in a romantic comedy, *Gigli*, which appeared in the summer of 2003, only weeks before their planned marriage in Santa Barbara. *Variety Film* declared the two were "thoroughly engaging in their smartly calibrated opposites—his lost boy under a tough, Vinnie-from-the-block exterior to her sensually purring Zen warrior." The review contended that "Lopez has not been this good since *Out of Sight.*" Most critics, however, mercilessly panned the film and its stars. *Rolling Stone* termed the movie "jaw-droppingly awful" and declared that Lopez and Affleck "display zero chemistry" while finding "themselves adorable. They're so taken with each other they don't need an audience. Good thing, because they're not going to get one, not with this swill." The *San Francisco Chronicle* declared the movie "dead on arrival," proclaiming it "the most thoroughly joyless and inept film of the year, and one of the worst of the decade." Reel.com contended that Lopez, "a warm, likable screen siren who can be glamorous and earthy . . . deserves better." Less than two months later, apparently after stories floated that he had been spotted at a strip club, Lopez and Affleck called off their wedding and soon split altogether. The media posed the question of whether Lopez would return the expensive engagement ring, which she eventually did. Following her breakup with Affleck, Lopez began dating the singer-actor Marc Anthony, who had separated from his wife, Dayanara Torres, a former Miss Universe. On June 5, 2004, Lopez and Anthony declared their vows at a secret wedding and set up their domiciles in tony BelAir on the west side of Los Angeles, on Fisher Island, and on Long Island.

That same year Lopez appeared in both *Jersey Girl* and *Shall We Dance.* She had only a minor although very well-paying part in *Jersey Girl*, which co-starred Affleck and had been shot before they ended their relationship. The *Village Voice* opened its review with the observation that "*L'affaire Bennifer* gets one last airing" in the film. The *Miami Herald* indicated that the scenes between the two actors, "the subject of much speculation and derision" after the last year's "marriage-derailing" *Gigli*, were "actually terrific . . . displaying a convincing chemistry." *Shall We Dance*, starring Lopez as a dance instructor and Richard Gere as a lawyer who becomes interested in the ballroom dancing she teaches, amassed mixed reviews. *Premiere* affirmed it was "Gere's movie" and that both Lopez and Susan Sarandon, who starred as Gere's wife, "graciously let him dance away with it." Terming the film "a listless, Hollywooden affair" featuring uninteresting "generic characters," *The Hollywood Reporter* complained that Lopez's "severely underwritten character" possessed "a lot less to grab onto than costume designer Sophie de Rakoff Carbonell's elegant, form-hugging creations." Claiming the film was "miscast, misguided and woefully misbegotten," the *Village Voice* charged that "Lopez primps and poses instead of acts." She appeared in the finale of the television program, *Will and Grace*, as she would in the ensuing season's initial episode.

In 2005 Lopez remained in the spotlight as a major American popular cultural figure although her luster appeared to further dim a bit despite the fact that her personal wealth was estimated at over $250 million. Then her studio album, *Rebirth*, appeared on March 1, debuting in the second spot on the *Billboard* 200 and featuring the hit single, "Get Right." Even more successful, her Hollywood film *Monster-in-Law*, co-starring Jane Fonda, proved a blockbuster. Reviewers proved less enamored than the public, however, with the *Los Angeles Times*' Carina Chocano comparing how "cool and poised" Lopez had been in *Out of Sight* and complaining how miscast she appeared in the new movie as a would-be fashion designer who worked as an office temp and dog walker. Chocano suggested that Lopez was pretending to be teen star Hillary Duff, but Mick LaSalle of the *San Francisco Chronicle* delighted in the pairing of the young Latina and Fonda. *Slate* proclaimed Lopez, paid $15 million for her part, "the multiplex draw" in her role "as a lilting ingénue." Lopez also starred with Robert Redford and Morgan Freeman in *An Unfinished Life*, in which she played a down-and-out-on-her-luck widow who felt compelled to return with her young daughter to the small Wyoming town where her grumpy father-in-law resided. In a somewhat typical review, the *Los Angeles Times* bemoaned the film's quality, notwithstanding "the presence of high-wattage talent." *Rolling Stone* contended that "Lopez looks lost and out of her league" performing with the male heavyweights while the *Washington Post* suggested that "whenever she's onscreen, *Unfinished Life* feels like one of those dramatic preambles to a music video." The August 22, 2005, issue of *Time* contained a write-up on Lopez, whose "place on a list of most influential Hispanics" was said to be "a no-brainer." The one-time "anonymous background dancer" on a "second-rate sketch-comedy show" was now "known by two syllables." Lopez, *Time* continued, "has an outsider's hunger and a native's assumption of infinite possibilities. She works hard and dreams big." Her clothing line, fragrances, album sales, and movie salary combined to make her among the twenty richest individuals in the country under the age of forty, *Fortune* reported.

In April 2006, *Harper's Bazaar* released shots of its impending summer fashion issue, which included a cover and inside photographs of the smartly dressed Lopez. The magazine quoted her as stating, "I'm bleeding! I'm bleeding for fashion!" and reported that "If any actress could—or would—shed blood over a dress, it would be Jennifer." She acknowledged, "You know me—I love all fashion. But this red Galliano dress makes me feel like I want to run through fire." Designer John Galliano revealed, "The romance and rebellion of this gown is perfect for Jennifer, as she is such a strong yet seductive icon. The dress is like an inflamed flamenco dancer, and only someone with real passion could carry it off. She is such an inspiring woman of our times. She is unstoppable!" Lopez admitted, "Now that I do my own collections, I look at the work. There are dresses, and then there are *dresses*. These have beading on top of paillettes on top of major construction. They're incredible, elaborate creations." Designer Giorgio Armani contended, "Jennifer is a chameleon of style who can capture the street or the red carpet with equal panache." When queried about who had inspired her sense of fashion, Lopez responded, "Anybody who's fearless. Women who've started their own trends, who don't care what other people are thinking. I admire Gwen Stefani's style and Madonna's. Those two have blazed their own trails." Complimented by Lopez for designing clothes that fit the body, Donatella Versace responded by saluting the actress:

> Jennifer, whom I've dressed for red carpets and also for her wedding, has the most perfect aura. She has a profound sense of her own body, and she moves with such self-confidence that even if she's not a tiny size 0, she looks fresh, romantic, and irresistible. She gives to couture the personality we all crave—a sexy, iconic approach. I adore her.

In May 2006 MTV approved of Lopez's reality show, *Moves*, produced by Nuyorican Productions, which she founded, intended to track six would-be dancers as they sought to make their professional mark. Nuyorican also had two major films in the works starring Lopez: *El Cantante*, costarring Marc Anthony, a biography of salsa singer Hector Lavoe, who died of AIDS, and *Bordertown*, directed by Gregory Nava. Lopez starred as an investigative journalist tracking the killing of hundreds of women in a Mexican border town. "Since first hearing of these atrocities in 1998, when Gregory Nava came to me with this project, I desperately wanted to tell this story," Lopez revealed. "I began working to ensure we made this film in order to bring the attention of the world to this tragedy and to pressure the Mexican government to bring to justice those responsible for these horrible crimes."

People en Español magazine featured her on the cover of its "50 Most

Beautiful" issue. As of early 2007 Lopez seemed to be the embodiment of the American Dream. Boasting a far more authentic rags-to-riches tale than the characters in Horatio Alger novels, she had become a type of Latina Oprah Winfrey, a multidimensional artist who had turned into a financial powerhouse. In largely singular fashion, Lopez had demonstrated that a Latina could remain on the Hollywood "A" list, be a top recording artist, and operate as a major player in the corporate world, with her perfumes alone pulling in over $500 million annually. At the Berlin International Film Festival in February 2007, Nobel Peace Prize recipient Jose Ramos Horta presented Lopez with the Artists for Amnesty International award "in recognition of her work as producer and star of *Bordertown*." Horta declared, "She's a remarkable woman and a true inspiration." The next month Lopez released her first Spanish-language album, *Como Ama Una Mujer*, with the hit single, *"Que Hiciste,"* establishing a record for Spanish debut albums. She also worked on another studio album, explaining that it would contain "dance, funk, R & B, hip-hop . . . all mixed up together to make some great pop music." Her intricately developed website contained information about her movies, clothing line, jewelry, fragrance, and a new Jennifer Lopez Video Player, among other items. To the delight of her fans, Lopez appeared on *American Idol* in April 2007. *Forbes* magazine placed her ninth on its list of the 20 Richest Women in Entertainment, with an estimated estate of $110 million, and indicated that she was both the wealthiest Hispanic in Hollywood and the most influential Hispanic performer in the United States. In late September 2007, Lopez and her husband Marc Anthony began a six-week tour titled *Juntos en Concierto*. In October she released another album, *Brave*, with the hit single "Do It Well." On February 22, 2008, she gave birth to twin boys, Max and Emme. The cover of *People* magazine on March 20 displayed a beaming Lopez with her sleeping babies nestled against her. A lead article contained twelve pages of photographs of Lopez, Anthony, and their month-old children.

Bibliography

Bondy, Filip. *Tip Off: How the 1984 NBA Draft Changed Basketball Forever*. Cambridge, Massachusetts: Da Capo Press, 2007.

Duncan, Patrician J. *Jennifer Lopez: An Unauthorized Biography*. New York: Macmillan, 1999.

Gallick, Sarah. *J-Lo: The Secret Behind Jennifer Lopez's Climb to the Top*. New York: HarperCollins, 2003.

Greene, Bob. *Rebound: The Odyssey of Michael Jordan*. New York: W.W. Norton, 1999.

Halberstam, David. *Playing for Keeps: Michael Jordan and the World He Made*. New York: Broadway Books, 1999.

Jackson, Phil. *More than a Game*. New York: Simon & Schuster, 2002.

Jordan, Michael. *Driven From Within*. New York: Simon & Schuster, 2006.

———. *For the Love of the Game: My Story*. New York: Crown, 1998.

———. *I Can't Accept Not Trying: Michael Jordan on the Pursuit of Excellence*. New York: HarperCollins, 1994.

LaFeber, Walter. *Michael Jordan and the New Global Capitalism*. New York: W.W. Norton, 1999.

Leahy, Michael. *When Nothing Else Matters: Michael Jordan's Last Comeback*. New York: Simon & Schuster, 2005.

Lopez, Jennifer. *Jennifer Lopez: This Is Me . . . Then*. Indianapolis: Hal Leonard, 2003.

Porter, David L. *Michael Jordan: A Biography*. Santa Barbara, CA: Greenwood Press, 2007.

Sailes, Garry A., ed. *African Americans in Sport*. New Brunswick, NJ: Transaction, 1998.

Smith, Sam. *The Jordan Rules*. New York: Pocket Books, 1993.

Tracy, Kathleen. *Jennifer Lopez*. Westport, CT: Greenwood Press, 2008.

Wiggins, David, and Patrick B. Miller. *The Unlevel Playing Field: A Documentary History of the African American Experience in Sport*. Champaign: University of Illinois Press, 2003.

Index

About the Author

Robert C. Cottrell is Professor of History and American Studies at California State University, Chico, where he is a past winner of the Outstanding Professor Award and the system-wide Wang Family Excellence Award. Professor Cottrell is the author of numerous books–, including biographies of I.F. Stone, Roger Nash Baldwin, and Rube Foster–, and co-author (with Blaine T. Browne) of the two-volume *Lives and Legacies: Biographies in Western Civilization* and *Modern American Lives: Individuals and Issues in American History Since 1945*. He also has taught in London, Moscow, and Puebla (Mexico).